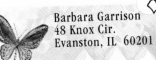

Barbara Garrison
48 Knox Cir.
Evanston, IL 60201

W9-ClO-993

MR. LANGSHAW'S
SQUARE PIANO

Mr Langshaw's square piano

MR. LANGSHAW'S SQUARE PIANO

The Story of the First Pianos and
How They Caused a Cultural Revolution

MADELINE GOOLD

Jacket design by Stefan Killen Design

Cover art top: after Samuel Scott (c. 1702–1772), A View of the Thames with the York Buildings Water Tower, c. 1760–70, Tate Gallery, London, Great Britain. Photo credit: Tate, London / Art Resource, NY

Cover art bottom: George G. Kilburne (1839–1924), The duet, Haynes Fine Art Gallery, Broadway, Worcester, Great Britain. Photo credit: Fine Art Photographic Library, London / Art Resource, NY

Published in Great Britain by Corvo Books Ltd

Library of Congress Cataloging-in-Publication Data

Goold, Madeline.
Mr. Langshaw's square piano : the story of the first pianos and how they caused a cultural revolution / Madeline Goold.
p. cm.
First published in Great Britain in 2008 by Corvo.
Includes bibliographical references and index.
ISBN 978-1-933346-21-2
1. Square piano—England—History. 2. Square piano—Social aspects—History. 3. Square piano—Economic aspects—History. 4. Langshaw, John, 1763-1832. 5. John Broadwood and Sons Limited. 6. Piano makers—England—London—History—18th century. 7. Piano—Construction—England—London—History—18th century. 8. Piano—Identification—Case studies. 9. Piano—Collectors and collecting—Case studies. I. Title.
ML678.3.G66 2009
786.2'1909—dc22   2009031824

First published in North America in 2009 by
BlueBridge
An imprint of
United Tribes Media Inc.
240 West 35th Street, Suite 500
New York, NY 10001
www.bluebridgebooks.com

Printed in the United States of America

10 9 8 7 6 5 4 3 2 1

To my parents, Frederick and Amy Freeman,
who bought me my first Broadwood piano

Music, the greatest good that mortals know,
And all of Heaven we have below

Joseph Addison, 'Song for St Cecilia's Day'

CONTENTS

vii

1

JOURNEY

EARLY ONE SUMMER *morning in 1807 a horse and cart loaded with two oblong wooden boxes stood waiting at the porters' lodge in the gateway from a yard in Bridle Lane, near Golden Square in London. The driver of the cart was the first porter that day to leave the premises of John Broadwood and Son, piano maker to the King of England.*

'Morning, Mr Thorpe,' he called respectfully, and an older man looked out of the lodge's small window.

'Good morning, William.'

'Two squares.'

Mr Thorpe, who would not be rushed, glanced down at the open page of a large leather-bound ledger on the desk in front of him.

'Now then, William, come in and sign.'

The driver, a tall, well-built man, got down from the cart. He wore strong shoes and thick breeches and a waistcoat, even though it was July. His stockings and coarse linen shirt were clean, much washed and mended; they were all he had. His own hair was tied loosely at the back.

Taking care to keep clear of two large dogs growling at the ends of their chains, William walked round his cart to the lodge. As he did he threw the core of an apple he had been eating at the pink snout of a bear standing in a large cage on the other side of the gateway; the brute dropped to all four paws and snuffled to find it in the rubbish and ordure on the floor of the cage.

William stood in the doorway to the lodge while Mr Thorpe gave him his first orders for the day. 'These two for Pickfords at Paddington, William, and on your way back I want you to collect a square that's been taken out to Mrs Wharton, in Great Cumberland Street. Then go to number sixteen Bulstrode Street and meet Clarke; he'll tell you what to do next.'

The ledger clerk took a quill pen, dipped it in a pot of black ink he had just filled from a quart jar, tapped it on the side of the pot to remove the excess and gave it to William, pointing to the place in the ledger where he was to sign.

William had great respect for Mr Thorpe's ledger, although he could not read it; the patterns were so beautiful. Neither of the other clerks, Mr Benson or Mr Rose, made the patterns as beautiful and neat as Mr Thorpe; not even Mr James Shudi Broadwood, young Mr Thomas Broadwood, nor old Mr John Broadwood himself.

The big man stepped forward, took the pen gingerly and carefully made his mark, a tick like Mr Thorpe had shown him, in the small box the clerk was pointing to on the left-hand side of the ledger page. William's expression was rueful. It was always the same: however hard he tried, he could not control the ink and his ticks were always so much thicker and darker than Mr Thorpe's.

'Get a move on now,' said the older man, not unkindly, and William returned to his cart. Mr Thorpe wiped the quill and felt the point. It was no longer as sharp as he liked. He took a small penknife from his waistcoat pocket and, holding the back of the quill down on a block of wood on the desk, cut diagonally across the end. Then he entered the numbers of the two square pianos in the ledger from a slip of paper William had given him.

Clicking to the patient mare, William manoeuvred the cart out of the yard into the dust of Bridle Lane, then into Great Pulteney Street. As he passed the sign of the Plume of Feathers fixed above the doorway of a tall redbrick house of four storeys, he glanced into the window of the 'Dining Room' (as Broadwood's showroom was always called) at one of his master's grand pianos displayed there; and

William felt proud, not only that everyone in London from the Prince of Wales down wanted to buy Mr Broadwood's pianos but that he, William, was the only porter who could deliver a grand by himself. He headed towards the north of town. Here and there he recognized one of Mr Pickford's supervisors patrolling the streets to make sure that none of his carters slacked on their delivery rounds. By the time he could see fields at the edge of town and had turned into the New Road – what is now Marylebone Road – it was already crammed with carts. It was a busy Monday morning in the forty-seventh year of the reign of King George III. Pickford's boats from the north had been arriving at the Paddington Canal Basin since two o'clock that morning. Unloading had begun at four, and small goods such as boxes of hats and silk from Macclesfield had already been sent into the city, many to the docks for export.

Now the heavier goods from all parts of the country had been unloaded, and William saw great wagons loaded with coal and timber drawn by eight horses going in the opposite direction; he had to drive carefully to avoid the deep ruts they made. The New Road was forty feet wide and had been opened half a century earlier to stop drovers taking their animals through the fashionable West End streets. Smaller carts pulled by men were carrying all manner of foodstuffs into the city. He saw one piled high with cheeses for Fortnum's, the grocers; another was loaded with barrels that might have contained rum or gunpowder, William wasn't sure. Porters like William were the delivery vans of Georgian London; it could not function without them. One day he might have his own cart and join the ranks of independent porters for hire, but on the 9s a week that Broadwood's paid him that day was far off. An escaped ox stumbled between the carts, almost colliding with one filled with guano. William called to a mate pulling a cart filled with bales of old rags from Lancashire for paper-making. A flock of sheep made everyone pause, and William watched carts carrying earthenware, flints and casks of ale into London, the capital city, principal port and largest centre of income and consumption in the kingdom. With a population of a million people it was many times larger than any other city and it dominated the country. It was the most rapidly expanding capital city in Europe and arguably the commercial capital of the world.

Many of the carts going in William's direction were carrying London-made consumables. The two square pianos on his cart were Broadwood's most popular model and, like all the others he had taken to Paddington, the docks and the different carriers' starting points all over London, they would carry the capital's cultural influence with them wherever they went. All William knew about it that July morning in 1807 was that he had to get to Paddington on time. Pickfords operated fly boats that ran to a schedule and departed promptly, whether they were full or not. They were pulled by relays of horses and were faster than the ordinary stage or 'tramp' boats. A fly boat could make four miles an hour between locks, where it was given priority.

Encouraging the placid mare, he found a way through the crush of carts at the entrance to the canal basin. It was the biggest inland port in the country, 400 yards long and 30 wide, with boats going to and from all parts of the kingdom, day and night. William drove past the hay and straw market, the animal pens and several warehouses until he came to the bigger carriers' wharfs. After he had unloaded the two square pianos at Pickford's new, second wharf, he turned and drove back into town.

———

Pickfords must have moved mountains in their 250-year history. Like Broadwoods, the company survived into the twenty-first century and still operates all over the world. At the end of the eighteenth century Matthew Pickford, who had taken over from his father, had 20 barges, 50 wagons and 400 horses operating out of wharfs the length of the London-Midland canal routes to Manchester and the developing industrial centres of northern England. He had moved with the times: a single horse and cart could take only a 300-pound load, although a wagoner's team of eight could pull much more, but a canal barge pulled by one horse could carry a 50-ton load. Since 1793 war with France had given impetus to a spate of canal building. All over England gangs of Irish immigrant labourers known as navigators, or navvies, dug canals to make a network of inland waterways that linked north to south and converged on London.

Long years of war with France and the hazards of coastal shipping guaranteed the success of canal transport. Canals linked waterways and roads, production centres and ports at a time of huge increases in manufacturing. Cotton production in the north was distributed largely by canal; exports from there rose from £355,000 in 1780 to £9,753,000 by 1806, and at the end of the eighteenth century there were fifty-two mills in Manchester alone. Matthew Pickford was the biggest commercial canal carrier, with boats concentrated on the main north-south run of the Grand Junction between Manchester, the Midlands and London, after which their cargo was taken on through a network of northern canals.

As Pickford's fly boats had priority at locks, this could lead to some wrangling, but his were not the boats found drifting out of control with the crews in a drunken stupor; his men were not thieves who, mistaking barrels containing gunpowder for kegs of rum, blew up the boat; if his crews were poachers, as some boatmen were, they still managed to arrive on time. Pickford's reputation was built on the speed of his deliveries; no one carried goods between the industrial north and London more quickly.

Mr William Wright, Pickford's agent at Paddington, watched the two boxes from Broadwoods being carried on to the barge. While his men worked quickly to get the boat loaded on time, the horse, one retired from the road haulage side of the business, was harnessed and brought forward. When all was ready Mr Wright gave the signal and, prompt to the timetable, the horse took the eighteen-ton strain. Slowly the long boat began to move out of the canal basin. It gained momentum and the two square pianos in the hold, each wrapped in its linen cover and packed with six turned legs in a deal case, started their journey. They travelled first along the thirteen-mile stretch of the Paddington Arm towards Bull's Bridge, where the horse was changed at Pickford's depot. Then the boat joined the Grand Junction Canal and turned north.

It was a quiet journey. Within a week they would have reached the canal network of the industrial North-West, where the two square pianos parted company. The one for Mr Collins, organ builder of Liverpool, was carried west along the Liverpool-Leeds Canal and thereafter its history is unknown. The other piano continued north. When it reached Walton Summit, just south of Preston in Lancashire, it was unloaded and carried four miles by iron tramway through the Ribble Gap, then reloaded on another boat to complete the last thirty miles on the Lancaster Canal.

The Lancaster Canal had been opened in 1797 to carry limestone and slate south, and coal north from the Wigan coalfields. The intention of the enabling statute had been 'to procure a line of inland navigation from Kendal to London,' with its southern end feeding into the Liverpool-Leeds canal; but the project ran out of money. The aqueduct over the River Lune at Lancaster had cost £48,000 and the Kendal link was not built for another twenty years. The southern end was completed by the cast-iron tramway.

The square piano travelled 235 miles from London to reach the musician who was waiting for it in Lancaster – Mr Langshaw. It was the beginning of a journey that would last more than two centuries.

———

Square pianos were *the* domestic instrument of the late eighteenth and early nineteenth centuries. They were in fact oblong rather than square, looked like a sideboard when closed, and were sometimes called box or table pianos. They were small and charming and although the earliest sounded as much like a harpsichord as a modern piano, they were something new: the sound they made depended on hammers striking strings rather than quills that plucked them as in the majority of keyboard instruments at the time. Unlike the harpsichord with its dynamically unchanging pluck, the square piano's striking action was capable of dynamic variety and greater expression. They started a fashion for pianos and a new industry grew from their early, phenomenal popularity. They had a light, bell-like tone and it was not until iron was introduced into the frame in the 1820s that they began to sound fuller, fruitier, more modern. They were unrivalled in their elegant proportions and reflected the highest quality furniture of the period. Hundreds have survived. The core of the classical piano repertoire, Mozart, Haydn and early Beethoven, was written for the early, wooden-framed fortepiano, and the music of the Classical and early Romantic composers played on a square piano evokes the sound of their era as no other keyboard instrument can, magically transporting the listener back in time.

Their mechanism is simple: when depressed, the key flings a key shank up to the string stretched horizontally above. In no other piano is the hand of the performer as directly in contact with the source of sound. The grand piano, based on the flugel shape of the harpsichord, followed in the early 1780s. The grand had an intermediate lever that enhanced the sound, but at the expense of the square's direct touch. Grands were bigger, louder, often opulently veneered or decorated. At first the new instrument was known by several names: fortepiano, forte piano, pianoforte, piano forte. In Europe all wooden-framed pianos, whether square or grand, were called fortepiano. In England and North America they were known as pianoforte, which, by 1800, had already been shortened to 'piano.' Nowadays the term fortepiano generally refers to any early piano with a wooden frame. The familiar upright piano was not manufactured until the 1820s, and it gradually replaced the square; in North America the square piano remained popular until the late nineteenth century.

For about sixty years from the time of its first appearance in London in 1768, the square piano dominated the piano market. People at many levels of society bought and played one. It was a link between the keyboard instruments of the eighteenth century and the modern piano, and bridged the time from when only the very wealthy could afford a keyboard instrument, to the mass production of the mid-nineteenth century.

In Britain in the late eighteenth century the piano carried the privileged music culture of the Royal Court out into the concert hall and the upper-class drawing-room and thence into the parlours of a newly industrialized society. At first it was an exclusive, musical diversion, but it rapidly acquired serious musical status and social significance, and as industry and commerce generated wealth in the most intense phase of the Industrial Revolution it became a commercial commodity. Perhaps nowhere can the relationship between new urban wealth and the commercialization of culture be seen more clearly than in the progress of the piano. In the last twenty-five years of the eighteenth century the courtly culture associated with the harpsichord was reinvented, and the piano in its many different forms became the sine qua non of sociocultural advancement for an emerging, many-stratified middle class, known at first as the 'middling sort.' In the process the piano, particularly the square piano, so charming and convenient in size, became a symbol of domestic harmony, and an ability to play one the defining attribute of a lady.

John Broadwood (1732–1812) was the first to make square pianos in serious commercial numbers, and he became the most successful piano maker in late Georgian London. He was a businessman of genius who recognized the all-important social distinctions of the day and made pianos in a range of styles and prices to suit them. His innovative marketing, pricing and production by division of labour increased sales and kept costs down. People at many levels of society bought his square pianos: lowly paid provincial organists as well as kings and queens, military men and fashionable women. The daughters of earls and farmers played them, as did teachers and clergymen, actors and industrialists and anyone with social aspirations. John Broadwood's square pianos graced palace and drawing-room, enlivened schoolroom and parlour and found their way eventually into terraced house and public house.

His father-in-law's fashionable harpsichord business provided the foundation for a piano enterprise that became, in Broadwood's lifetime, a global industry. For two hundred years John Broadwood & Sons was the premier British piano maker and a Broadwood piano was a potent symbol of the British way of life. During that time, wherever the British went – and they went almost everywhere – they took their pianos with them, carrying the voice and values of their culture to every known part of the globe.

The Broadwood Company's records for the entire period still exist. They reveal how at a very early stage Broadwoods were selling their pianos through a network of national and global distributors. At the end of the eighteenth century their name carried as potent a cachet in the drawing-rooms of America's Eastern Seaboard as in London. Two of the founding fathers had been harpsichord customers of Broadwood – Francis Hopkinson of Philadelphia and Charles Carroll of Maryland; and Thomas Jefferson visited Broadwood in London in 1786. John Jacob Astor was their first piano agent in America – an instrument from one of his shipments can be seen in the collection at Vassar College – and other agents followed in Charleston, Philadelphia, Boston and Virginia. By the early nineteenth century Broadwood pianos were distributed from the Far East to the West Indies.

The Broadwood Archive in Woking outside London is like an imaginary musical mansion, filled with many famous people, monarchs and statesmen, lords and ladies, prelates and princes. Everyone who was anyone bought a Broadwood piano. Other, lesser-known characters bought them too and, on better acquaintance, they were as interesting as their more famous contemporaries.

One of them was Mr Langshaw – an organist and music master

from Lancaster in the north of England struggling to make a living and educate his children in the early years of the Industrial Revolution. Mr John (Jack) Langshaw's life (1763–1832) was contemporaneous with the heyday of the small, square piano. His early musical apprenticeship was at the hands of his father, also named John (1725–98); Jack completed his training in London with the sons of the Reverend Charles Wesley, brother of John Wesley, the founder of Methodism. During three periods of study between 1778 and 1784 young Jack became a well-loved visitor to the Wesley household, where he met John Wesley and other leading Methodists. During his time with the Wesley family Jack also experienced the fashionable world of the Georgian subscription concert, and became acquainted with the new square pianos made by John Broadwood.

After London, Jack Langshaw returned to Lancaster, then one of the busiest ports in England, where he was appointed organist. Mr Langshaw, as he was then known, married, and his children followed in his musical footsteps. He spent the rest of his life in Lancaster, playing the organ, composing music and teaching. He also distributed Broadwood pianos at the rate of two or three a year for fifty years. Although he occasionally supplied a grand piano to one of his more illustrious pupils, most of his customers were less well off people who bought plain squares at the most inexpensive end of Broadwood's range. He brought music to a part of northern England where no one before him could even play Handel's keyboard lessons, let alone teach them. In doing so Mr Langshaw was instrumental in bringing about the social changes that accompanied the piano.

The business relationship between John Langshaw and John Broadwood was a microcosm of the process by which the piano culture helped to shape modern life; it was part of a much bigger picture, a frieze of far greater significance than any individual story. Their enterprise helped to make the square piano at once a commercial commodity and an instrument of socio-cultural democracy. A piano was and is a social instrument that draws many different people into its harmonious ambit. In an era when social change was often accompanied by violence, Mr Langshaw and many other forgotten organist music-masters – and a few music mistresses – who also distributed square pianos for Broadwood brought about the quiet revolution that is the story of the piano.

2

REVIVAL AND RESTORATION

MR LANGSHAW'S SQUARE piano had come my way almost 200 years after he had purchased it in 1807. At first I knew nothing about its past. But a clue inside it made me curious about its story. My search would show that history is not a regular progression of monarchs and statesmen, of wars and causes, riot and revolution. Initially, it seemed as if the people who had built and played my square piano were erratic travelling companions whose faces, once glimpsed, disappeared again into the over-populated ether of the past. Like fleeting images forming and re-forming in reflecting glass, they would fill a sudden moment then fade until they were no more than shadows behind a distant window.

But the square piano led me to many archives, and as its story unfolded a group of people past and present, some famous but many forgotten, began to appear more clearly, and before long a host of characters surged forward out of the past. It was as if they had been waiting in a long-lost music room while the main acts of history played. Now it was their turn to step into the light and I was their only audience. Without my square piano no one would ever find them again; the people who had built and played it would return to oblivion unless I recorded my search to find them.

I had first come across this square piano some years ago. It had been on a Sunday, one of those March days that belong more to winter than spring; an indoor day for a lazy read of the papers. My eyes surfed the pages, drifting over print while my mind wandered off. Suddenly, my mind came to heel as I registered the words 'Two Square Pianos' listed between a flight of chemist's drawers and a French commode in the announcement of a local sale of antiques the following Saturday.

Earlier that year my piano tuner, observing the early music scores stacked on top of my Welmar upright piano, had suggested looking for a second-hand harpsichord. During the search, which had so far been unsuccessful, square pianos had been mentioned, but only ever dismissively: they were either Victorian warhorses or wooden-framed instruments that had warped. 'Square pianos are a minefield,' one dealer had warned.

The day before the antiques sale I went to the preview. The auction rooms, in a nearby county town, were a collection of industrial units in a maze of back streets. A small lobby was littered with piles of magazines, boxes of books and odds and ends of china heaped in baskets. A woman handed me three sheets of paper with the lots listed on them and disappeared. There was no mention of square pianos, only 'An early nineteenth century Spinetti Piano,' Lot 408 and 'A piano,' Lot 409. In the auction room about a dozen people were picking over hundreds of items set out on tables: bundles of teaspoons, knives and forks, more magazines, stacks of long-playing records, embroidered tray cloths.

But where were the pianos? The woman eventually sent me along the street to another building where an ancient man sat directing people to their quarry. To avoid attracting attention I began to look without his help. The building was freezing, the atmosphere predatory. Pallid salesroom habitués sidled out of shadows and stalked the alleyways between stacks of furniture, heads turning anxiously. Eyes widened in the gloom. There was muttering and sniffing. The big cats had had the rich pickings;

these were the remains, the tag end of history. I had no clear idea what I was looking for. There was nothing remotely like a piano.

I sat on a stripped pine pew to collect myself. I glanced at a home-made chicken coop on my left, a long box on legs made of weathered wood with chicken wire stapled over the open top. The inside was littered with stained feathers and dried excrement. I stared at the white sticker. It was Lot 409, 'A Piano'– transformed into a chicken incubator by some creative eccentric who had rigged up a light where the piano's action had once been. I turned away in disgust. What a waste of time. In the past few weeks I had seen some of the finest harpsichords ever made, now here I was on a wild goose chase for an instrument I had hardly heard of, had never seriously thought of playing and could not recognize. I got up to leave.

On my way out I saw some turned legs lying on the floor beside a long, flat box propped up on end. There were six slender legs; I picked one up. It was tapered to an inch at one end and fitted with a brass castor; the other end, about three inches in diameter, had been turned to form the threads of a wooden screw. The legless box was wedged in between two wardrobes. Could this dusty coffin be a piano? It was about six feet long with what looked like a slit in the top and a hinged section of lid.

By crouching I managed to lift the lid up and out about four inches, enough to see a small keyboard inside, running half the length of the piano. I touched a key. It was loose and made no sound. I pushed the lid further back and touched another key higher up the keyboard. This time a muffled, sour little note came out. It was the oldest voice I had ever heard. I touched another key and heard it again. Time stopped.

Then I peered further in. This was no Spinetti piano. The name board behind the keys was in shadow and it was difficult to read what was written there. My eyes fastened on the copperplate script and I recognized the familiar shape of a name I had known since childhood: John Broadwood. There were other words and a date, either 1801 or 1807, I could not be sure.

I closed the lid. Broadwood! In my mind's eye I saw a van with a big black upright piano in the back pulled up outside my child-hood home – my father had gone to a house auction to buy a dining table – and I heard my mother's voice saying, 'We haven't even got lino on the floor and you buy a piano.'

The Broadwood upright stood on the boards of our front room until I was old enough to have lessons. Occasionally my father would play it. He couldn't read music and would move his hands over the keys finding chords of his own devising until, mysteri-ously, from the mesh of sounds a tune emerged.

'Let's have *The Student Prince*,' he would cry, modulating through the keys and fitting chords together until he found his favourite tunes. Sometimes we played a duet in which he vamped chords around a sequence of notes he had shown me on the upper keys. Papa Oom papaa, Papa Oom papaa, Papa Oompa, Oompa, Oom papaa. But he hadn't bought the piano for himself; he'd bought it for me. He wanted me to be a lady, and an ability to play the piano was, even in the mid-twentieth century, still one of the attributes of a lady; it still carried a whiff of high-class culture that went back to the eighteenth century. We did not know this; only that a Broadwood was, as my father said, 'the Rolls Royce of pianos.'

Lessons began on my eleventh birthday. The elderly Miss Lilian Niblet, pronounced Niblette, who lived round the corner, had studied 'under a Big Frenchman,' she told me. But by the time I became her pupil her fingers were stiff with arthritis. She gave me a nineteenth-century tuition manual and while she chain-smoked and rehearsed the litany of her teachers' teachers, tracing her musi-cal pedigree back to Chopin himself, I struggled through heroic five-finger exercises, endless scales and a frosting of Victorian par-lour pieces of which one was 'Love's Ritornella' and another, 'O Beauteous Isle of the Sea,' was a duet reserved for one of Miss Niblet's rare performances.

My father's efforts on the piano transported him out of the drab realities of post-war rationing into a world of student princes and

Bohemian romance, of Persian markets and monastery gardens. I trailed after him with Bach and Beethoven, Schubert and Chopin. The previous owner's prescription, 'What this piano wants is playing,' was fulfilled. The £50 Broadwood in the front room gave more pleasure and many more laughs than a dozen dining tables.

When I saw Lot 408 wedged in between two wardrobes in the saleroom and heard its muffled voice, the love kindled by my father's impulsive purchase so many years before flared up again. People who fall in love with old pianos see the shadows that linger round them; they hear music in the silence. With love comes a desire to rescue, to prop up shaking legs, to hear a tired voice sing again and, most of all, to possess. Falling in love with a piano is a *coup de foudre,* and like all great amours it changes our lives.

Next day at the sale Lot 408 was knocked down to me for £100. Two months earlier I had set out to find a second-hand harpsichord. I now owned a John Broadwood square piano instead, bought for less than the value of its brass castors.

The legs of the square piano buckled under its weight and two men were needed to carry it. When we got it home we covered it with a blanket and left it resting on an old computer table in the barn. The square piano was about six feet long, three feet wide and ten inches deep. A section of the lid folded back on seven small brass hinges to form a music rest and in the centre of the nameboard behind the keys there was a satinwood cartouche in which the piano maker's details were written in black ink in a mixture of Gothic and copperplate script:

John Broadwood and Son, Piano makers to His Majesty and the Princesses, Great Pulteney Street, Golden Square, London. 1807

It had a range or compass of five and a half octaves, from the third F below middle C to the third C above (FF – c"").There were sixty-eight keys, twenty fewer than a modern piano; the forty-eight ivory naturals were still white and there were twenty black sharps. The keys in the middle of the piano felt more worn than the rest. A few of the upper notes clunked with the same sour sound I had heard in the saleroom; most of them were unresponsive and silent, but they were all there.

I raised the lid, propped it open with the two struts at either end of the piano and lifted out a thin sheet of wood painted cream with a black border that rested over the piano's action. Underneath a tangle of broken strings there was a horizontal row of hammers covered in pale grey leather, each about the size of my thumbnail, held in position by a row of wooden shanks hinged with leather to a hammer rail. The edges of the hammers were dented where they had struck the strings many times. It looked as though this piano, now stiff with age, had once been played a lot.

It was dilapidated but there did not seem to be anything missing. The scarlet wool under the rusty hitch pins that secured one end of each string to the soundboard was faded and moth-eaten, but the case itself had not warped, probably because the strings had broken long ago and released the tension. The other ends of the broken strings were still wrapped round the small iron wrest pins fixed in pairs – there were two strings to each note – along the wrest plank at the back of the piano. By turning the wrest pins a string can be adjusted to the desired pitch. In a small compartment to the left of the keyboard I found a tuning lever made of boxwood; it was about the same size as an old-fashioned corkscrew. I placed it over a wrest pin. There was comfortable room to use it in the confined space of the angle formed between the raised lid and the back of the piano. A longer modern lever would have needed the lid to be pushed further back, putting strain on the small brass hinges. It was the correct tuning lever for this piano.

The compartment also contained a small metal instrument

about two inches long with a disc at one end on which the notes of the scale were etched. The disc felt as if it could be turned, but it too was stiff with age and I was afraid to force it. The words 'Eardley's Patent' were stamped on the side of the tube. I blew into the open end. There was no sound and I decided that Eardley's Patent was a string gauge. At the back of the compartment I found a 1937 copper penny, four brass screws, a cigar band and one jet bead.

Recalling the advice of Charles Dickens's Mr Dick about the thing to do with a waif and stray I washed the piano and, like poor David Copperfield, it began to look better. I polished it. The mahogany case was crossbanded with a double border of satin-wood outlined with ebony. The lid had been cut from a single plank of mahogany and the grain across the hinged sections was well matched. I swept out the dust and dirt from inside with a soft brush, and looked more closely.

There was writing by at least three different hands inside the piano. The most obvious was the writing on the wrest plank.

Square piano 10651 before restoration

Someone had written the name of every note in Indian ink next to the corresponding pair of wrest pins. The writing was in cursive copperplate letters more than a centimetre high. There had been no attempt to conceal them; they were meant to be seen. Why?

Keyboard instruments with wooden frames are affected by changes in temperature and humidity and need frequent tuning. Someone playing such an instrument would need to know how to tune it. Whether tuning with a modern digital tuner or by ear, finding the correct wrest pin for the tuning lever can be a problem; matching key, string and wrest pin for every note can double the tuning time. Some musicians put a felt collar on all the C wrest pins as a quick guide; others press a key and track the vibrating string. The writing on the wrest plank showed at a glance where to put the tuning lever for any note; it was also a stringing guide.

It would have been impossible to write on the wrest plank beneath taut strings; the note names must have been written there before the piano was strung. It is not unusual for early pianos to turn up for restoration with the notes so marked, and restorers suggest that it was done in the maker's workshop as a stringing and tuning guide. Nonetheless I wondered if a piano would have left Broadwood's marked in such a bold and apparently carefree fashion and whether the writing on this wrest plank was put there some time after the piano was sold, perhaps for a pupil by a teacher who was also a technician and knew how to re-string.

The cursive copperplate writer had also written a five-figure number at the right-hand end of the wrest plank. Only the last two digits, 5 and 1, were legible. The number was important: every piano, like every car engine, has a unique serial number that is the key to its history.

Another hand had drawn a diagonal line across the key shanks, numbered them just above the line and signed the fifty-eighth shank, the third D above middle C, with his name: Fraser.

Fraser the keymaker had secured the prepared piece of limewood to his bench. Although steam power had made rapid headway since the

1790s and woodworking machines had been patented ten years earlier, almost everyone at Broadwoods still worked with hand tools in 1807. The light, fine-grained wood had been shaped and smoothed; he had chiselled the arcaded front edges of the keys and marked them out on the block in parallel lines just over an inch apart. He smoothed his hand across the wood. Before he started to cut the keys he drew a diagonal line in pencil across the shanks and numbered every key in Indian ink just above the line as a guide for whoever assembled the piano or repaired it in future. Further back he scored another diagonal to mark where he would gimlet the holes for the iron rods that would push the hammers up to the strings when the key was pressed down.

Adjusting the middle bar of his frame saw to just over an inch from the blade to allow for the width of his cut, Fraser grasped the handle at the top of the blade with his right hand and the bar with his left and began to work up and down through the wood from front to back, following his line and keeping the bar at the edge of the block. He worked carefully. If the key shanks were not accurate they would make a noise when the piano was played and he could not afford mistakes. A set of keys for a square piano required eight feet of limewood at 6d a foot – the cost of a good dinner with bread, cheese and ale – and he was paid £1 a set. To finish he would cut a square hole in every shank for the key rod on which the key would pivot.

I looked at Fraser's small numerals and his discreet signature in the shadow of the soundboard. It was the writing of a careful, neat man.

As I replaced the dust cover over the strings, I noticed another number, 10651, written in a third hand on a strip of paper glued diagonally across the underside of the cover. These copperplate numerals were two centimetres high and the ink was unfaded, having always faced down inside the piano. It seemed reasonable to assume that the dust cover was numbered when it was allocated to its piano and I decided to work on 10651 as the piano's serial number.

My desire to hear and play square piano 10651 was becoming irre-sistible; finding someone who could restore it proved more complicated. There are still many square pianos around and most have had someone 'have a go' at them at some time. Original actions have been replaced by modern ones, cases have been painted, lacquered, converted into dressing tables and cutlery cab-inets; no indignity seems to have been omitted by well-intentioned handymen. 'Play?' asked a lady in an antique shop, as if that was the last thing to be done with her highly polished Georgian square. 'They can all tell a story,' one piano dealer remarked. In every piano workshop there were tales of men who could carry a grand piano upstairs unaided, about theatrical pianos, prison pianos, pianos that had never been played, pianos with the lid nailed down. 'Square pianos are a minefield' – I was beginning to see why.

There was a listing for Broadwood Pianos in the London tele-phone directory, and when I phoned a woman told me they had stopped making pianos in 2003, but still tuned and repaired them. She gave me the name of a Broadwood workshop in Birmingham: 'They're your nearest and they're great at repairs. That's your start-ing point.'

When I visited the Birmingham workshop, the august presence of three magnificent Broadwood grand pianos, and the slow, sure movements of the three craftsmen attending them, created a wel-come atmosphere of calm.

'Repairs we can do,' Alan, the workshop gaffer, told me.

'But I've never had a go at a square. Pianos,' he confided, 'have all gone to China now, but we've got some of the last Broadwoods made in England in our showroom. Go and try them.'

Afterwards he told me that twentieth-century instruments were his forte; historic instruments needed a specialist approach.

'You might be interested in one of these though' – and he gave me a programme for the pianist Melvyn Tan's 1992 concert tour with the grand piano that Broadwoods had presented to Beethoven in 1818.

The programme gave a brief history of the famous piano. In 1817 Thomas Broadwood, the second son of John Broadwood, had visited Beethoven in Vienna. He later described how ill the composer was: 'His table supported as many vials of medicine and golipots as it did sheets of music papers.' A year later he presented the composer with the six-octave grand piano. It had a case of Spanish mahogany inlaid with marquetry and ormolu, and its brass carrying handles were in the shape of laurel wreaths. The nameboard was inscribed with the words 'Hoc instrumentum est Thomae Broadwood londini donum propter ingenium illustrissimi Beethoven.' Beethoven wrote to Broadwood: 'As soon as I receive your excellent instrument I shall immediately send you the fruits of the first moments of inspiration I spend at it.'

The piano was shipped to Trieste, then taken 200 miles overland by bullock cart to Vienna, where the *Vienna Gazette of Arts* described it as 'perhaps the best [piano] ever constructed.' Beethoven referred to his Broadwood as 'a beautiful piano . . . sent to me as a present from London . . . It is a handsome present and has a fine tone.' That summer he composed the 'Hammerklavier' Sonata, Opus 106, of which he said, 'It will keep performers busy and challenged for fifty years,' and which is still, artistically and technically, one of the greatest tests of pianist and instrument.

Thomas had intended the piano as a mark of his esteem, but stories about the gift inevitably added lustre to the Broadwood reputation. Beethoven's increasing deafness made him hard on pianos, and seven years later Johann Andreas Stumpff, a London harp maker who had visited him in Vienna, wrote to the *Musical Times* describing the sad state of the Broadwood: 'What a spectacle offered itself to my view. There was no sound left in the treble and the broken strings were mixed up like a thornbush in a gale.'

After Beethoven's death a dealer sold the piano to Liszt, who bequeathed it to the National Museum of Hungary. It is now in the Beethoven House in Bonn.

At the back of the programme there was an account of the

restoration of the piano written by David Winston, the man who had done it. He was pictured in his workshop in Kent with the historic piano in pieces. Would he be prepared to look at piano 10651?

————

'Of course it's worth restoring,' he answered when I phoned. 'They make delightful instruments.' He would do it, he said, if no one else had had a go at it.

David Winston looks after some of the world's most celebrated historic pianos for museums and special collections, and I was surprised that he was prepared to visit me to look at an unknown square.

'They're serious instruments ... and you never know who might have owned it.'

Some venerable ancestors of the modern piano had passed through his hands, instruments by the great makers – Broadwood, Erard, Pleyel, Clementi, Longman and Broderip – and while he was in the barn inspecting 10651, I wondered whether this humble square was worthy to join so distinguished an ensemble or, more worryingly, if it had ever suffered any clumsy repairs.

Early square pianos made between their invention in the 1760s and the introduction of iron in the 1820s had wooden frames. The wooden construction was at once their charm and their weakness. It would not allow great string tension, about 80lb a string; a modern grand can have an overall tension weight of eight tons. But it was enough to make them warp and most of them, standing under tension, warped beyond repair – 'like bananas,' according to square piano expert Michael Cole. As pianos were used more and more in virtuoso concert performances and as the makers realized the piano's potential for playing arrangements of increasingly popular orchestral music, piano makers searched for ways to make an instrument with a louder, fuller tone. Bigger hammers were needed and strings had to be stronger to take the heavier blows. To keep the same pitch, strings had to be pulled tighter, causing ever-greater tension on the wooden frame. The early squares could not take it. With the introduction of iron supports in the frame and steel strings in the 1820s, their light, edgy sound changed to a fuller, louder, more recognizably modern one.

A very old piano is a historical document of musical sound and style. After years of neglect and more recently central heating, those that have survived need varying degrees of attention to restore their authentic voice. If a period piano is ignorantly repaired or over-zealously restored, what it can tell us about the music and culture of its age is lost.

A good restorer will have studied historic instruments and the music written for them and will have gleaned information from contemporary images and literature. He or she will understand the historical context and methods of construction of a piano's action and use authentic woods, veneers and inlays, metals and strings, ivory and ormolu, leathers and felts, and will have accumulated patterns and even spare parts from pianos that have passed through the workshop. For example, the open fretwork at either end of the keyboard on square pianos is fragile and often damaged; a replacement section should be made from a matching wood, usually fruitwood, following a historically correct pattern from the restorer's fretwork 'library.' Authentic glues to complement the ones already present should be used in such a way as to allow removal of the parts for future repairs. At least four different metals were used for strings – iron, brass, tin and copper – and different makers used different fixing methods: a string 'eye' for the hitch pin on a Clementi square piano, for example, is different from the small butterfly fitting on a Broadwood. It is better to support original parts to extend their life and function than replace them. Essential replacements should be with parts saved from other contemporary instruments that are beyond restoration or with carefully replicated parts in authentic materials. A restorer needs therefore to be aware of any contemporary technical information. Original replaced parts should be returned with the restored instrument and nothing should be irreversible.

Pianos are individuals with unique souls and just as a good pianist will find his or her way to each soul and play music that suits it, so a sensitive restorer will avoid imposing his or her will on an old piano, but let the piano itself guide the way back to its original voice. A good ear, keen eye and delicate hand are needed, as well as sensitivity to the character of each individual piano. Ideally a well-restored piano should look and sound, not necessarily as it did when new, but as if it were played in. If it has hardly been played, that is the condition to maintain. Signs of the restorer's intervention should be few.

After fifteen minutes David reappeared.

'It's never been touched.'

He told me that the number 10651 written on the underside of the piano's dust cover was likely to be the instrument's correct serial number. I asked if there was any way of finding out who had bought the piano in 1807.

'The number should tell you. You could easily find out from the Broadwood Archive in Surrey. They will look up serial numbers of old pianos.'

He offered to take the square piano with him and start preliminary work on the cracked soundboard. As we slid it into the back of his estate car he warned that restoration is unpredictable and he could not say when it would be ready.

'Depends on what I find in there. Possibly by Christmas.' He looked forward, he said, 'to getting this lovely piano working again.'

And then he drove away with 10651, a piano that now had a future as well as a past.

I wrote to the Surrey History Centre in Woking that holds the Broadwood Archive and asked for a search on piano 10651 made in 1807. The reply indicated it was not so simple: 'Unfortunately the surviving Number Books in the Broadwood Company records . . . cover only pianos produced after 1817. We do, however, hold the

Porters' Book for the date of your piano. The Porters' Books are a daily record of pianos coming into and going out of the Broadwood Factory and Workshops. They give the name and address of each customer. You are welcome to come and search through the Porters' Books yourself.'

The prospect was intriguing. The old piano was a miraculous survivor. It had escaped the teeth of time for two hundred years and kept its secrets safe among the worn hammers and broken strings. If I could find a match for the five numerals in the Broadwood Company records then I might be able to re-create the past and bring the story of the square piano into the here and now.

3

BROADWOOD PIANOS

THE SURVIVAL OF the Broadwood Company records, like so much else connected with pianos, has been a matter of chance. Some time in the middle of the twentieth century, probably during the Second World War, the Broadwood Company books containing two centuries of business, music and social history were taken from London to the family's country estate at Lyne in Surrey. They remained there until 1977, when they were given to the Surrey Record Office after the death of Captain Evelyn Broadwood. Lyne House had been empty for two years and was by then almost derelict. Staircases had collapsed and ceilings had fallen into rooms full of the detritus of generations, including a wrecked piano. Ledgers and papers strewn about the house and stables were water-stained, some had mould growing on them, spines and covers were missing, marbled end papers had faded and sewing had been bitten through. Pages were soiled at the edges or stuck together; some disintegrated at the touch. Repairs with sticky tape had dried out and left brown stains. The county archivist worked through the debris and photographed books and papers where they lay before taking them away. The earliest, most damaged ledgers were microfilmed, which was fortunate, for it would be twenty-nine years until conservation was complete and there could be full access to them.

The archive is vast and complex. Separating personal papers from the business records was difficult because many members of the Broadwood family had been involved over the centuries, as partners, trustees, employees and beneficiaries. The 175 ledger books recording the day-to-day business of John Broadwood and Sons from 1798 until 1977 contain details of the five main aspects of the company's business during that period: piano manufacture, sale and hire, tuning and repair. John Broadwood's Scottish thrift and the good management of his two sons James Shudi and Thomas set the tone of the business from the start. It is no exaggeration to say that for 200 years no scrap of paper was thrown away. Every purchase, from quills and quarts of ink to tons of Honduras mahogany, every sale, from spare strings to six-octave grand pianos and every other aspect of the company's activity, was recorded and bound in the great leather ledgers.

Sales ledgers before 1800 showed both wholesale and retail (or 'chance') trade – the latter being individual customers who bought from the 'Dining Room' in Great Pulteney Street or ordered by letter. Wholesale customers, usually music warehousemen or musicians, had separate sales ledgers after 1800, though several are now missing. There is one surviving book of business correspondence, the Letter Book (1801–1810), number books from 1817 to 1952, and porters' books (called day books after 1857) which run from 1798 to 1977. The porters' books were a daily record of every piano that passed through the porters' yard. The serial number of every piano is given, as well as the customer's name, a brief description of the instrument, the type of transaction and the transport arrangements. Pianos made after 1817 can be traced by finding the serial number in the relevant number book, then looking it up in the related porters' book.

The archive catalogue is on the internet; the contents are not. A piano made before 1817 and its original purchaser can only be found by searching through the porters' book for the relevant period of manufacture. Fortunately the porters' book for September 1806–April 1808 was available.

The porters' book for September 1806–April 1808, a heavy folio ledger measuring about 16" × 22", had been rebound in 1997. What remained of the old cover was inside and there were traces of a label on the front. The new covers were made of millboard and decorated with a double, blind-tooled border. The original spine had been constructed from leather and cloth strips and the folio pages sewn on to four vellum slips, which were split and laced into the hard vellum cover. There were several hundred foolscap pages and many thousands of transactions.

Each page had an inch-wide margin on the left ruled in red ink in which the customers' names were recorded. Next to the name running across the page were details of the transaction. A line was ruled under every entry and a thicker line under the end of each day's business. The next day continued on the next line of the same page. The entire ledger was written in the same small copperplate hand in Indian ink, which had faded to pale amber. The writing was tightly packed on to every page; not an inch of John Broadwood's foolscap paper was wasted. The porters' book was a model of meticulous book-keeping and a historic document of beauty.

The dispatch clerk had used abbreviations: 'Spf' for a square pianoforte and 'Gpf' for a grand; 'add' referred to a piano's additional keys, and 'Dp' referred to the foot-operated pedal that lifted the dampers off the strings. Every piano's serial number was entered and whether it was packed in a deal or a tin case; deal for delivery to the home market, deal and tin for shipment by sea. The delivery and collection arrangements were a study in early nineteenth-century transport. There were no railways in 1807; pianos went by road, canal or sea. Every ledger entry named a carrier, wharfinger, shipper, or ship and its captain. Shipping costs, duty and insurance were all noted and at the end of each entry there was a name, one of the same small group: William, Clarke, Larkin, Jefford and others. These were Broadwood's porters, the men responsible for taking the pianos from the company's premises in

Great Pulteney Street to the carriers' starting points, the coaching yards, wharfs and quays of Georgian London, and who also carried the pianos sold or hired out to and from the houses of London customers.

The piano serial numbers in the porters' book were not in sequence; pianos were not sold in strict numerical order, but picked from stock as required. A further complication was that pianos let out on hire appeared several times in the records before being sold off. One piano sold in 1807 had been made in 1798. If piano 10651 had been hired out its eventual sale and the name of the purchaser might not appear until several years after 1807.

The porters' book was as entertaining as a gossip column: on 22 June 1807, a grand pianoforte had been sent to Josiah Wedgwood at Etruria in Staffordshire. Who was Mrs Fearon, whose piano was delivered to her on 28 May at the 12th Light Dragoons stationed on Hounslow Heath? What story lay behind the entry for 3 July, 'removing Harp from Mrs Gordon's, 29 Garrard Street to Captain Rainstorm, Kew Green,' and who or what was Mrs Go to bed, 15 Norfolk Street Strand, who bought a Best square piano for thirty-two guineas? These were the daily minutiae of Broadwood's business with the great and the not-so-great of Georgian London.

A more methodical approach was needed to find piano 10651. The first entry for 1 January 1807 recorded a shipment of pianos to John and Michael Paff of New York: two grands and four squares, with serial numbers in the early ten thousands.

> . . . to go to Mr Farlow's, Hungerford Market to ship on 'The Enterprize' under Captain Jacob Packwood, for New York. £2 10 0 shipping expenses and lading bills. Insurance and Duty £14 8 0.

Patterns began to emerge from the entries. Ruffords generally carried pianos to the Midlands, starting from London's Bull and Mouth Inn. Farlow of Hungerford Market was the regular overseas shipping agent: pianos bound for New York, for example, were sent there for onward shipping, usually on *The Enterprize* under Captain Packwood. A Mr Hodges appeared frequently; the pianos he distributed to the West Country through his music warehouse in Bristol were picked up at The Swan at Holborn Bridge and carried by Lye's wagon. Mr Corri was an Edinburgh distributor. Pianos for his warehouse were sent first to Miller's Wharf on the Thames, then on the Fife packet under Captain James Cummings, who carried them up the East coast to Leith docks throughout the Napoleonic Wars. The ledger showed that by 1807, despite the predations of French privateers, Broadwood was selling pianos in many places overseas as well as throughout the British Isles.

In 1807 the square piano was their best-selling model; by the end of the year serial numbers had reached the twelve thousands. Square pianos were sold, 'taken out' on hire, 'received' from hire, carried across London from one customer to another, repaired and tuned and shipped all over the world.

British currency was then divided into pounds (£), shillings (s) and pence (d), with twelve pence to the shilling and twenty shillings to the pound. Pianos were usually referred to in guineas (a guinea was one pound and a shilling and had a superior cachet), and noted in guineas in the porters' books. In sales ledgers prices were expressed in '£ s d.' This was further complicated by additional sundries such as cases, covers and transport costs. There were plain squares at twenty-four guineas and best squares with decorative brass mouldings at thirty-two. Second-hand squares that had been out on hire, such as the one sold for eight guineas on 23 September, also passed through the porters' yard and were duly recorded. By 1807 most squares had additional keys and a damper pedal, and turned legs rather than the Sheraton-influenced straight, tapered ones of the late eighteenth century.

Square piano 10650 had been hired out to a Mr Young at 36 Suffolk Street, Hay Market, on 27 April. Two months later Number 10652, packed in a deal and tin case for Messrs Gow and Shepherd

– Music Warehouse Edinbro', was delivered to Miller's Wharf by the porter Lovell:

> ... and ... goes off ship – Fifeshire Packet. Captain James Cummings for Leith and paid Wharfage and Suffrance 3/6d.

Later that summer square piano 10650, the one hired to Mr Young in April, reappeared. It was brought back by Clarke and Lovell, the porters' book dispatch clerk noting as they carried it through the yard, 'Rec'd in a very bad case.' Every entry told a story. What was behind the double entry for 20 August, when piano Spf. 10625 was recorded as having been taken 'to the Marchioness of Salisbury Nr. Saxmundham, Suffolk,' as well as 'to Miller's Wharf for Mr Corri's Edinburgh warehouse'? Was this a mistake or a hanging matter best left undiscovered after 200 years?

By September 1807, square pianos in the 10670s and '80s were appearing in the porters' book. But where was square piano 10651?

⊶•⊷

Gradually some of the details in the porters' book became clearer. Beneath every customer's name in the left-hand margin was a small tick that was thicker and darker than the rest of the entry. The piano serial number in many entries was also darker. The ticks in the margin were roughly formed; the piano numbers were in the dispatch clerk's elegant hand. Most likely he had written his day's delivery schedule in advance, and as a piano was taken out through the yard in Great Pulteney Street, he inserted its number in the relevant ledger entry; then the porter who was to carry the piano signed for it with a tick and did the same when he brought one back in. While the men were out delivering, the dispatch clerk worked on the following day's schedule.

In addition to many private customers in 1807, Broadwood had a well-established distribution network for its pianos, both at home and abroad. The names of music warehousemen such as

Hodges of Bristol and Corri of Edinburgh, Thomas Beale of Manchester, Mr Rudge of Wolverhampton, Jacob Eckhardt of Charleston, Harmon of Philadelphia and Michael Paff of New York all occurred regularly. On the same ledger pages as these men of business were the names of musicians, organists and music teachers who were also buying and distributing pianos. For example, there were several references to Francis Sharpe, organist and music master of Knutsford in Cheshire, to Mr Collins, organist and organ builder of Liverpool, and to Mr Churchill, music master of Southernhay, near Exeter.

In an era of nicely observed social distinctions, high and low rubbed shoulders in the porters' book. The dispatch clerk's entries read like a *Who's Who* of late Georgian Society and reflect his view of the social standing of John Broadwood's customers. He always reserved his most rococo capitals for the names of the nobility and wrote their names in full; Lady Anstruther and Lady Lonsdale occupied a full line each. The name of Lady Williams Wynn was written in letters twice the size of plain Miss Morgan of Kensington Gore, while His Royal Highness the Prince of Wales had capital letters twice the size of any others. Though lesser mortals and provincials were entered more modestly, they still mingled with the mighty on the Broadwood ledger pages. People were buying pianos as a business, to supplement their living, for social and cultural status, for pleasure, and Broadwoods were delivering them to the mansion house of the earl and the terraced house of the organist, to the plantation houses of the colonies and the barracks of the military who defended them, to the manse of the clergyman and the townhouse of the cake baker. In 1807 people from many walks of life were buying Broadwood square pianos.

The porters' book was rather more than a Georgian *Who's Who*, however. Although many of the people whose names were recorded there may have had little to do with one another, they all had something in common: they were all playing music on much the same instrument. By 1807 Broadwood had made over 11,000 square pianos and almost 4,000 grands. A piano was a social instrument that drew many into its ambit. Seventy years earlier Daniel Defoe had identified seven social classes in England; in 1807 Broadwood's customers came from most of them. Music was no longer the preserve of the Court and the Church, of the great who lived profusely and the rich who lived plentifully; rather it was enjoyed by the middle sort who lived well, the working trades who laboured hard but felt no want, and farmers; even the poor who fared hard, such as country organists on 100 guineas a year, bought Broadwood square pianos.

It was also more than a business history; it was a catalogue of social change. In the early years of the nineteenth century the piano, particularly the square piano, played a socio-cultural as well as a musical role in Britain. A musical culture that until a few years before had been the preserve of the Court and the great was moving into many levels of society, and into the rest of the world, which was opening through trade and colonization. Unlike the changes forced on society in France by the instrument erected in the Place de la Concorde fifteen years earlier, those brought about by the piano in Britain came about less obtrusively, but were longer lasting and just as widespread; the piano re-channelled the social aspirations of a volatile society into a more harmonious activity. The evidence for this lies in the Broadwood porters' books, in the day-to-day entries of the copperplate dispatch clerk, which show that the hands and minds of many men and women from different levels of British society were joined in making music on the same instrument.

The identity of the man who had unwittingly recorded this quiet revolution was revealed in a ledger entry for 7 August 1807. On that day James Shudi Broadwood's coachman Richard drove up to town to collect a square piano to take back to his master's country house at Lyne in Surrey. No porter being needed to deliver this one, the dispatch clerk signed out Spf. No. 10710 himself. In his smallest copperplate he wrote his own name at the end of the entry, J. Thorpe.

Mr Thorpe and his team of porters lived and worked in the rapidly expanding infrastructure of late Georgian London. His ledger entries give details of the range of pianos and products his employer, John Broadwood and Son, was making in 1807, how they were sold, selected, packed, shipped and delivered. His record of the names of those who bought them, what they paid, where they lived and their station in life reveals something of Mr Thorpe's attitude to the social hierarchy of his day. His fastidious script shows the logistical economy of his piano delivery schedules and it immortalizes the porters who carried those pianos around London.

William was the only porter who could deliver a grand by himself; he appears most often and carried the biggest workload. Clarke and Lovell often delivered and collected together. Jefford and Robert tended to work solo and Larkin and Lovell seemed to be the juniors. There were also Chandler, Ross, Cranfield and Coomes. With countless others they served the demands of a voracious capital city in the early years of the Industrial Age at the beginning of the nineteenth century. They lived and worked and died anonymously and were forgotten until one of their pianos re-emerged after 200 years to testify to their day-to-day existence.

Monday, 27 July 1807 was a typical working day for them. There were fifteen ledger entries relating to fourteen pianos – ten squares and four grands. Mr Thorpe had organized his team as follows: at the start of the day William set off alone for Paddington with two new square pianos to be sent north; Clarke went to Summer's Quay on the Thames with a superior square, packed in a deal and a tin case. It was on the order of Mr Dominicus of India House, for shipment to Captain Eyles of Bombay. On his way back he met William, who had collected a square from Mrs Wharton's at 1 Great Cumberland Street on his return journey from Paddington. Together they collected another square from Mr Rutlidge at 16 Bulstrode Street, then loaded a grand from Lady Camden's in fashionable Arlington Street and another grand from Lady Viner's house at 30 Dover Street. All four pianos had been out on hire and

*Dispatch record of square piano 10651 to Mr John Langshaw,
27 July 1807, Broadwood Porters' Book, 1806–1808. Reproduced
by permission of Surrey History Service.*

the two porters brought them 'home' to Great Pulteney Street.
Then, while young Lovell went to deliver some sheet music to
Mr Tingcombe from Plymouth, who was staying at The Golden
Cross at Charing Cross, William went out again to deliver another
new square to Southampton Row. There, at The Bedford Hotel, he

met Lovell and they unloaded a square piano for Mr Gilbert Briggs. Meanwhile, Robert delivered three more new squares; he took two to The Bell in Friday Street to go by Russell's wagon to Exeter for Mr Churchill, the music master at Southernhay, and the third to The George Inn at Smithfield, to go by Jolly's wagon to Mr James Crosbee of Birmingham. Jefford's task, which took all day, was the removal of Lady Lonsdale's square piano from her house in Somerset Street to Broome House in Fulham. Chandler's only outside job that Monday was to deliver a packing case for a square piano to Lady Anstruther in Albermarle Street.

Some entries gave prices in the left-hand margin. Mr Churchill's standard squares with additional keys, six legs and a damper pedal were twenty-four guineas each. The superior square for Captain Eyles in Bombay was thirty-six guineas; it had six reeded legs, brass inlay and decorative brass mouldings. Captain Eyles was Commissary of Stores in Bombay; whatever became of him and his elegant square piano?

The two new squares William had taken to Paddington that morning were standard squares at twenty-four guineas each. One was for Mr J. Collins, organ builder of Liverpool. The other was piano 10651. Mr Thorpe's ledger entry read:

Langshaw   A SPF add 6 legs D.P. N10651 & case, addressed
~ 24 ~   Mr J Langshaw, Organist, Lancaster – delivered at
           Pickford & Co. Warehouse, Paddington, and goes by
           their boat.

                                                 William

4

THE TWO ORGANISTS

LANGSHAW, JOHN, was employed about 1761, under the direction of John Christopher Smith, in setting music upon the barrels of an organ, of much larger size than had been theretofore used for barrels, then being constructed for the Earl of Bute ... In 1772 he became organist of the parish church of Lancaster, and died in 1798.

His son John was born in London in 1763, in 1779 he became a pupil of Charles and Samuel Wesley 'from whom he received great kindness', and in 1798 succeeded his father as organist at Lancaster. He composed many hymns, chants, organ voluntaries, pianoforte concertos, songs and duets, and made numerous arrangements for the pianoforte.

George Grove (ed.), *A Dictionary of Music and Musicians*, 1936

John Langshaw junior, the second Langshaw organist at the parish church of Lancaster, bought square piano 10651 in 1807, two years after the Battle of Trafalgar. The battle and the name of Nelson entered the world's consciousness and remained there; such men and events are the great bones of history. Apart from the brief entry in an early edition of Grove's *Dictionary of Music and Musicians*,

John Langshaw's name appears in no history book. But details such as those from the porters' book about Mr Langshaw's piano, how much he paid for it, how it was transported to Lancaster, are like the metatarsals of history: find them, fit them together and history lives.

How could the story of an obscure organist and his piano in late eighteenth-century Lancaster be found?

'John Langshaw? He's here in our churchyard; him and his father,' the churchwarden of Lancaster's priory church replied to a phone call, speaking as if the two organists were alive and well in Lancaster. Why not pay them a visit?

The view from the top of Lancaster's Castle Hill is worth the hard climb up the narrow path through Vicarage Fields. It is easy to see why Agricola had built a garrison hill fort here at the bridgehead over the River Lune in AD 70. England stretches away to the south and there is a commanding view of the road from the north taken over many centuries by invading Scots, until the last Jacobite rebellion under Bonnie Prince Charlie was crushed by the Duke of Cumberland in 1745. Draconian punishment for dissidents and wrongdoers guaranteed the more stable political climate that followed and Lancaster, like many other English towns, experienced unprecedented economic expansion in the second half of the eighteenth century.

It became a prosperous town of merchants and sea-faring men with trading interests, great and small, in the New World. Since the end of the seventeenth century, a small group of Quakers in the town that included John Lawson, a sugar-baker, and William Stout, an ironmonger and merchant, had traded with the West Indies and Virginia. Ships that sailed with everyday items such as clay pipes, candles and shoes brought back molasses, tobacco, fustic and mahogany. Young Lancastrian men were sent as factors to represent the interests of the merchant families. Mr Langshaw's brother Benjamin, also a musician, went to the island of

St Thomas; John Lowther had mercantile interests in St Kitts, as did Thomas Worswick, who had a furniture-making enterprise there with Moses Altman. Abraham Rawlinson made a fortune out of the sale of candles, mainly to Barbados, and became a Member of Parliament. Perhaps best-known was the cabinet-maker Robert Gillow, who made fashionable furniture from imported West Indian mahogany and shipped a good deal of it back to the New World. The organ in St John's, Lancaster's merchants' church, that is still played today, was built in 1785 by the two Langshaw organists from what is thought to have been some of the first mahogany shipped into Lancaster.

The Georgian warehouses on the quayside of the River Lune below Castle Hill are testament to the spirit of enterprise in the two organists' day that took men out in their small ships upon the treacherous waters of Morecambe Bay and the Lune Deep, when around fifty ships a year sailed out to trade with the New World.

On top of the hill, next to the Castle, is Lancaster's historic parish church, the Priory Church of St Mary. The old gravestones in its churchyard have been tiered up into ten parallel pavements across the western slope. Some of the inscriptions have weathered away but most are still legible. They commemorate members of the priory congregation from the two organists' day, people Mr Langshaw and his father would have known: James Booth, Collector of Customs at Lancaster's port; James Fisher, shipwright; William Ashburner, sailmaker. There are many women who had died young, such as Isabel, wife of Captain John Read, and even more children who had not survived infancy: Nathaniel Calvert, three months old in 1789; Isabella Threlfall, seventeen weeks in 1808; and young William, infant son of the solicitor Thomas Thompson and his wife, Mary.

Three stones in on the second pavement from the top is a single slab of moorland stone. It is deeply incised and bears the Langshaw name.

John Langshaw Organist died 1798 aged 73
George his son died 1782 aged 18
James his son died 1784 aged 10
Joseph his son died 1785 aged 10
Mary his wife died 1800 aged 67
Sarah Langshaw his grandaughter died 1816 aged 12
Jane her sister died 1817 aged 7
Frances her sister died 1824 aged 12
John Langshaw, Organist, son of the above
John Langshaw, who died Dec. 12th 1832
Aged 69 Years and 9 Months
Sarah Langshaw, who died Jan. 26th 1865
Aged 90 years and 7 months.

In the two organists' day St Mary's church looked much as it does now, having been rebuilt in the sixteenth century after the Dissolution, and the tower replaced early in the eighteenth. The interior would have been lighter then, without stained-glass windows, and there were box pews. The Gothic choir stalls, the organ and pulpit have been moved several times since, depending on the emphasis given to music and preaching. The present organ is a replacement for one built at the start of the twentieth century. The bells of the priory still gladden the listener's heart as they did in the two organists' day; the present organist hurries home to tea down the same church steps, and eerie shadows still haunt the alleyways around Lancaster's old town hall next to the public library.

———

The Langshaw file in Lancaster City Library is a slim folder containing five items. A family pedigree written out by a Colonel Chippindall in the early years of the twentieth century contains very little relating to the two organists. There is a handbill announcing the sale in 1795 of old John Langshaw's book collection, and a copy of a ballad for pianoforte or harpsichord accompaniment composed in 1802 by John Langshaw. The words are by the poet Robert Bloomfield.

> Dear Boy throw that Icicle down,
> And sweep this deep snow from the door,
> Old Winter comes on with a frown,
> A terrible frown for the poor.
> In a season so rude and forlorn,
> How can age, how can Infancy bear,
> The silent neglect and the scorn
> Of those who have plenty to spare.

According to Chippindall's pedigree, the Langshaw family had originated in Wigan, near Manchester, in the seventeenth century, and local records and the inscription in the churchyard confirm his dates. In the world of the archives everything is topsy-turvy, telescoped into unreal time, and disconcerting to an uninvited

St. George's Quay, Lancaster, showing Gillow's Custom House and the Tonnage Warehouse, and St Mary's Priory Church on the far left, 2007. Author's photograph.

observer. Records turn up information in any order; a tragic death can appear before the victim's birth, children become orphaned before the announcement of their parents' marriage.

A sketch in a local history book by an Emily Langshaw (1814–94), who was married to the second organist's youngest son Pearson, leads to the Austin-Paley Archive in Lancaster's Maritime Museum. Among dozens of plans of Arts and Crafts churches from the nineteenth-century architectural practice founded by Emily's brother, there is an uncatalogued cache of material that had belonged to the women in the family. It contains a folder of Emily's botanical studies, four of her sketchbooks and many loose drawings and water colours. The record she left of her long life includes a drawing of Bath from her schoolroom window, and intense botanical studies from teenage years that contrast with gentler scenes made in later life. She was an observant and gifted woman. Her views of Lancaster are an interesting record of how the town developed; the notes she left on colour mixing and technique – 'look through half-closed eyes' – are still relevant. The sketchbooks and letters record her joy at her infant son's first steps, her grief at his death twenty years later. Emily's daughter Fanny had kept a scrapbook of newspaper cuttings and old photographs that was continued by her granddaughters until the 1960s. It contains references to Fanny's grandfather, Mr Langshaw, and even to old John Langshaw, the first organist, in the eighteenth century.

Mixed up with the Austin-Paley architectural plans are loose drawings by other artists. One is a half portrait pencil sketch of Miss Bessy Langshaw, the second organist's first daughter, aged twenty. The artist, the son of a local professional artist, James Lonsdale, had signed the portrait 'R. Lonsdale, aged thirteen, fecit, 1820.' An attractive young woman with a determined profile gazes out to the left of the paper. She wears a high-waisted dress with a dark satin collar and a muslin frill at her throat. Her abundant dark hair is arranged on top of her head. A note in Chippindall's

Mr Langshaw, c. 1820; drawing by R. Lonsdale. Reproduced by permission of Lancaster Museum Service.

pedigree says that she became the wife of the vicar of Halton, a village near Lancaster.

A few church plans later there is another drawing by Master Lonsdale, also dated 1820. This one is of the young woman's father: 'Mr. Langshaw.' It shows a man in middle age wearing a dark, high-collared coat, his arms folded awkwardly in front, his shoulders slightly hunched, his hair short and brushed forward carelessly.

Mr Langshaw has an air of impatience. His tightly closed lips, upturned eyes and his back hardly touching the chair all indicate a busy man with more pressing things to do. Yet he has made time to sit for an aspiring young artist, despite his organist's duties, his teaching and performing commitments.

This unexpected encounter with the man who bought square piano 10651 in 1807 is a shock; the incised slab of moorland stone on Castle Hill is not Mr Langshaw's only memorial, clearly there is much more to him than had first appeared.

———

A phone call from Mr Langshaw's great-great-great-grandson Tim Austin, who has learned from Lancaster Library of a stranger's interest in his ancestor, brings the offer of old family photographs and letters, and Bible entries going back to the two organists' day. These lead, via the Broadwood Archive in the south of England, to libraries and collections in the north, to the British Library in London and the Bodleian Library in Oxford, where the three oldest Broadwood books reveal surprising information about John Broadwood's early piano-making enterprise and the Langshaw's part in it. The story of Mr Langshaw's youthful days in London with the Wesley family emerges from the John Rylands Library in Manchester, from the Reverend Charles Wesley's notebooks in the Royal Academy of Music in London and finally from the Wesley-Langshaw letters at Emory University in Atlanta.

These different sources eventually reveal a story that goes back to the middle of the eighteenth century, to old John Langshaw, the first organist, and John Broadwood, the piano maker – two men of ideas and action who personify the inseparable enterprise and inventiveness that characterize the spirit of the second half of the eighteenth century. Both had used their talents and skills in an age when the doors to advancement were opening to men of merit. Music had offered them their opportunity, and they had both traveled south to London to make the most of it.

5

KEYBOARD MAKERS

WITHIN A FEW years of the Jacobite uprising of 1745, John Langshaw, the first organist, set out for London from the Lancashire town of Wigan. He was part of the vast immigration to the capital from provincial England in the middle of the eighteenth century that made London the fastest-growing city in Europe. Like many thousands of others he was going there to make a better future for himself. Although he was only in his early twenties he walked with some difficulty. John Langshaw was lame, but there was not a man in the district of Scoles where he was born or indeed in the whole of Wigan with hands as clever and as capable as his.

Those hands would record in the family Bible that he had been born in Wigan, a town of skilled metal workers, on 11 July 1725, to a family of pewterers who had been there since the sixteenth century. He should have followed his father (after whom he, the eldest of nine children, was named), ready to support his mother, Ann, and the little ones if necessary. But he did not. Making pewter was a hazardous occupation. Lead and tin were smelted into a new compound from which utensils of all kinds were made in the days before modern materials, including china, were readily available. Pewterers were craftsmen; they also engaged in more dangerous activities, like roofing. Wigan records speak of a Langshaw in the previous century 'laying lead on the Chancel roof,' and in 1732 John's father had bushed the rollers of eight new bells for the parish church of All Saints. The cause of John Langshaw's accident is not known, but his lameness affected the course of his life and all his descendants. In old age he would write that he had always received good for ill, but when he looked to the first cause he could never feel truly thankful.

He learned the art of music and on 2 October 1742, when he was seventeen, he petitioned a court leet in Wigan where there was a vacancy for a wait, or municipal watchman.

> The Humble Petition of John Langshaw, son of John Langshaw, of Wigan ... Pewterer, Sheweth, – that your Petitioner, being the son of a freeman of this Corporation, and having the misfortune to become lame, he has with great pains and Industry learned to get an honest Livelyhood, and to prevent himself from being troublesome to your Corporation.

His petition was allowed and the pewterer's son joined the Wigan Waits, a wind band that attended the night watches, raised alarums and performed on civic occasions. Their music was rough and rousing, far removed from the elegant English baroque then the fashion in the capital 200 miles to the south, but for many it was the only music they heard, apart from at church. Wigan Waits were appointed annually and the following year John Langshaw successfully petitioned again, adding that he had:

> ... learned to play upon the violin and that last year he had the honour to go through Your Corporation in the night time as one of the Waits thereof and has given great satisfaction not only as one of the Waits but also in having a diligent watchful eye upon all strolling idle persons that opportunism gives in the night of committing any robberies or mischievous acts and constantly will use his utmost endeavours for the detecting of all such villainy and preventing of any such crimes in your Corporation.

He did not apply again in 1744. He was a gifted natural musician with a good ear and his ancestors' manual skills, and as well as playing the rustic instruments of the Waits band he had also learned to play the church organ.

At first he may have done no more than pump the bellows while others played. He learned the carefully guarded secrets of the organ loft, possibly on the All Saints' organ, a simple finger instrument built in 1708. In the days before electricity it took three to tune an organ and a clever musical youth would soon have graduated to playing the notes while someone else worked the bellows and the organist tuned the pipes.

His hands always obeyed him and he became an accomplished keyboard musician, as adept at playing and maintaining the harpsichord as the organ. With his reputation as an ingenious mechanic and his natural musical ability he must have had high hopes as he set forth on what was described by another eighteenth-century traveller, Arthur Young, as the 'infernal road,' south of Wigan. He probably travelled on horseback as there was no regular stage from Lancashire to London before 1760.

London absorbed him. For some years he laboured in obscurity, honing his technical skills, and by 1754 he had added composition to his musical credentials. Two of his pieces, 'A Hymn for Christmas Day' and 'Say Mighty Love, An Epithalamium [Wedding] Ballad,' appeared in *Apollo's Cabinet: or The Muses Delight*, a collection of music by nine English composers published between 1754 and 1756 by John Sadler of Liverpool. It was a prestigious publication with a two-colour title page; it included seven pieces by Handel and another contributor was the blind composer John Stanley. John Langshaw met the leading organ builder of the day, John Snetzler, and made friends that he would never have had as a pewterer in Wigan. By this time he was thirty and part of a close-knit circle of London musicians, organists and inventors, with Handel at its centre. Handel's influence radiated out through friends such as Stanley and his pupil the librettist John Christopher

Smith – whose father, Johann Christoph Schmidt, had been Handel's secretary and factotum for many years. Smith and Stanley continued Handel's oratorio series at Covent Garden after his death in 1759.

John Langshaw's abilities began to be noticed in high places. At the end of the decade his fortunes took a dramatic turn for the better when John Smith was commissioned by the Earl of Bute to build a self-playing organ (see Chapter 6). Bute was the favourite of the young King George III and exercised a powerful influence over him. The organ was to be the largest of its kind ever made and pinning the barrels that would make it play was a skill that required the highest musicianship and technical dexterity. John Langshaw was the best man for the job and it kept him employed for a remarkable twelve years. The resulting instrument was a triumph of mechanical inventiveness that became a musical *succès d'estime*.

In 1762, with the prospect of continuing work for a patron who was the second most powerful man in the land, John Langshaw married twenty-nine-year-old Mary Haydock, from the parish of Hawridge in Buckinghamshire, not far from Luton Park. Her parents, George and Mary, were north-country folk who had also moved south. For the next eight years he, Mary, and a growing number of children lived in lodgings in Soho while he worked on the earl's machine organ. At the same time, a short distance away in the workshops around Great Pulteney Street and Hanover Square, the first English pianos were being made.

———

Agreeable as the prospect of marriage to Mary Haydock was, John Langshaw's mind must often have been on other things as he worked out how to pin the barrels of the earl's machine organ to make it play for long enough and sound as if an organist were sitting at the keyboard playing it. Living and working in the vicinity it would be surprising if he had not often made his way along Bridle Lane into Great Pulteney Street. With his head full of music and mechanics, he may not have noticed on one such occasion a man only a few years younger than he was, standing just inside the archway leading to the workshop of Burkat Shudi (1702–73), the king's harpsichord maker.

That man was John Broadwood. His journey had started at the Scottish village of Oldhamstocks, thirty miles south of Edinburgh. John Broadwood's father, a carpenter who had given him a decent education and an apprenticeship, now had younger sons to think about and John came to London from Scotland in 1761, having first secured a letter of introduction to Shudi from the local laird. He carried little with him apart from the letter, a desire to use his cabinet-maker's skills in a new way and his ambition. He was twenty-nine, a strong, fresh-faced man, fair, with small, deep-set eyes. Waiting at the porters' lodge to the premises he would one day own, he saw people of every kind and degree pass by and he watched them with that patient observation of the world without which he would never achieve the success in business that was his destiny.

Over all the noise of the streets of Soho his keen ear picked up gutteral accents not unlike his own coming from the workshop across the yard. In Shudi's household German was spoken – the old master himself had been an immigrant from Schwanden in German-speaking Switzerland forty years earlier, and recently he had employed refugees from the Seven Years War in Europe. Hostilities between Prussia and Saxony had prompted a number of musical-instrument makers, sometimes known as the Twelve Apostles, to leave for London. The capital's social and cultural expansion, the work opportunities and commercial possibilities attracted refugees, particularly those with skills to make the artifacts that both old and new money wanted.

One of these men, Johann Zumpe, was about to leave Shudi to set up on his own account and there was a vacancy. John Broadwood, already a skilled cabinet-maker, joined Shudi's workshop as the master's journeyman, or senior craftsman. While he would have smelled the familiar scents of a woodworking shop – the shavings and sawdust, the warm animal glue – the sights that met his eyes would have been less familiar: planks of a pinkish wood he knew to be mahogany, costly veneers, rare satinwood, elaborate open fretworks, key-cutting saws with adjustable frames, and the fine, small tools of the harpsichord maker. There too he would have seen rails and jacks waiting to go into unfinished harpsichords, whose birdlike shape he remembered from the laird's drawing-room.

Burkat Shudi was one of London's two leading harpsichord makers. As a young man in London in the 1720s he and his rival, Jacob Kirkman, had been apprenticed to Hermann Tabel, another Swiss, who had learned his craft in Antwerp with Ruckers. For two centuries the Ruckers family were Europe's master harpsichord builders. 'A Ruckers harpsichord ranked as a Cremona violin by Stradivari,' Shudi's grandson, James Shudi Broadwood, would one day write, tracing his firm's connections back to the finest keyboard maker in Europe. Shudi had married Catherine Wild, the daughter of a Swiss timber merchant, in London and started his own harpsichord business in 1728.

Johann Christoph Schmidt, Handel's manager, had lived in the same street as Shudi in Soho, and Broadwood tradition has it that both he and Handel were Shudi's friends and frequent guests. In 1729 Handel presented a Shudi harpsichord to the soprano Anna Strada del Po after a successful season at the King's Theatre. It made Shudi's name and gave him the entrée to court circles that all musicians and musical-instrument makers then needed. Secular music-making in the early eighteenth century was largely confined to the Court and nobility. The harpsichord maker waxed prosperous. After making a harpsichord for Frederick, Prince of Wales, in 1740 Shudi received the royal warrant and began trading under the Plume of Feathers. The construction of the instrument, still in

Kew Palace, and another from 1742 at Chirk Castle show the Tabel-Ruckers influence. Such instruments laid the foundation of a successful keyboard business that would last for more than 250 years. More immediately they prompted a move to larger premises. A notice in London's *Daily Advertiser* for 5 October 1742 announces: 'Burkat Shudi, harpsichord maker to the Prince of Wales, has moved from Meard's Street in Dean Street, Soho, to Great Pulteney Street, Golden Square.' Three years later he commissioned one of the then fashionable conversation pieces and hung it in his new showroom, the 'Dining Room.'

The painting by the German Marcus Tuscher is now in the National Portrait Gallery. Its brilliantly coloured, dramatically arranged draperies leave no doubt about Shudi's success. Pride of place is given to one of his harpsichords, possibly the one he made for Frederick the Great of Prussia the same year. Background pictures of the Prussian king and Frederick, Prince of Wales, lend royal endorsement to the magnificent instrument at which the harpsichord maker sits, tuning fork in sensitive hand. The case of polished mahogany rests on a lavishly gilded trestle, supported by three griffins. The prosperous craftsman and his family are richly

Burkat Shudi and his Family, 1745, oil painting by Marcus Tuscher.
© *National Portrait Gallery, London.*

dressed in silks of gold and blue. His comely wife holds what is thought to be her father's will, which left the family comfortably off. Shudi wears pink silk slippers. He and his wife and their two well-behaved, clean children and the cat are all recorded in an informal atmosphere that is thoroughly English. They may have originated in Switzerland, but they are depicted as English gentlefolk. It is a scene of earthly harmony reflecting the harmony of Heaven, symbolized by the harpsichord. The tone it set continued to define Shudi's business long after his death. Long after the firm he had founded no longer made harpsichords the picture remained in the 'Dining Room,' and everything it represented was transferred to the pianos made by his descendants.

For ten years after Shudi took John Broadwood on as his journeyman in 1761, the two men worked on some of the finest English harpsichords ever made. A Shudi harpsichord was a luxury. The intricate musical parts and costly wooden case were made by craftsmen; it was not an instrument capable of being mass produced. His clients were among the most notable figures in Georgian society and his harpsichords were part of an exclusive, elite culture. When other makers he had trained started their own businesses they invoked his name. When the boy Mozart performed in Ranelagh Gardens in Chelsea in 1765 he played a Shudi harpsichord, and Frederick the Great ordered three more for Potsdam.

In 1769 the journeyman married his master's twenty-year-old daughter Barbara, and two years later he became a partner in the business. Shudi and Broadwood made between twelve and fifteen harpsichords a year and they were very different instruments from their Ruckers antecedents. The basic structure of the case and the underlying principle were the same: a jack plucked a string. But with their rich cases, multiple sets of strings, stops, couplers, and Venetian swell, these late Shudi-Broadwood harpsichords had a grandeur in keeping with the social standing of their wealthy clientele and a sophisticated mechanism that reflected changing tastes in music and brought the harpsichord as close as it ever came to doing something it could never do: play piano e forte, soft and loud. The Venetian swell patented by Shudi in 1769, for example, was a series of wooden louvres inside the lid that could be opened and closed to give an effect of overall loudness and softness, with sudden rushes from one to the other in the fashionable galant style.

During the partnership years John Broadwood kept in touch with what other instrument makers were doing in the workshops around Great Pulteney Street, most particularly with Johann Zumpe, the German craftsman he had replaced in Shudi's workshop.

This diagram gives an outline of the piano's development during the eighteenth century until its first appearance in London in the 1760s:

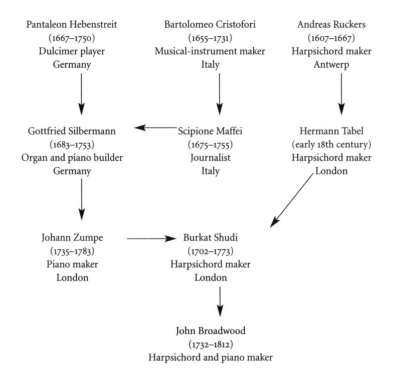

Pantaleon Hebenstreit	Bartolomeo Cristofori	Andreas Ruckers
(1667–1750)	(1655–1731)	(1607–1667)
Dulcimer player	Musical-instrument maker	Harpsichord maker
Germany	Italy	Antwerp

Gottfried Silbermann	← Scipione Maffei	Hermann Tabel
(1683–1753)	(1675–1755)	(early 18th century)
Organ and piano builder	Journalist	Harpsichord maker
Germany	Italy	London

Johann Zumpe	→ Burkat Shudi	
(1735–1783)	(1702–1773)	
Piano maker	Harpsichord maker	
London	London	

John Broadwood
(1732–1812)
Harpsichord and piano maker

When Johann Zumpe had left Shudi he had carried to his new premises in Hanover Square a keyboard-making tradition from the Continent that went back to the beginning of the eighteenth century and the charismatic figure of a dulcimer player by the name of Pantaleon Hebenstreit.

Hebenstreit's dulcimer was a monster. Descriptions vary, but it is thought to have been about nine feet long with 186 gut and metal strings. Holding double-headed mallets of wood and cloth he leapt around his instrument (he had been a dancing master), striking the strings loud and soft at will and damping them by hand, rather as players of the Hungarian cymbalum still do. The strings vibrated freely in a wall of sound that captivated all who heard it. He was taken up by the French court, where pastoral themes were in vogue. The dulcimer, with its folksy connotations, could not fail and King Louis XIV was so entranced he renamed the instrument the pantaleon.

Throughout the eighteenth century French language and culture were de rigueur in many European courts, nowhere more than in the conglomeration of German kingdoms and principalities. The King of Saxony, Augustus the Strong, lured Hebenstreit and his pantaleon to the hedonistic Dresden court by appointing him Royal Pantaleonist on the same salary as the king's kappellmeister, an income and a position that always eluded the local man, the cantor at St Thomas's School in Leipzig, Johann Sebastian Bach.

The zeitgeist took wings across the Alps to Italy where, around the year 1700, Bartolomeo Cristofori, keeper of musical instruments at the court of Prince Ferdinand de Medici, invented a new instrument played by striking rather than plucking strings stretched over a soundboard. Cristofori's instrument had a keyboard that controlled a row of leather-tipped hammers. He gave each note two strings and strengthened the case to take the increased tension. When a key was pressed an intermediate lever launched the hammer towards the string then dropped away, leaving the hammer free to strike and fall back. The string sounded until the key returned to rest and lowered a damper. By exerting different pressure on the key a performer could vary the velocity of a hammer's flight to the string and so control the quality of each note. Cristofori's concept of the free-flying hammer and the intermediate lever or escapement was one that piano makers would refine and reinterpret for the next 300 years.

In his endeavour to make a keyboard instrument with a range of dynamic shading that could 'sing' like the human voice or stringed instruments played by bow – this was the golden period of Stradivarius – Cristofori had made the first fortepiano, a term that came to be used to describe a wooden keyboard instrument with leather-covered hammers.

He called it a harpsichord of new invention that plays loud and soft – *Un Arpicembalo . . . di nuova inventione, che fa' il piano, e il forte a due registri principali* – with two sets of strings. He made several more, three of which survive: one in New York, one in Rome and one in Leipzig, all still playable. They were the same shape as the harpsichord but they did not have the same brittle, plucked sound; they did not sound like a modern piano either, but a mixture of the two. In 1722 he introduced an una corda lever that could reduce the sound by directing the hammers at only one set of strings. Cristofori may have thought of his new instrument as a new kind of harpsichord, but unlike the harpsichord where the plectrum always plucks with a fixed force, his was capable of dynamic expression. It did not catch on in Italy, where music continued to be dominated by opera and the expressive stringed instruments made in Cremona, and it took almost sixty years for his invention to be appreciated as an instrument with its own unique character rather than as the poor relation of the harpsichord.

King João of Portugal bought several Florentine instruments that subsequently influenced keyboard making and music in the Iberian Peninsula. Domenico Scarlatti knew of them and some of his many keyboard sonatas, dedicated to his patron, the Queen of Spain, may have been written with them in mind.

The eighteenth century was a time of great travel. Men and women, ideas, books and journals moved with surprising freedom. Some time in 1725, back over the Alps in Saxony, Gottfried Silbermann, organ builder of Freiberg, read a German translation with working drawings of an article about Cristofori's invention. It had been written some years earlier by the Italian poet and playwright Scipione Maffei, who recognized the unique appeal of the new instrument:

> . . . those skilled in the art of music know that . . . the secret of especially delighting their listeners is the differention of soft and loud . . . either in theme and its response, or when the tone is artfully allowed to diminish little by little, and then at a stroke made to return at full blast.

In speaking of propositions and responses Maffei had identified what the fortepiano could do that the harpsichord could not, namely play soft and loud with varying degrees of dynamics in between. A performer could thus emphasize one phrase of music over another, or shade and contrast notes and chords to give the music expression as in sung or spoken dialogue:

> The production of sound depends on the degree of power with which the player pressed the keys . . . hence the sound is greater or less at the pleasure of the player.

The article was timely. Silbermann had become disenchanted with the dubious honour of maintaining and reproducing the Dresden court pantaleon and he began work on the fortepiano that continued for the next twenty years. Like Cristofori he gave his instruments an escapement – free-flying hammers and a stop or lever to raise the dampers and give a pantaleon-like wash of sound. Johann Sebastian Bach tried one and was not impressed; keyboard players of plucked instruments were not used to having to vary their touch. The new instrument was seen as an inferior harpsichord, less suited to reproducing clear even tones in the interwoven parts that form the complex, overlapping textures of polyphony. Maffei, one of the few who recognized the singularity of Cristofori's invention from the start, continued:

> One must understand how to take things for what they are and not judge with regard to one purpose something that has been made for another ... Being a new instrument it requires a person who understands its virtues ... so that he may regulate the varying impulses that he must input to the keys.

At this stage almost nothing had been written for the new instrument. A set of sonatas for 'The keyboard of soft and loud commonly called Little Hammers' was composed in 1732 by Lodovico Giustini of Pistoia. It was essentially music for harpsichord with a few dynamic markings to demonstrate how the new instrument worked. Recognition and exploration of the new instrument's potential came slowly. Until the middle of the century the fortepiano remained a curiosity, the amusement of kings and privileged court musicians.

Silbermann persevered. His improved fortepianos caught the attention of King Frederick the Great and his chamber harpsichordist, Carl Philipp Emanuel, Bach's second son. C. P. E. Bach was one of the most original keyboard artists of the eighteenth century, who early on composed music that could be played on either harpsichord or fortepiano. His Prussian Sonatas, Opus 48, written in 1742 and dedicated to Frederick the Great, are playable on either instrument. The Andante second movement of the first sonata has a harpsichord-like praeludium; the singing line of the Andante second movement of Sonata No. 5 is more suited to the piano. His compositions were in the *Empfindsamer Stil*, a sentimental style which took the expressive human voice as its model. 'Music must speak,' he said. He liked the fortepiano and thought it had 'many fine qualities although special painstaking study is required to master the touch.' His *Essay on the art of playing keyboard instruments* (1753) advised the aspiring keyboard player: 'Lose no opportunity to hear artistic singing . . . In doing so the keyboardist will learn to think in terms of song.' His cantabile style anticipated pianoforte technique and opened the door to the eventual ascendancy of the piano over the harpsichord at the end of the century.

The learned system of counterpoint was challenged and it was on the fortepiano that the contest was played out. One evening in 1747 in the royal palace at Potsdam King Frederick confronted C. P. E.'s father, Old Bach, with a difficult sequence of notes and invited him to harmonize them on a royal fortepiano made by Silbermann. Counterpoint is the art of writing one or more lines of music against another, usually given, melody or subject. It is divided into five orders of increasing complexity which can be worked in two or more parts according to strict musical principles. Four or even five parts is usual. In composing, the number of parts is limited only by the skill and ingenuity of the composer. Bach declined to go to six parts for the king and the incident became a musical legend. It also prompted Bach's 'Musical Offering,' a set of harpsichord variations based on the king's piano theme.

Changes in musical taste reflected a changing social order. The learned counterpoint and its jealously guarded principles was thought to reflect the underlying harmony of a divinely ordered universe. In the mid-eighteenth century that order was investigated and questioned by both natural scientists and philosophers. The value placed on individual rationality by science and invention had its counterpart in music. As people began to entertain aspirations beyond the accepted social order, so recognition of the capabilities of the fortepiano made it possible to turn away from accepted tenets of composition. Instead of a wave of voices woven together in polyphonic harmony, the expressive voice of the new instrument could reflect the dramas of individual experience. As musical taste was gradually re-shaped, the reciprocal interplay between social change, technical invention and musical composition became the story of the piano.

During the second half of the century the relationship between keyboard makers and composers also changed. In the years between Bach's 'Musical Offering' and Beethoven's 'Tempest' Sonata, Opus 31, No. 2, written in 1802, a rigid social order was questioned and challenged by the chaos of revolution. Music that reflected divine order and appealed more to the intellect was replaced by music that expressed human feeling and moved the emotions. Haydn acknowledged his debt to C. P. E. Bach: 'I believe music must first and foremost stir the heart.' By the time Beethoven was writing his revolutionary keyboard sonatas at the end of the century it was he, the composer, who was pushing the inventiveness of piano makers rather than simply responding to the possibilities they offered.

Unlike Mozart or Haydn, Beethoven was his own master; his music was not written to order. His first eight keyboard sonatas for 'clavecin (harpsichord) or Pianoforte' were written when he was better known as a performer than composer. The three Opus 31 sonatas written at the turn of the century were revolutionary in style and vision, his personal response to the social and political upheavals of the time, to the terrifying forces of nature that were beyond even Enlightenment man's control, and to the inner turmoil of his own spirit. Such introspective music with its dramatic dynamics, its sforzandos and pianissimos, its sudden contrasts of mood and colour, also reflected the personal drama and tragedy of his deafness. The extraordinary series of contrasts in the 'Tempest' Sonata, for instance, needed all the dynamic range the piano makers could give him. The search for a fuller, more powerful tone continued and within twenty years, by the time Thomas Broadwood presented Beethoven with the six-octave grand in 1818, the piano had become the sensually lush voice of the Romantics. The 'Hammerklavier' was written for the modern piano; the

'Tempest' played on a modern grand by any other than a master's hands is like hearing early Beethoven through Liszt.

Back in Germany in the mid-eighteenth century there had been, in addition to Silbermann's royal pianos, a tradition of more simple keyboard instruments. In the houses and schools of the Lutheran Church, where music was an accepted adjunct to worship, the relatively inexpensive clavichord was popular. The dynamic control over the little metal hammers or tangents set it apart from other keyboard instruments of the time. There were also pantaleon clavichords, which had a moveable felt strip that could be lifted to allow the strings to vibrate, and small table pianos with wooden keys, some with no dampers at all in deference to the continuing taste for the pantaleon's wash of sound.

The clavichord had not been made much in England, however, and as harpsichords were a luxury that did not cope with dynamic shading, the stage was set for a keyboard instrument with the power of a harpsichord and the expressiveness of a clavichord. According to a note left by James Shudi Broadwood, John's eldest son, 'Sometime about 1760 Johan Zumpe, a German, who worked for Shudi, on returning from a visit to his native country, brought with him a piano, the first one in England, and immediately began to manufacture his square piano.'

Whether Zumpe actually brought a piano back with him or not, he certainly brought piano know-how, and some time in 1766 he launched his new keyboard instrument. He kept the clavichord's oblong shape and layout and adapted the small, wooden-hammered pantaleon, giving it a compass of five octaves with heavier strings in a sturdier case. He retained Cristofori's principle of the free-flying hammer as handed down by Silbermann, but dispensed with the intermediate lever and came up with his own unique hybrid: the English single-action square piano.

As a key was pressed down it lifted a metal pin with a leather knob set in the other end of the key shank. This in turn pushed the hammer shank up and launched the small leather-covered hammer towards the string above. A pad of leather under the key stopped it being fully depressed, leaving the hammer to fly free and strike the string. The string vibrated freely, the hammer fell back and a damper that had been raised by the action of the key shank was lowered back on to the string as the key came to rest.

Zumpe's single-action piano was simple and it could be played piano e forte – not just overall soft and loud, but relatively soft and loud – legato (smoothly) or staccato (abruptly). Varying degrees of soft and loud could be produced depending on how hard the keys were struck. The touch of the performer controlled a range of dynamic effects. Musical phrases could be shaped and emphasized, and lines of music could be made to sing out against an accompaniment. Musical ornaments and devices like Venetian swells and string couplers were no longer needed, although the lush, undamped sound that went back to Pantaleon Hebenstreit and his dulcimer remained popular. Mozart used it to effect in his Fantasy in D Minor (1782), as did Beethoven in the first movement of the 'Moonlight' Sonata (1802). The hand stop that Zumpe gave his piano to raise the dampers was eventually replaced by a knee lever and finally by the sustaining, or 'loud,' pedal that has been the refuge of so many amateur pianists ever since.

John Broadwood watched developments from the workshop in Great Pulteney Street and left a description of a Zumpe square piano, passed on many years later by his son James Shudi Broadwood.

> They were in length about four feet, the hammers very lightly covered with a thin coat of leather; the strings were small, nearly the size of those on a harpsichord; the tones clear, what is now called thin and wiry.

At this early stage there was still no real conceptual change from the harpsichord to the piano and the two were closely related in the minds of early piano makers. They thought in terms of a hammer harpsichord that could play soft and loud, depending on touch. James Shudi's description continues: 'his [Zumpe's] object being, seemingly to approach the tones of the harpsichord, to which the ear at that period was accustomed.' As mentioned, the new instrument was known by several names: fortepiano, forte piano, pianoforte, piano forte; and by the end of the eighteenth century, it was generally known as a pianoforte and often shortened to 'piano.'

———

Zumpe's invention had coincided with the arrival in London of the man who would promote it for him. Johann Christian, the youngest of Bach's sons, had appeared on the city's musical scene in 1762, the year after John Broadwood had arrived. He was taken up by King George III's young queen, the former Princess Charlotte of Mecklenburg-Strelitz, and appointed Master of the Queen's Music. Johann Christian preferred the pianoforte to the harpsichord and so did his royal pupil. He became the leader of London's musical society and his influence accelerated the popularity of the piano. George III and his household continued the Hanoverian enthusiasm for German music, and much of the success of the early piano, as well as the popularity of German-Viennese music, was also due to their early patronage.

Johann Christian met Zumpe and in 1768 he played one of his square pianos at the Thatched House in St James's Street. It was an immediate success. The musicologist Charles Burney later wrote in *The Cyclopaedia: or Universal Dictionary of Arts, Sciences and Literature*:

> ... the tone was very sweet, and the touch, with a little use, equal to any degree of rapidity. These, from their low price and the convenience of their form, as well as the power of expression, suddenly grew into such favour, that there was scarcely a house in the kingdom where a keyed-instrument had ever

had admission, but was supplied with one of Zumpe's pianofortes . . . In short he could not make them fast enough to satisfy the craving of the public.

Elegant, expressive music played on the pianoforte appealed directly to the emotions. People who had once socialized and walked about during fashionable concert evenings at the house of Mrs Teresa Cornelys in Soho Square went to listen to the queen's music master play the pianoforte. Operetta and musical comedy at the Covent Garden Theatre offered popular vocal entertainment, but Zumpe's invention opened the door to modern keyboard music in the German-Viennese style. The pianoforte played by J. C. Bach had the same emotional surge as the human voice; it spoke to the heart as much as to the intellect. London had heard nothing like it. At the time almost the entire keyboard repertory, apart from the organ, was for harpsichord, which generally accompanied opera and cantata or provided a rhythmic and harmonic framework for other instruments. Now the pianist moved to the front. J. C. Bach's Six Sonatas, Opus 5, indicated 'Cembalo o Piano e Forte,' music for either harpsichord or piano, and included both contrapuntal and melodic writing. It was the piano that people wanted to hear and within a few years Mozart would perform his piano concertos in propositions and response with the orchestra itself.

For twelve years J. C. Bach and another immigrant musician from Germany, the cellist Karl Abel, gave a series of popular public concerts in London. The Bach-Abel concerts were expensive – at two guineas subscription they kept hoi polloi out – but the aristocracy's grip on taste was loosened. Everyone who was or aspired to be *Someone* went to hear the new music on the new instrument and wanted to buy one.

The connection between Zumpe and J. C. Bach was crucial to the early popularity of the piano. As promoted by the queen's music master the fortepiano was no longer seen as an inferior harpsichord but as a serious musical instrument in its own right, and the endorsement of the royal household gave it an attractive social cachet. The square piano, the only model made at that stage, rapidly became a status symbol. Zumpe is thought to have charged J. C. Bach fifty guineas for his square – more than three times the price of a Shudi double manual harpsichord, then at sixteen guineas. It was a novelty and Zumpe could not make them fast enough. There were many inferior copies and even at twenty guineas the price was still desirably high. Square pianos were pretty and compact and their light silvery sound appealed to fashionable women whose private efforts to learn the new, touch-sensitive technique carried no taint of work. It was the chosen instrument of the queen; no woman of fashion or quality could be without one.

Although demand for Shudi's instruments remained constant for the next fifteen years, the harpsichord was as fully developed as it could be; its nemesis had arrived. When John Broadwood visited Shudi's fashionable clientele to tune their harpsichords and, increasingly, their square pianos, he had ample opportunity to observe other changes. A wide range of people could afford culture at many levels. Economic activity in Britain had shifted from the country to town and city, and more people worked in industry, trade or commerce than on the land. A growing middle class that included gentlemen, well-off artisans and some professional men on an income of between £50 and £100 a year represented 25 percent of the population. Though the gap between rich and poor was huge, in the 1760s there were many in between who could afford books, prints, theatre and music. As Dr Johnson asserted to James Boswell, whose acquaintance he made in 1763, a man could live on an annual income of £30 'without being contemptible.'

Zumpe's invention opened the way for a fortepiano of reasonable size and price that could be produced commercially. Art had led the way. Ideas about suitable subjects and traditional audiences were changing. Gainsborough painted his upper-class sitters in scenes based on observable nature instead of classical or historical backgrounds. William Hogarth had painted pictures of shrimp girls rather than princesses. He had shown the street life of London in all its gin-sodden squalor and exposed the lives of the upper classes as little better. His pictures in the form of prints reached a wide market in a new crossover between culture and commerce that anticipated the future of the piano industry.

John Broadwood's arrival in London in 1761 was no less propitious for the future of the piano than that of Zumpe and Bach. He saw the piano move rapidly from fashionable novelty to serious musical instrument. He saw Zumpe offer his square piano to an eager, open market rather than make individual instruments to order. He saw that performers and pianos could promote each other and he saw, earlier than most, that pianos could be made more quickly and in greater numbers than harpsichords; that they could be made by many pairs of hands; that the same basic instrument could be packaged in many different ways to appeal to people at varying levels of income and society. He saw that the piano could be the foundation of a grand enterprise and a private fortune, and if John Broadwood needed encouragement to act on all he saw he needed to look no further than the painting on the wall of his father-in-law's 'Dining Room.'

6

INVENTION AND ENTERPRISE

JOHN LANGSHAW, THE first organist, was late for his own wedding. As Pearson Langshaw would write to his cousin Eleanor Brabazon in 1891, 'Biographies do not always tell everything . . . no mention is made of my grandfather's great love of books – that on his wedding day he was not at Church in time and was sought for and found at a bookstall.' Despite the late start, however, John Langshaw married Mary Haydock at St James's Church in Westminster in May 1762, and their first child, John, known as Jack, was born nine months later, on 24 February 1763. It was Jack who would buy square piano 10651 forty-four years later.

Work had already started on the Earl of Bute's machine organ. John Stuart, the third Marquis of Bute, was also the premier Scottish earl. After the sudden death of Frederick, Prince of Wales, in 1751 he had become something of a father figure to Frederick's son, the future King George III. A man of taste and culture, he enjoyed immense riches from coalfield royalties inherited by his wife. After 1760 he was much favoured by the young king, who appointed him First Lord of the Treasury in 1762, making him effectively his prime minister.

The earl bought a lease of land to the south-west of what is now London's Berkeley Square for a proposed Bute House. Like many Scots around whom the whiff of Jacobinism still lingered, Bute was

Organ housing, c. 1760; drawn by Robert Adam, thought to be a possible housing for the Earl of Bute's machine organ. By courtesy of the trustees of Sir John Soane's Museum, London.

not popular. When James Boswell was introduced to Dr Johnson, he admitted that he came from Scotland, 'but I cannot help it.' Bute favoured north Britons for senior appointments and he was suspected of undue influence over the young king and improper friendship with Augusta, the Dowager Princess of Wales, whose confidence he enjoyed. The princess had harpsichord lessons twice a week from John Christopher Smith. Bute shared her taste in music. He also shared her son's fascination with inventive instruments. King George commissioned the scientific variety; Bute enjoyed the musical ones.

The age's spirit of enquiry was fostered by the enthusiasm and patronage of wealthy men, and London at this time saw a flowering of skills in the production of intricate and beautiful scientific instruments; it was also an important centre for musical-instrument making. For some years the idea of a self-playing organ had been mooted in musical circles as both an entertainment and a means of recording contemporary music, particularly the works of Handel. Bute had commissioned John Christopher Smith to orchestrate the building of 'a spectacular self-playing organ.' Alexander Cumming, who had charge of the organ some years later, wrote: 'In the year 1762 several of the most ingenious artists of the metropolis were engaged in building, for the Earl of Bute, a Machine Organ, on which no expense was spared and that was to have every improvement that art and ingenuity could bestow.' Cumming, who made a barograph for the king in 1765 for the enormous sum of £1,178, recorded that John Snetzler, the country's most eminent organ builder, was to make the organ's pipework and keyboard. The machinery was to be designed by William Pinchbeck, builder of the Theatre of Muses clockwork organ; Smith would programme the music and John Langshaw would pin the barrels. Robert Adam prepared plans for a grand organ room in Bute House with a large niche for the instrument, and drew up designs for appropriately lavish organ housings.

Before John Langshaw had made much progress, however, events overtook his patron. Bute had little taste for politics, his enemies were vociferous and he resigned in April 1763, his ministry having lasted barely twelve months. He bought land at Luton Park in Bedfordshire and in the late 1760s the machine organ 'was put up at his Lordship's Mansion,' in a revised organ room designed by

Adam. 'To that organ,' Cumming wrote, 'there were no fewer than sixty barrels of large dimensions, on which were set a selection from the choicest compositions of several of the first masters of the age.'

Barrel organs were not new: in John Langshaw's day they were known as singing or playing engines, sometimes as clock organs. They are wind organs operated by turning a handle that simultaneously turns a solid wooden cylinder or 'barrel,' and works a bellows inside the organ. The barrel, fixed horizontally, turns slowly because of a reducing gear connected to the handle. As it turns, so pins and staples fixed on to the surface trip levers that rise and fall and let air into the organ's pipes at intervals to play a tune. One complete turn plays the tune, and the barrel can be moved into different playing positions to play different tunes. There is usually a decorative case with dummy pipes at the front that conceal the real works inside.

They were used in country churches without an organist where they did not have to compete with a large choir. There were smaller, moveable versions with around sixteen pipes, and some even small enough to be slung round the neck. Smallest of all were serinettes, used for encouraging songbirds to sing.

Machine organs commissioned for the private pleasure of wealthy connoisseurs were more spectacular. They were much larger, often with combined finger and automatic mechanisms and elaborate architectural cases. The Earl of Bute's organ was one such – a great and beautiful machine that could be played either by keys by an organist or automatically by turning the barrels.

John Langshaw pinned all the organ's original fifty-six barrels. Each barrel was 4' 6" long with a diameter of 18". He solved the problem of playing longer pieces of music by spiralling the barrels. They played works by Corelli, Pergolesi, Vivaldi and Geminiani, but by far the greatest number, more than thirty-six barrels, were pinned with music by Handel. The Earl of Bute, the French musicologist F. J. Fetis wrote, 'asked Handel for some pieces for the instrument, the great musician wrote them and charged Langshaw with the duty of transferring them to enormous cylinders.' This assertion, written over one hundred years later, implies that John Langshaw was instructed directly by Handel. Whether or not it is reliable, there is no doubt that Smith had been close enough to the composer to know his musical intentions, and that John Langshaw worked closely with Smith on the job for twelve years.

How did he fix brass pins and staples into a wooden cylinder in all the right places to make the machine organ's levers rise and sound the notes in the correct sequence and tempi to reproduce a faithful performance of the finest music of the age? Where did he start? The conversion of a musical score to mechanical perform-ance was a closely guarded secret; sometimes it was done by writing a shorthand equivalent on paper, pasting it to the barrel and pricking the tune to the surface before pushing the pins and staples in place. But it is more accurate to mark the tunes on the barrel as it turns. To do this and mark each note and chord 'on' and 'off' without losing his place, John Langshaw would have needed to work undisturbed. There is no record of how he did the job; Cumming merely said that John Langshaw, 'organist and mechanic, pinned the barrels with such delicacy and taste as to convey a warm idea of the impression which the hand gives the instrument.'

This suggests that the tunes were not rigidly exact, as in musi-cal automata, but sounded like a live performance. Cumming continued, 'It was seen and heard by many of the best judges of music, and allowed by all very much to excel anything of the kind that had been produced before it.'

One of those hearers was the diarist Mary Granville, Mrs Delaney, famous in her day for her découpage creations and her friendship with the great and good of Georgian society, including Handel and the king and queen. She was an arbiter of taste, described by Edmund Burke as 'the perfect pattern of a perfect fine lady,' and she left the following account of hearing the earl's machine organ:

. . . a clock[work] organ, and plays an hour and a half without once winding up. There were thirty barrels [there were fifty-six] of which the principal are Geminiani, Handel and Corelli . . . the tone is mellow and pleasant and has an effect I could not have expected. It is a vast size and has a great many stops (for different tonal effects) and I'd rather hear [it] than any of their operas or printed concerts. Many parts are judiciously brought in – some parts of Handel's Choruses were tolerably executed.

Some years later, the earl in failing health moved to Highcliffe House on the south coast. He had Cumming install another machine organ there that worked by hydraulics (rising and descending buckets of water) and he took the barrels from Luton Park with him. The earlier organ was destroyed by fire in 1843. The one at Highcliffe passed to Bute's son and then to the Earl of Shaftesbury, who allegedly had the stairs of his London house removed to accommodate it and the barrels. Cumming eventually bought it back and it was last heard of many years after his death, in 1838, when 'An Hydraulic Machine Organ with sixty-four barrels' was advertised in a London newspaper, since when it and the barrels have disappeared.

But not entirely without trace. Before he died in 1814, Cumming had catalogued the contents of the barrels and noted the sequence and timing of every piece of music. Smith had programmed what were in effect mini suites arranged according to the taste of the day and in 1983 the musicologist William Malloch recorded them according to Cumming's catalogue and found that, 'each piece of music seems to grow out of the one that precedes it . . . the pauses between the pieces are short, measured beats rather than dead time [and make] . . . experiencing the rhythmic transformations more fun.'

The Luton Park organ was a marriage of art and technology informed by Smith and Langshaw's first-hand knowledge of the composers' intentions. They were both musicians, they understood and felt the music as participants who would have been familiar with contemporary interpretations of all the music on the barrels. Timings were not rushed or distorted to fit the available space on the barrels – there are gaps of more than two minutes on some of them; people then did not mind silence. Smith's arrangements and Langshaw's pinning was done, said Cumming, 'in so masterly a manner that the effect was equal to the most finished player,' and his catalogue is an authentic reflection of the taste and spirit that animated the music of the English baroque.

Did John Langshaw meet John Broadwood while he was living in Westminster and working on the organ? There was ample opportunity. His work placed him in the circle of keyboard musicians and inventors during the critical 1760s when the square piano first appeared in London. Many were the connections in that esoteric little world. Broadwood was working for Shudi in Great Pulteney Street and Zumpe was in Hanover Square, both only a few hundred yards from Bute House. John Christopher Smith was Shudi's friend, as his father and Handel had been. He had cared for Handel during the composer's last years when he had 'charged Langshaw with the duty of transferring them [the pieces] to enormous barrels.' Snetzler, the Swiss organ builder who had worked on the Bute machine organ and other projects with Langshaw, was Shudi's friend and executor. Snetzler lived in Oxford Road and Smith in Piccadilly. The spirit of invention was in the air and it is tempting to think that the natural affinity of like-minded inventors living and working at close quarters would have brought John Langshaw into contact with John Broadwood and the piano makers.

His marriage to Mary and the baptisms of his first five children are all recorded at St James's Church in Westminster, still referred to a century later by his grandson Pearson Langshaw as 'our old parish church.' The family lived in lodgings at Angel Court, off Windmill Street in Soho. As a musical artisan he would not have been well off; as an organist he at least made valuable contacts in

London's more traditional music circles, contacts that he would call upon when the time came to educate his sons.

A second Langshaw son, George, had followed Jack in 1764, then two girls, Mary and Ann, who both died in infancy. Elizabeth, who became the beauty of the family, was born in 1770, shortly before John Langshaw moved back with his family to his home town of Wigan, 'wishing to reside in the Country for the benefit of his health,' as his son would write in a biographical note fifty-four years later. His mother had already died and his father, who followed her a year later, was ailing; an eldest son had responsibilities. Repairs to the organ at All Saints Parish Church were needed. John Langshaw worked on it with the London firm of Byfield and Green, and stayed on as organist for two years.

The All Saints churchwardens' accounts and vestry minutes contain the following details:

29 August 1770	–	Organ being repaired			
3 August 1771	–	Paid John Langshaw for tuning the Organ during the year	4	0	0
Undated entry (between April 1770 and August 1771)	–	John Langshaw, another part of his salary	6	10	0
19 November	–	John Langshaw – half year's salary paid	10	0	0
13 April 1772	–	John Langshaw – half a year's salary paid	10	0	0

However, even with an additional £4 for tuning the organ, £20 a year was not much to keep a family on and in the spring of 1772, with another child on the way, John and Mary moved to Lancaster, where he had been appointed organist at the priory church.

He had been interviewed in London by the vicar of Lancaster, who gave him a somewhat perfunctory letter of introduction to the town's mayor:

Sir,

The Bearer of this Letter is the Person whom I have appointed
to be Organist of the Parish Church of Lancaster. I flatter myself
that he will be approved of by you and the Whole Town.
I beg my compliments to Mrs Fenton

April 7th 1772
   Your Sincere Friend and Humble Servant
   Oliver Marton

P.S. His name is John Langshaw

For his part John Langshaw signed an undertaking that set out his
organist's duties:

London, April 8th 1772

I John Langshaw do hereby promise the Rev'd Mr Oliver
Marton, to do the duty of Organist in the Parish Church of
Lancaster, by playing the Organ every Sunday and Holyday in
the Year, & also on every Wednesday & Friday, & every day in
Passion Week. Also to keep the Organ in tune after it is put into
sufficient Repair; to teach Miss Parrin [the previous organist's
daughter] to play the Organ & fulfill every other engagement
the late Mr Crompton undertook to do.

   As witness my hand
   John Langshaw

Mr Crompton had been the preferred candidate but he had died
before taking up the post. Possibly the prospect of teaching Miss
Parrin as well as the organist's other duties had been too much for
him; it did not deter John Langshaw. Collecting his final pay from
Wigan five days later, he started work in Lancaster on Easter
Sunday 1772.

Neither John Langshaw nor John Broadwood can have been unaware of the success of Zumpe's square piano as they worked in their respective workshops within a few hundred yards of one another in London during the 1760s. By the end of the decade John Langshaw had returned north; Shudi had more or less retired, and when he died in 1773 his son-in-law was already in the piano business.

John Broadwood still had the royal warrant for harpsichords and an enviable client list inherited from Shudi. King George III continued to patronize him, as did the royal family, members of the old aristocracy and some of the new manufacturing elite, of whom the china manufacturer Josiah Wedgwood was one. For another twenty years he continued to make harpsichords and ship them all over the world: to Josef Haydn in Vienna, to the Empress of Russia, to the plantocrats of the West Indies, to English grandees in Portugal, and to the citizens of a newly independent United States.

At the same time he stayed close to piano invention. As Charles Burney had noted after its success at the Thatched House concert in 1768, it was the square piano that people wanted. As with the machine organ, so with pianos: art and technology moved hand in hand. John Broadwood took advice in the science of acoustics and in the early 1770s he began, cautiously, to make the new instrument. He strengthened the case, moved the wrest plank or tuning pin block to the back of the piano and introduced arched 'peacock' dampers made of brass. Being a businessman, he patented his improvements, 'for a new constructed pianoforte . . . far superior to any instrument heretofore made.'

His square pianos had, according to his son James Shudi, 'greater power than those of Zumpe,' and just as Zumpe's square piano had been promoted by J. C. Bach, so Broadwood sought to attract prestige by enlisting the rising keyboard star Muzio

*John Broadwood, 1812; mezzotint engraved by William Say, after
John Harrison Jr. Reproduced by permission of
Surrey History Service.*

Clementi to perform on his. Clementi may not have been close to
royalty but he had a dazzling keyboard technique and he was an
inspired entrepreneur. For a time he and Broadwood backed both
horses. On 12 May 1781 Broadwood's 'shipped a Harp'd and a
p.forte for Mr Clemente to Paris,' and Clementi played them both
on his first promotional concert tour of Europe. At that time
Sébastien Erard was the leading Parisian piano maker. He made

elegant pianos for an aristocracy teetering on the brink of the abyss – the one for Marie Antoinette survived its mistress. He made squares like Zumpe's and there was concern that he would capture the piano market until, at the end of the decade, he was compelled to flee the Revolution and lost ground at a critical time.

The clients John Broadwood inherited from Shudi and the fortune that gave him an unchallenged market accounted only in part for his success in business. The three oldest surviving Broadwood books, now in the Bodleian Library, show that it was his own enterprise that carried his business successfully into the Industrial Age:

John Broadwood kept his personal accounts in a book that was small enough to fit in a greatcoat pocket (Bodleian Library, Ms Eng. misc. e663). Over time the vellum cover became darkened and polished with use. The first harpsichord sale he noted was in September 1771: '1771. Sept. 16th. Mrs Williams a double key'd Harpsichord 16-16-0.'

There seems to have been no consistent method of recording in this book, but the transactions noted on pages 2 to 6 show that by then harpsichord serial numbers had reached the 600s. The following year the Shudi-Broadwood partnership sold twenty-six harpsichords that ranged from sixteen guineas for a 'Double Key'd' fitted with Shudi's patented [Venetian] swell, such as the one sold to Sir Henry Dashwood in January, to a single manual with swell at ten guineas and one without at seven. These figures suggest that by then the partnership had already adopted more industrial methods of production – ten years earlier Shudi had made about fifteen harpsichords a year. At sixteen guineas their cost was not prohibitive and a great deal less than the square piano Zumpe had sold J. C. Bach a few years earlier. Old Shudi's wavering signature completed the entries for 1772.

John Broadwood's enterprise grew steadily during the 1770s. At the back of his pocket book he recorded the customers whose harpsichords he tuned and repaired and the fees he charged. Entries ceased in the mid-1770s when his wife, Barbara, died bearing their fourth child. They continued several years later with details of serious money-lending. One loan of £2,000 (about £100,000 in today's money) to James Gibson brought him interest at £125 a quarter. He loaned money to William Ware, organist of Belfast, one of his earliest overseas harpsichord distributors. A mortgage to a Mrs Fraser was repaid at £50 a year until 1817, five years after his death.

On the debit side he recorded payments to his shipping agent and to 'Mr. Compton for mahogany £62-6-11d.' He made regular modest payments to himself and to his mother-in-law, Mrs Shudi. He prospered. He could afford to hazard over £700 for a quarter share in several voyages of the brigantine *Duchess of York* and the ship *Sally*. But apart from a few second-hand piano sales in the early 1790s, his pocket book contained little information about his piano business.

Barbara Broadwood started keeping a household account book in 1769, the year she married John (Bodleian Library, Ms Eng. misc. c529). Everything befitting a prosperous craftsman's household is recorded: oranges, salad, anchova, French bread, oil and vinegar, candles and currants, shrimps and veal. She paid the washerwoman 1s 3d, bought chamber pots and soap at 1s 6d and ' Lost at Cards 4d.' Two years later she was recording business messages for her husband in the same book:

Lady Bracechurch of Somerset House to tune her harpsichord on Monday morning.
A pottle of Raspberries 7d. Porter – 10d.

There is an early entry for a piano tuning, denoted by the use of the apostrophe: '1772 March. Miss Douglas' Piano.' Whether the piano was a Broadwood is not clear.

Many early pages of Barbara's book had crumbled before conservators had worked on them. It had been rebound in vellum and the fragmented pages reassembled between manilla tissue. Some of the pages were incomplete and not all the fragments or pages had been reassembled in quite the right order. A scrap relating to personal linen ('3 Bed gowns, 30 shifts, 4 nightcaps'); a memo, 'My father gave me a present of a Ten Pound Note'; and a note saying what she did with it ('Lace 1-9-0, A Silk Petticoat 1-3-0, A Pair of Shoes – 9-8, 2 Pair of Stockings – 5-0, A wax Doll – 2-6') had all been reassembled on to a page dated 1785, nine years after she had died. Another piano entry, '1772 Miss Lowell for Pianos,' possibly relating to piano sales, appears on the same 1785 page.

These mismatched fragments are poignant and tantalizing. When had John Broadwood started making pianos? According to James Shudi's note on the origins of the piano, it was after the success of Zumpe's square piano in the late 1760s, and Broadwood family legend has it as early as 1770, when the family was still living on the premises in Great Pulteney Street. It is clear from Barbara's book that her husband's business was part of their family life from the beginning. She took messages and arranged appointments for him. Her entries are a mixture of domestic and business diary. Payments of eight guineas a year to her servant Elizabeth Powell and £1 12s 6d a quarter to her girl Jane Kennedy are entered next to notes of her husband's tuning appointments – mainly harpsichords, but pianos begin to appear in increasing numbers in the early 1770s.

The Broadwood Journal (1771–85), a day book measuring 6″ × 14″, contains 287 pages with an average 25 transactions to a page (Bodleian Library, Ms Eng. misc. b107). The early pages are filled with tunings and hirings of harpsichords and pianos interspersed with some harpsichord sales. 'Sept 16 1771 – Lord Spencer's Pianoforte – 2-6d' is clearly a tuning. The names of Lord Spencer and others such as Mrs Luther and Count Bruhl, the Saxon ambassador, who had a tuning contract with John Broadwood, appear regularly over several years. Some, such as 'Mr. Bach' (Johann Christian), had their harpsichord and piano tuned at the same time, for which they were charged 7s.

Other piano entries do not show a tuning fee. Could they be

sales, simply 'posted' into the day book as harpsichord sales were, showing no charge? There are no sales ledgers for this period, only the three Bodleian books. Another entry for 1772, 'Miss Pelham sent the piano home,' i.e. back to Broadwood's, seems to refer to the return of one of their own instruments, and there are similar references to Miss Lowell's and Miss Douglas's pianos in Barbara Broadwood's book in the same year. Even if these were tunings rather than sales, is it likely that they would have been tuning the pianos of other makers rather than their own?

By 1775 there are clear references in the journal to piano sales. A pianoforte was packed for a Miss Long and sent 'to the Country'; another was shipped to a Captain Scanen – destination unknown. A year later Sir Alexander Leith bought a pianoforte for his lady and Mr Ware had one sent to Belfast. Piano hirings and tunings and harpsichord sales continue. It is difficult to be accurate about sales at this time because of the lack of sales ledgers, and because numbering was inconsistent at first. But in 1779 the journal shows a distinct movement of pianoforte sales to London customers who already owned a harpsichord, such as Lady Mary Duncan and the Bishop of Worcester. First they hired a piano; then they bought one. From the early 1780s, sales of 'Small' pianos delivered by 'Chair-men' [sedan] within London appear increasingly.

The pattern of Broadwood's overseas sales was similar. Shipping procedures for harpsichord sales were already in place in Jamaica, Oporto, Philadelphia, Barbados, Copenhagen, Dublin, Quebec and 'Ruschia'; existing harpsichord agents, like Mr Ware of Belfast, started buying pianos and became conduits for piano sales. In 1784 the number of piano distributors increased to include Corri and Sutherland in Edinburgh, Orpin in Bath, Brooks in Oporto and Liotard Cazenove in Paris, and the first recorded Broadwood business in the United States appears.

Broadwood's earliest recorded business in America was a harpsichord, with Robert Bremner in London acting as agent (or 'friend,' as they came to be called): '1784 June 28 Bought by and sent to Mr Hopkinson Philadelphia A Double Key'd Harpsichord with five stops and two pedals & patent swell mahogany case. 73 10 00.'

Francis Hopkinson was one of the signers of the Declaration of Independence, a Philadelphia lawyer and amateur musician of repute who prided himself on his musical inventiveness. In November 1784 he informed the Philosophical Society of Philadelphia that Broadwood of London had made him a harpsichord, 'quilled according to my method,' incorporating improvements already described to an earlier meeting. He thought that although the 'Forte Piano, was free from the harpsichord's jingle or tinkling between the quills and wires,' it was inferior in every other respect. How could he have known this? Had the fifteen guinea 'Piano-forte with brass dampers,' recorded at the end of the dispatch note for the harpsichord, also been for him? The Broadwood Journal is not clear.

When Hopkinson later substituted leather for quill plectra on his harpsichord, he wrote to his friend Thomas Jefferson, then minister to France in Paris, telling him that he had 'sent this Discovery to a friend [Broadwood?] in England.' In spring 1786 Jefferson visited Broadwood in Great Pulteney Street, and later wrote to Hopkinson: '[I] conversed with him about your newest jack. He showed me instruments in his shop with precisely the same substitute quill, but I omitted to examine whether it had the same spring on the back.' Broadwood claimed to have made the change before he was aware of Hopkinson's, but the latter felt he had been 'defrauded of both the money and credit' (he had offered it to Broadwood for £50). The following year Hopkinson and Jefferson ordered harpsichords from Kirkman, Broadwood's rival. (When Jefferson became the third president of the United States, he bought a piano made by George Astor of London.) The disagreement did not deter others in North America from buying Broadwood instruments. Charles Carroll of Carrollton, Maryland, another signer of the Declaration of Independence, ordered a Shudi & Broadwood two-manual harpsichord in 1785.

Pianos were already known in America. In March 1775 John

Behrent, a German immigrant to Philadelphia, had advertised in *Dunlap's Pennsylvania Packet* '. . . for sale, an extraordinary fine instrument by the name of PIANOFORTE, of mahogany in the manner of a harpsichord, with hammers and several changes [stops].' However, local piano-making progressed slowly until the end of the century, by which time Broadwood already had a number of piano agents along the Eastern Seaboard.

For a time after the Revolutionary War, whatever was in fashion in London found its way into drawing-rooms in Philadelphia, Boston, New York and Charleston as shippers and merchants, lawyers and statesmen sought to emulate an elevated, transatlantic taste personified by Jefferson. While such wealthy Americans bought the finest of London's musical instruments, there were others who sensed, as Broadwood did, a growing preference for the piano over the harpsichord. In 1783 John Jacob Astor had sailed for America. Since leaving Walldorf in Germany for London five years earlier to join his brother George Astor, a well-known maker of musical instruments, he too had seen the early popularity of the pianoforte. Recognizing that music and money could be made from pianos at every level, he settled in New York and began shipping furs to Europe while bringing musical instruments, including Broadwood pianos, back to the United States.

The year 1784 was a turning point in John Broadwood's piano enterprise, the first year when more than 100 square pianos were sold. He was now supplying the public rather than just making them for individual customers. People of the First Consequence bought them, including the Duchess of Norfolk and the Duke of Ancaster; People of Distinction also bought from him, including Lord Clive and Admiral Piggot; other customers included People of Consequence – Mr Garrick and Dr Johnson, the painters Thomas Gainsborough and Sir Joshua Reynolds – and there were also People of Fashion, like Mrs Luther and Miss Bull, both of whom had been harpsichord customers since Shudi's day. A number of society music teachers, professional musicians and organists also bought them. The queen's cake baker, Mrs Horton, bought a square piano; so did Lord Spencer's housekeeper and her employer.

In the same year John Broadwood launched his grand piano. During the 1770s he had brought together the disparate talents of a number of instrument makers. One of his apprentices, Robert Stodart, and the Dutchman Americus Backers had invented the English grand action, the basis of the grand piano, for which Stodart took out a patent in 1777. Broadwood was privy to these developments and began making his own grands. In April 1782 a Mr North hired a 'Large pianoforte'; later that year a 'Grand Piano-forte' is mentioned for the first time.

The price of Broadwood's harpsichords had risen considerably since Shudi's day, as these extracts from the Journal show:

1772

A Double Key'd Harp'd with Patent Swell	16	0	0
A Single do with Swell	10	0	0
A Single do without Swell	7	0	0

By 1778 annual output had increased from fifteen to twenty-six harpsichords a year. Broadwood employed more men and continued to put his harpsichord prices up. Twelve years later he had positioned his harpsichords at the top end of his range:

1784

A Double Key'd Harp'd in a mahogany case	68	0	0
A Large Double Key'd Harpsichord for Miss Crew	89	5	0
A Harp'd with a Swell [Single] sent Mr Brooks Oporto	44	2	0

Even a second-hand harpsichord 'late the property of Lady Leith' was sold for £68 5s. At the same time he priced his basic small piano at 16 guineas and the improved model with the wrest plank at the back at 21. Another model 'in a veneer'd case' cost 26 guineas and the one he sold to Clementi was 31.

A year later he sold a 'large p.f with two pedals . . .' to Mr Tyler of Bath for £48 6s and a 'Grand Piano-forte' to Mr Glover of Cambridge for £63. By positioning both harpsichords and his appropriately named 'Grand Forte pianos' at an elevated price level, he guaranteed the exclusive top end of his market while meeting demand at the lower end with a range of squares starting at 16 guineas. He understood the concept of the inverted demand curve whereby the desirability of certain products increases not only with material value but also with a high price that reflects other, intangible qualities. With their richly-veneered cases and more sophisticated action, his grands and his harpsichords were positioned in the upper sector of the market, where well-to-do people who attended exclusive concerts wanted to pay a desirably high price. He could sell to the popular market without alienating his fashionable customers. Everyone was satisfied.

John Broadwood's great skill was to supply the instrument everyone wanted while ensuring that the all-important social distinctions were maintained. His pricing strategy meant that Lady Cavendish could still have her 'Large Double Key'd Harp'd' at eighty-eight guineas, while Mr Warner the engraver had his 'Plain Pianoforte' at sixteen. A wide band of customers in between had their veneered pianos, their superior squares, their single manual harpsichords, their second-hand trade-ins, and grand fortepianos that were nudging seventy guineas. His reputation as a harpsichord maker remained high, but it made business sense to promote pianos. Astute positioning ensured impeccable status for them and wide market penetration. All of his pianos at every level, with their courtly harpsichord provenance and understated appearance, acquired a brand identity synonymous with their maker's name. A Broadwood became *the* English piano, to which generations would remain loyal.

In 1785 John's first son, James Shudi, joined the business. He was thirteen, and it was nine years since his mother had died. He wrote 'I am your humble servant James' in her household book and took over responsibility for tunings (at 5s) and hirings (at 6s 2d for a small square piano). He also made a list, 'Wagons Set Out,' showing the main road carriers and starting points in London from which Broadwood pianos were transported to other parts of the country. Carriage by road was mainly to towns in the south of England, but they also delivered as far north as Stafford and Northampton. Others were shipped by sea to Hull and Edinburgh. The fashion for pianos had started to spread outward from London to the provinces and overseas, where the pattern of Broadwood's earliest piano sales was repeated: existing harpsichord customers started buying pianos.

James Shudi was soon recording chance piano sales to London clients: 'Lady Ancaster, Mrs Thomas's School, Mme Krumpholz, Capt. Green,' and the youthful doodles that decorated his first few pages became fewer. A surviving Broadwood square piano, made in 1787, is number 768. For the last fifteen years of the century, as more people made more money, particularly in the new manufacturing towns of the Midlands and the North, the demand for pianos increased. Canals built for the transport of coal, cotton, iron, timber and food also carried pianos out of London, and British naval supremacy would ensure their safe delivery to all parts of the globe. Commerce and culture went hand in hand.

James Shudi had joined his father's business when it was changing from a harpsichord workshop to a piano-manufacturing enterprise. Within five years production was almost entirely in pianos and the last third of the household book is given over to serious Broadwood piano business. Increased demand required more modern methods of output, and piano parts made by many pairs of hands were assembled by many others. He introduced sales ledgers and double-entry book-keeping, and built up a global distribution network. John Broadwood and Son were taking their business into the Industrial Age, and in the process the piano became a cultural commodity.

7

THE LANGSHAWS
OF LANCASTER

WHILE JOHN BROADWOOD was promoting his piano enterprise in London, John Langshaw and his family began to establish themselves in Lancaster. Earlier in the century Daniel Defoe had visited the town on what would become his *Tour Through the Whole Island of Great Britain,* and described it as lying in its own ruins with little to recommend it – 'only a decayed castle and a more decayed port . . . little or no trade and few people.' Fifty years later, on Easter Sunday morning 1772, if the new organist had glanced into his organ loft mirror when he played his first service at the priory church, he would have seen Lancaster's wealthy merchants and their families sitting in the best pews and recognized that he had come to a boom town with good prospects.

The port's position on the north-west coast, though never good for trade with Europe, was well situated for the Baltic and West Indian markets. Port Commission records show that the years 1750–1800 were Lancaster's golden era of shipping. In his *Outlines of an Economic History of Lancaster 1680–1860* (1946), M. M. Schofield writes that at this time 'The rise of shipping interests in Lancaster was the work of small merchants speculating in shares and ships and their cargoes, hoping to gain profit from the sale of the tropical produce of the New World.'

A period of unprecedented prosperity based on maritime trade followed the suppression of the Jacobite uprising of 1745, and in the more settled second half of the eighteenth century a fleet of about fifty ships operated out of Lancaster. Some plied the Irish Sea ports for wool and others brought wood and flax from the Baltic for shipbuilding and sailcloth, but when the Langshaws arrived the port of Lancaster was the fourth busiest in the country engaging in the West Indian trade. Lancaster merchants depended on the plantation economy, though few were engaged directly in the slave trade. Schofield quotes from *England Described, or the Traveller's Companion*, an anonymous work first published in 1776, which says of Lancaster:

> . . . it is more remarkable for commerce than agriculture, being at present a thriving corporation with a tolerable harbour and custom house . . . vessels of tolerable burden go from hence to America with earthen and hardware, woolen manufactures etc. and import from thence sugar, rum cotton etc.

Building had started at the bridgehead on the dramatic ox-bow in the River Lune at the foot of Castle Hill in 1751, and twenty years later St George's Quay was in full commercial use. It looks much the same now as it did then: 200 yards of granite warehouses five storeys high, with Robert Gillow's custom house at the centre, opposite stepped quays leading down to tidal High Water, and the Lune estuary and the open sea about a mile away. Today the warehouses, with the exception of a harpsichord workshop, are filled with loft apartments.

John Langshaw's appointment at the ancient parish church of one of the most prosperous towns in the north of England was prestigious, if somewhat unexpected at a time when there were few

Map of Lancaster, 1778; drawn by Stephen Mackreth.
Reproduced by permission of Lancashire Record Office, Preston.

openings to men of humble birth from the artisan class; but he had worked with the most reputable organ builder of the day and set the music of the first composers on a great machine organ for one of the most powerful men in the land and so had earned a reputation as a first-class musical technician. In London he had known some of the finest musicians of the age and he always maintained his contacts in musical circles there. He stayed in Lancaster until he died twenty-six years later, in 1798.

What was he like? After his petition in 1742 there is no further mention of his disability. He was a gifted, self-taught musician with an inventive capacity that was perhaps stronger for his lack of formal education, and he loved learning with the intensity of a clever man denied schooling. He 'received few advantages from education, but his uncommon assiduity had amply compensated for this defect,' says his obituary in *Gore's Advertiser*, a Liverpool paper. The handbill in Lancaster Library announcing the sale of his books in 1795 lists only part of his collection of 'upwards of 1700 Volumes, small books, pamphlets etc ... the prices marked in every one and fixed very low. Chiefly commentaries on the Scriptures, Sermons, Books of Piety and the controverted points between the Established Church, the Deists and different denominations of Dissenters.' They included such worthy tomes as *Stebbing's Tracts*, *Pearson and Stackhouse on the Creed* and *Strype's Memorials of Cranmer,* all no doubt fascinating in their way, but to the modern mind so dry that only a reader earnestly bent on self-improvement would struggle through them. But read them he did, and in doing so he acquired an 'extensive knowledge of civil and Ecclesiastical History', also referred to in the obituary.

The letter written by Pearson Langshaw to his cousin Eleanor Brabazon almost a hundred years later, in 1891, refers to his grand-father's fondness for 'reading books on Divinity ... [He] published a pamphlet ... on Baptismal Regeneration – which was thought so good that the Bishop of Sodor and Man offered him a living.' Another of Pearson's anecdotes in the same letter concerns a visit made by his grandfather to an atheist in Lancaster Gaol: he took an armful of books with him, bent on saving the man's soul, only to emerge three hours later saying, 'I have made no impression on him whatever.'

John Langshaw's interest above all else was to give his children the education he lacked. As priory organist he was paid £100 a year, this at a time when Mrs Muttlebury, the royal wet nurse, was paid £200 and a £100 annual pension for life. He had to use his contacts. In May 1772, one month after his interview in London for the Lancaster appointment, his second son, George Langshaw, then aged eight, was nominated for a place at London's renowned Charterhouse School by the Earl of Bute, who as a governor was entitled to propose one Poor Scholar a year. Had John Langshaw lobbied him? At some time during his two years in Wigan he had started work on another machine organ for the earl which was to be given to the earl's daughter, Lady Lonsdale. Working with the same team as before, he continued pinning the barrels in Lancaster and sent each finished barrel by sea to William Pinchbeck in London. A letter he wrote on 29 October 1773 gives a lively impression of his resourcefulness:

My dear Friend,

I am afraid you will be uneasy that you have not got the Barrel before now. I send this to let you know that no ships have gone out these six weeks from Lancaster, owing to the wind being against them, about a fortnight ago the vessel with our Barrel got out with a little favourable wind, but it blew her back in a few days after, she lies about 30 miles from me, and bad to get to, or I wou'd send this second barrel, I finished it last Monday but one, it wou'd be three days in going to the other barrel, in which time the ships may be gone, therefore I shall send it by the first ship to Liverpool, & there are ships often going to London, & by going to Liverpool there will need no land carriage.

I hope they will get safe, the musick of these two barrels has a better effect than any I have set lately.

I hope this will find you all well. I shall now go to writing my Lords Musick.

From your most obed.t Servt.

TO BE SOLD.

A LARGE COLLECTION OF BOOKS,

IN THE ENGLISH LANGUAGE,

Confifting of upwards of 1700 Volumes,

(Belonging to Mr. JOHN LANGSHAW, of Lancafter.)

Chiefly Commentaries on the Scriptures, Sermons, Books of Piety and the controverted points between the Eftablifhed Church, the Deifts and different denominations of Diffenters.

IN THE FOLIOS ARE,

PATRICK, Lowth and Whitby's Commentaries on the Old and New Teftament
Hammond's Works
Kidder on the Meffias
Bingham's Works
Leflie's Theological Works
Jos. Mede's Works
Bp. Hopkin's Do.
Sanderfon's Sermons
Littleton's Do.
Bp. Taylor's Do.
Bp. Tillotfons Do.
Bp. Sma ridge's Do.
Dr Clarke's Do.
Nichoils' and Comber on the Com. Prayer
Burnet on the 39 Articles
Pearfon and Stackhoufe on the Creed
Stackhoufe's Body of Divinity
Bp. Taylor's Polemical Difcourfes
——Rule of Confience
Eufebius' Church Hiftory
Dr. T. Jackfon's Works
Prefervative againft Popery
Heylin's Tracts

Dr. John Edwards' Works
Bp. Andrews on the Commandments
Bp. Hall's Works
——on Hard Texts of Scripture
St Cyprian's Works by Marfhall
Wood's Athenæ Oxonienfes
Lindfey's Vin. of the C. of England
Stebbing's Tracts
Clarendon's Do.
Collier's Church Hiftory
Strype's Memorials of Cranmer }
     Parker, Grindal and Whitgift }
Strype's Annals
Bp. William's Life
Bp. Ufher's Do.
Whitlock's Memorials
Dugdale's fhort view of the Troubles in England
Walker's fufferings of the Clergy
Chillingworth's Works
Stillingfleet's Origines Britannicæ
Hooker's Ecclefiaftical Polity
Several Treatifes on Irifh Affairs, during the Reign of King Charles the 1ft, by P. Walfh, of the order of St. Francis and Profeffor of Divinity. *very fcarce*

N. B. Several hundreds of fmall Bound Books, Pamphlets, &c. from 1d, to 6d, each: The Price is marked in every Book and fixed very low.

☞ *Any perfon willing to purchafe the whole will have a confiderable abatement.*

LANCASTER, JULY 20th, 1795.

Handbill for Sale of a Large Collection of Books, belonging to Mr John Langshaw, of Lancaster, 1795. Reproduced by permission of Lancaster Library.

As well as producing additional income, the work ensured that the Langshaw name was kept before the earl. George Langshaw duly went up to Charterhouse four years later in 1776 when he was twelve. He went as a Poor Scholar with the written endorsement of the Earl of Bute and an allowance of £20 a year from the school.

In his determination to get his sons a good education John Langshaw always kept up with life in London. He read the *Gentleman's Magazine* and maintained his friendships and his contacts. One of these was the man he referred to as 'my good friend,' Sir John Hawkins. Sir John was a founder member of Dr Johnson's Literary Club, whose members, described by Johnson as a 'miscellaneous collection of conspicuous men without any determinate character,' were among the most culturally influential men of the day. He was a musicologist, but his four-volume *General History of the Science and Practice of Music* (1776) was less popular than his rival Charles Burney's *General History of Music from the Earliest to the Present Time*, published in the same year.

Nonetheless, Sir John had influence and music was his passion. He was a conservative, an adherent of early music and mid-century English baroque by composers such as Thomas Arne, William Boyce, Joseph Kelway and John Stanley, all of whom were represented in *Apollo's Cabinet*. John Langshaw may have met him when the collection was put together, or it is possible that he knew him through the Academy of Ancient Music, a private club founded in 1726 to which Sir John had belonged for many years. Its members met at The Crown and Anchor in the Strand for supper, convivial male company and an evening's music, mainly vocal, and from an earlier age or by conservative contemporaries. This was at a time when it was unusual for works to remain in performance for more than a generation. Many choral singers and organists from London's leading churches were also members and John Langshaw could have been either a visitor or a performer. Whichever it was, he occupied a much lower station in life than Sir John; working musicians were then still regarded as artisans and attitudes were little different from earlier in the century when J. S. Bach had been made to serve in livery in Weimar.

After leaving London John Langshaw had kept the family name in front of Sir John too. He sent him one of his pamphlets from time to time, and suffered the Great Man's rebuffs:

... the M.S. you sent me ... is written in a hand as far from being plain as it is from stiffness and would be a discouragement even to a young person to read it with attention.

Sir John Hawkins to John Langshaw, 16 February 1782

Coming from Sir John, a master of the heavy hand, this seems harsh, but it was tempered by the interest he took in young George Langshaw:

I sometimes send for your son George to spend a day with me and my family and am pleased to find him likely to prove a sensible and sober young man ...

Sir John Hawkins to John Langshaw, 26 February 1778

In the spring of 1778 all seemed set fair for John Langshaw's second son, who was doing well at Charterhouse and had the endorsement of an earl and the patronage of a Great Man. Langshaw could now look to further the education of his first boy. Things, however, did not run quite so smoothly for Jack Langshaw: he had been formed in a different school.

When the family had moved to Lancaster in 1772, Jack, then aged nine, had been sent to the old grammar school, which offered places to boys who could 'read pretty well.' At the same time his father taught him to play the organ so that he could take over responsibility for the family if necessary. It was usual then for a first son to be named after his father and to follow his trade or profession. Life in those days was precarious and it was not uncommon for an older brother to take care of his siblings in the event of their father's demise; John Langshaw's disability must have made such a consideration ever present. Jack was always expected to take care of the family.

The Langshaws lived in the neighborhood of Skerton on the

north side of the river, within the sound of Robert Gillow's cabinet-making workshops. The age of mahogany had begun; traditional English oak and walnut furniture was being replaced by the hard, richly coloured wood from Jamaica and Honduras. Gillow supplied the best houses in England and shipped quality pieces back to the great houses of the West Indian plantocracy. Heavier timber from the Baltic was used at John Brockbank's shipbuilding yard on the Green Ayre, the tongue of land formed by the River Lune's ox-bow. The days were filled with sawing and hammering, the ring of heavy hammers on metal and the shouts of men as the creaking windlass turned a boat slowly over. There was the hiss of steam from the forge of the anchor smith Joseph Sharp. Within a few hundred yards there were several ropewalks, and on Lawson's Quay on the north side, barrels of molasses from Barbados rolled and rumbled over the stones to John Lawson's Sugar House, where muscovado was refined and made into sugar loaves. The sweet smell of boiling sugar was carried on the air with the aroma of pungent pitch from Brockbank's and the stench of rendered tallow drifting over from the town's candle and soap factories; the merchant family Rawlinson exported more candles to the West Indies than any other product. There were exotic scents from tobacco and snuff works, and the odours of cattle being driven up St Leonardsgate to the moors and from a town sanitation system that would not be modernized for a hundred years.

These sensations would have assailed Jack Langshaw as he crossed the old bridge and walked to school on the south side of the river. He would have heard the strange tongues of sailors working the Baltic and North Atlantic routes. German from men working in Lawson's Sugar House would have mingled with the Creole of West Indian sailors calling to Jeremiah Skerton perhaps, from Lancaster's community of baptized former slaves. As Jack walked on into town he might have heard the brogue of Irish immigrant labourers working on new buildings and the edgy vowels of men from Glasgow and Manchester bringing in manufactured goods for export. In town the streets would have been busy with the affairs of shippers and the tradesmen and business-men who depended on them, some of whom had travelled by coach for sugar or cotton sales. There too were the lawyers and lit-igants who came to the assizes, and the clerks and servants who attended them. And above all the many sounds and sights of men, Jack would have heard the timeless cries of seabirds.

The castle and priory dominated the town then as they do now. Georgian Lancaster was being built, and Jack might have dawdled to watch Roman coins or human bones being dug out of one of the cellars in Church Street, as old properties of wood and straw were being replaced by new buildings made of stone from the moor. In 1776 Arthur Young on his six-month tour of the North of England visited Lancaster and noted: 'It is a town that increases in buildings; having many new piles, much superior to the old streets, and hand-somely raised of white stone and slate.'

Stephen Mackreth's map of Lancaster published two years later and dedicated to the town's merchants gives a good idea of the changes taking place in Jack Langshaw's day and the men respon-sible for it. It shows the house of Thomas Covell, who had tried the Pendle witches a century before, The King's Arms coaching inn, and Penny's Hospital, where twelve poor men lived. The Assembly Rooms, where Jack's father sometimes performed on the harpsi-chord, had recently been built and so had Queen's Square, with its safe, open spaces between handsome town houses that are now occupied by professional practices. There was a market square with a grand town hall, now the City Museum. A grander civic square was proposed on land owned by the Dalton family. Mackreth's map shows the orderly plots of a proposed new high street and new streets on the Skerton side, all part of the design for a late-eighteenth-century rational and orderly new town with buildings that would be landmarks of Lancastrian prosperity.

The old Lancaster Grammar School was down Nip Hill to the west of the castle and the priory. As Jack hurried up Windy Hill towards the castle he might have remembered seeing a red-robed judge and the High Sheriff process to the assizes, and the public hangings that followed their visit. School began at six in summer with prayers by the headmaster, the Reverend Dr Watson. Lessons followed until eight, when Jack ate the breakfast he had taken with him. At first he would have been in Low Side, the room where the usher taught; then, as an older boy in High Side, he would have been given an unvarying diet of Classics from the headmaster. The two rooms were divided into 'forms,' the benches at which ten or so boys sat. While the master taught one form, the others got on with their work. If Jack's work was slovenly he would get a rap on the hand; bad behaviour was punished by the cane, but birching, though common in other schools at that time, was not resorted to at Lancaster Grammar School. During the winter, Jack would end his day's lessons by the light of his own candle.

The poet William Cowper's charge that 'Pedantry is all that schools impart' was not true of Lancaster Grammar School in Jack

Old Lancaster Grammar School, late eighteenth century; engraving by R. W. Johnson. Reproduced by permission of Lancaster Library.

Langshaw's day, for two reasons: it was supported by the corporation of a thriving mercantile port who recognized that boys who were likely to go into trade needed something more than Classics; and for twenty years between 1764 and 1784 William Cockin was the writing master and presiding genius of the writing school in the grammar school's upper room. He taught mathematics and accounts as well as writing for which the corporation paid him £10 a year; and he was allowed to charge an additional five shillings a quarter for teaching his pupils, including girls, book-keeping, geometry and navigation.

After the slog of Latin translation downstairs, the pupils could take flight upstairs. Like Jack's father, William Cockin was a self-educated man and his interests ranged widely. They included science and travel – he wrote *A Theory of the Syphon*, and edited *West's Guide to the Lakes*. He was also a poet, and his 'Ode to the Lakes' and other poems inspired his pupils to write their own poetry. His investigative paper *An Extraordinary Appearance in a Mist Near Lancaster* no doubt added to the writing master's charisma. He was known best, however, for his school textbook *A Rational and Practical Treatise on Arithmetic*, published in 1774, whose exercises caught the imagination and taught practical accounts in a memorable way:

Suppose a dog, a wolf, and a lion were to devour a sheep, and that the dog could eat up the sheep in an hour, the wolf in 3/4 of an hour and the lion in 1/2 an hour; now if the lion begins to eat 1/8 of an hour before the other two, and afterwards all three eat together, the question is in what time will the sheep be devoured?

A lad having got 4,000 nuts, in his return was met by Mad-Tom who took from him 5/8 of 2/3 of his whole stock: Raving-Ned light upon him afterwards and forced 2/5 of 5/8 of the remainder from him: Unluckily Positive-Jack found him, and required

7/10 of 17/20 of what he had left: Smiling-Dolly was by promise to have 3/4 of a quarter of what nuts he brought home: How many had the boy left?

The writing master's exercises stood Jack in good stead for the rest of his life. For fifty years as an organist and music master he managed the details of his financial affairs meticulously, and his habit of good book-keeping, inculcated by William Cockin, endured even to the dispositions in his will.

The priory organ was another ever-present influence in Jack's life. A note in Fanny Austin's scrapbook described it as having been built in 1729 by Gerard Smith, 'a three manual instrument . . . which contained eight stops on the Great, four on the Swell and four on the Choir.' It was briefly famous in 1745 when an officer in Bonnie Prince Charlie's retreating army played 'The King shall have his own again' on it. Later in the century, £100 was raised from public subscription to repair it, but after it was patched up again in 1772 at a further cost of £60 – which John Langshaw had pronounced 'incomplete and insufficient' – it was in constant need of the repair and attention that was a major part of the organist's job.

Jack's father was his first music teacher. There were no schools of music for professional musicians then; ancient universities were concerned more with the theory or 'science' of music, a more highly regarded branch of the art. One way to study music at a practical level was to serve an apprenticeship, usually starting at thirteen, with an organist and choirmaster, and at that age Jack began his formal training. His daily regime would have been strict. At four thirty in the afternoon, when the other boys ran off to swim in Dalton's Dam on the Lune, or fool around in the priory churchyard, he would have walked up the hill to help his father with the temperamental organ. Apprentices were trained from the start to make minor repairs and to tune. Changes in temperature as well as playing affect the pitch of organ pipes, and they require frequent adjustments. While the bellows blower pumped away at the back of the organ and Jack played or held the notes called out by his father, John Langshaw would have gently tapped the head of the tuning wire to increase or reduce the length of the vibrating part of the tongue of the reed and so tuned the organ.

A lesson might have followed. Jack Langshaw was nurtured on the music of the English baroque. His father imbued in him a lifelong love of the works of organist composers such as Maurice Greene and John Stanley, William Boyce and Joseph Kelway, the Italians Geminiani, Corelli and Pergolesi, and the music of Handel. No man in England knew Handel's music any better than his father, and what became known as Ancient Music formed the core of Jack's musical education. If the first organist had to leave, perhaps to prepare for a concert in the Assembly Rooms, Jack might have stayed on in the priory to practise, entrusted with the priory keys to lock up afterwards. Apprentice organists have always assumed great responsibilities at an early age.

Jack's instructions would have continued in the evenings with practice on his father's keyboard instrument at home or lessons and exercises in harmony and counterpoint. 'I am sure,' wrote Thomas Henry Collinson, an apprentice organist at Durham Cathedral a century later, 'it is the diligent study of counterpoint only that makes the thoroughly practical musician and composer.'

Above all else – above the sights and sounds of Lancaster, the polyglot community, the Latin declensions of his headmaster, the flights of fancy of the writing master; above the play and the squabbles of his younger brothers William and James, the twins Joseph and Benjamin and his sister Elizabeth; above the demands of the priory organ and the strict rules of counterpoint – the most lasting influence on Jack Langshaw was his father. Many years later when Jack was an old man and, as Mr Langshaw, had been priory organist himself for twenty-six years, he was asked by John Sainsbury to write something about himself and his musical life for *The New Biographical Dictionary of Musicians*. He responded with a letter that opened with an account of his father's achievements in London:

... this ingenious organist and mechanic, my father, was engaged by the late Earl of Bute to set the Barrels for his celebrated organ ... and continued in his Lordship's sole employ for above twelve years ... The Barrels were set ... in so masterly a manner that the effect was equal to that produced by the most finished player.

John Langshaw to John Sainsbury, 3 January 1824

This letter, giving precedence to Jack's father, the first organist, became the entry for the two organists in Sainsbury and the basis of the entry for them both in Grove's dictionary.

It is not surprising that the first organist had such a strong influence. His obituary would note his strong and vigorous mind and 'his conversation lively and instructive.' It is not hard to imagine the middle-aged father recalling the days of his youthful London triumphs to his son as they worked together on the troublesome old organ; all the important people he had known, his noble employer the Earl of Bute, the great George Frideric Handel, the London organists and organ builders, the exciting days of keyboard invention in the 1760s, the influential Sir John Hawkins. His stories made a lasting impression on Jack. All the anecdotes related by his grandson Pearson, Jack's youngest son, more than a hundred years later, can only have come from Jack, since Pearson was not born until 1814, sixteen years after his grandfather had died. The words 'ingenious organist ... so masterly a manner ... effect equal to that produced by the most finished player ...' became family legend, expressions of approval passed down by John Langshaw to his son Jack, who repeated them to his son and to the compiler of a musical dictionary fifty years later.

Jack probably heard the story of the Earl of Bute's organ many times as he helped his father and learned the art, mystery and skills of the organ loft, and he might have heard it yet again as he watched him working on a much smaller barrel organ that is now in the Judge's House Museum in Lancaster.

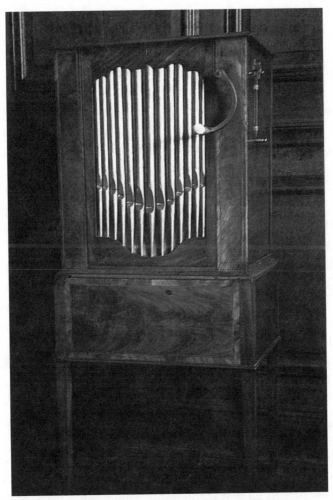

Barrel organ made by John Langshaw, late eighteenth century.
Reproduced by permission of Lancaster Museum Service.

This barrel organ is quite small, about four feet high, contained in an elegant mahogany case probably made by Gillows towards the end of the 1780s. Like all barrel organs, it is wind-operated. The rank of gilded pipes at the front is for show only; the real ones, four ranks of pipes made of wood and thin tin or pewter, are inside. An ivory handle is turned to work the bellows and rotate the barrels at the right speed. The tune depends on the length and spacing of the staples pinned on to the barrels.

Thomas Arne's 'Rule, Britannia' played on Langshaw's barrel organ fills the main room of the museum. The familiar verse begins with a single line of notes. The first line of the chorus adds a bass line. Three-part harmony is brought in for 'Britannia rule the waves,' and 'Britons never, never, never shall be slaves' is rounded off in full, four-part harmony. Trills and turns ornament the music throughout, cleverly compensating for any extra air used to sustain the important notes. Composers often left ornaments to the individual performer's discretion; they would have been part of the musical vocabulary of a musician like John Langshaw, who played both organ and harpsichord, and his interpretation of the well-known air is lively, light and joyful. He pasted a label saying 'John Langshaw, Organ Maker, Lancaster' on the barrel before he pinned it and another inside the lid listing the thirty tunes on the three barrels.

They were the popular tunes of the day, all no doubt well-known to him and his family by the time he had finished the job: 'La Belle Catherine,' 'Blaise et Babet' and 'The Assassin.' There were military airs: 'London Military Dance,' 'Captain Mackintosh' and 'Soldier's Joy'; tunes to dance to: 'Carlisle Minuet', 'Slingsby's Allemande' and 'Fisher's Hornpipe'; and music for fun: 'Charming Fellow' and 'What a Brave my Granny is.' Langshaw's barrel organ was the automatic music of the late eighteenth century, and the barrels were its CDs. It is still in tune and when it plays 'See the Conquering Hero Comes' it is probably as authentic a Handelian sound as one can hear. Few people then or now, armed only with hammer, nails and pliers, could produce music so delightful, so enchanting.

Yet for all his efforts John Langshaw was always dependent on Lancaster Corporation for his employment as priory organist, and he had to look to his contacts and friends in London to further Jack's musical career. Having got his scholarly second son away to one of the best schools in London, he was determined to secure a capital education for his eldest boy. Sir John Hawkins's continued patronage of young George Langshaw made him an obvious ally, and in a letter written in February 1778 Sir John looks forward to a proposed trip south by the Lancaster organist. Later that year John Langshaw did go to London, and by the autumn Jack, then fifteen, had started life there as a pupil of Dr Benjamin Cooke. Cooke was a friend of Sir John's, a member of the Academy of Ancient Music and the organist at Westminster Abbey.

8

——•◦••◦•——

JACK IN LONDON

LONDON IN 1778, when Jack Langshaw first went there, was as glamorous and dangerous, as unique and ever-changing, as it is today. It was the largest city in Europe, with a population of almost one million people. Its demographic explosion during the eighteenth century was due not to an increased birth or survival rate but to the huge influx of provincial immigrants from a rural economy in decline. This ever-expanding population had an insatiable need for raw materials, food, consumer and luxury goods. Daniel Defoe, in his *Tour Through the Whole Island of Great Britain* (1724–26), had written of 'the general dependence of the whole country upon the City of London, as well for the consumption of its produce, as the circulation of its trade.' London was a vast consumers' market. It lived by trade and commerce. Goods from overseas and all parts of the country were shipped in daily by sea, road and increasingly by canal. It was the centre of government, and, with the most important seaport in the country and the world's most sophisticated system of banking, it was the commercial and cultural capital of the country and of the whole colonial empire. In Defoe's words, 'It is not the kingdom which makes London rich, but the city of London makes all the country rich.' It was the greatest emporium in the world, and the

Strand was the nation's shop window where manufactured goods made in the city's workshops and from all over the country were displayed. In the streets, traders sold everything from live lobsters, eels and shrimps to pottles of raspberries.

It was a city of riches and a city of poverty. The influx of Defoe's 'working trades,' 'the poor' and 'the miserable' had caused the westward drift of wealthier people across the city; as James Boswell noted, 'one end of London is like a different country from the rest in looks and manners.' The social distinctions separating the west from the east end of town were reflected in the architecture. The most fashionable addresses, where a number of Broadwood customers lived, were in Westminster and St James, Marylebone and Piccadilly, in new streets such Arlington Street and elegant, open squares. Master craftsmen, journeymen and entrepreneurs like John Broadwood also lived there, close to their patrons. Unskilled workers, the chairmen, porters and coal haulers lived to the east in a belt of waterside parishes along the shores of the Thames, at Shadwell, Whitechapel and Bethnal Green. There the houses were old, the streets narrow; there was overcrowding, poverty and disease. St Katherine's and Southwark were dangerous places where vagrants, beggars and the destitute eked out miserable lives in a constant struggle to survive the violence and wretched conditions.

In those parishes, and in the rookeries and thieves' kitchens off Holborn and Long Acre, mortality was high. The poor, it was said, lived on bad bread and cheap gin and many starved to death. Drunkenness, crime and prostitution were the result both of living conditions and the indifference of the governing class, some of whom, at the highest level, set a heroically debauched example of their own. William Hogarth's print *Gin Lane* gave a picture of the degradation caused by the widespread abuse of cheap gin in the middle of the century, a social problem on a huge scale that declined but slowly as gin shops were replaced by ale-houses. In 1780, at the time of the Gordon Riots, the most violent and savagely repressed riots in London's history, Horace Walpole wrote that there were 'more persons killed by drinking than by ball or bayonet.'

Sporadic outbursts of rioting were often signs of underlying class resentment, of the enormous differences between rich and poor. The Earl of Mornington thought he needed £50,000 a year to begin to live like a gentleman, while a prosperous tradesman's family lived well on £350. Others worked punishing hours for subsistence wages: a journeyman cabinet-maker earned between 15s and £1 a week, an assistant organist received £15 a year and a Spitalfields silk girl was paid as little as 3s a week. The lowest paid of all were female domestic workers: Barbara Broadwood paid her servant Elizabeth Powell 8 guineas a year. At the same time 6d would buy enough meat and drink for a journeyman's dinner, 1lb of candles cost 2s 10d, a ticket for the *Messiah* at the Foundling Hospital was 10s 6d and a set of false teeth with gold springs at £73 10s cost more than a harpsichord; little wonder that many got dead drunk on gin for 2d.

Between these extremes were many levels of the middle ranks of society. People with incomes of between £50 and £200 a year who could afford some of life's pleasures constituted about a quarter of the population. Wealth was no longer measured only in terms of land. In the cities and towns of England, industry and the accumulation of money generated a range of entertainments and pursuits to suit every pocket or purse. Whereas French culture in the years before the Revolution was dominated by the Court, in London there was something for everyone at every level.

High and low life mixed at Vauxhall and Ranelagh Gardens, where diversions of all kinds were offered for a shilling: music, fireworks, balls and masquerades, the social scene. 'There is nothing in all the world like these two gardens,' noted Leopold Mozart when he brought his son to perform in London in 1765; 'People constantly moved about elegantly dressed. Gentlemen wore silk stockings and shoes with silver buckles, carrying their three cornered hats under their arms and their swords at their sides. Ladies wore long dresses and huge hooped skirts.' James Boswell was bowled over by the scene: 'Went to Ranelagh,' he wrote. 'This is Fashionable entertainment peculiar to London. The noble Rotunda all surrounded by boxes to sit in and such a profusion of well-dressed people walking round is very fine.' Ladies with hair as high as steeples and men in short-tailed perukes attended exhibitions at the Royal Academy at Somerset House or walked in the parks of St James and Kensington Gardens, to see and be seen. 'Here,' according to Boswell, 'a young man of curiosity and observation may have a sufficient fund of entertainment and may lap up ideas to employ the mind in old age . . . [he] can have the most lively enjoyment from the sight of external objects without regard to property at all.'

By the 1770s there were over a hundred papers and journals, and men of affairs met in coffee houses all over the city to read them and discuss and settle the questions of the day. One of the most influential journals throughout the eighteenth century was the *Spectator*. In conveniently short essays it advocated a system of polite behaviour by which men could accommodate the complexities of modern life and live in harmony by cultivating good taste and regulating and refining their natural passions to a greater Elegance. Gratification of the passions was effeminate, in the sense of womanish; intellectual pursuits were deemed manly. Though there were many notable exceptions to the good manners of 'Mr Spectator,' in late-eighteenth-century England such manners were promoted as the key to civilized living. Politeness was a modus vivendi, essentially urban, sociable and cultured.

It had its counterpart in popular pastimes of extreme violence: bull and bear baiting, cock fighting and 'throwing.' There were bare knuckle contests between men and fights between men and dogs; 'Bruising Peg' was one of many women pugilists. Such spectacles, reeking of stale sweat, tobacco, bad breath, ale and old clothes, were also opportunities for the most popular pastime of all: gambling. At the highest level fortunes and reputations were won and lost at private parties and in White's and Brooks' clubs by some of the leading figures of the day: at the age of twenty-four Charles James Fox had gambling debts of over £140,000 paid for him by his father; the Prince of Wales had his paid by Parliament. The most violent and popular of all entertainments, usually designated a fair day, were the executions at Tyburn, which remained public until 1868.

London was a cosmopolitan city with an increasingly European taste in music. People went to hear it in the city's great churches, at the Hanover Square Rooms where Bach and Abel's concerts were still the most prestigious. At the Pantheon, where Marks and Spencer now stands in Oxford Street, music was only part of the varied entertainment. Entrance to Handel's oratorios was by open ticket, Italian opera at the King's Theatre in Haymarket cost 3s and there was popular light operetta at Covent Garden. Music as spectacle was also on offer. Three-year-old William 'Little Billy' Crotch, for example, a cobbler's son from Norfolk, was brought to London to perform as 'the Self-taught Musical Child.' He could play anything by ear, name every note in a chord of twelve and, although his span was a mere six notes, he played with his knuckles, tumbling his hand over the keys. If there was to be any element of music's former exclusivity, the courtly culture that once surrounded it had to be reinvented.

There were still gentlemen's concert clubs, but people, especially women, who cared passionately about the social distinctions had to look elsewhere to hear their music in a venue that set them apart from what was available commercially and reflected their social standing. The wife of a man who was in the process of making a fortune might buy a Court Kalendar, as Barbara Broadwood did, to follow the progress of the royal family, and practise her French in anticipation of arriving socially; her husband might sell his best harpsichords to people of the highest quality, but that did not mean she would be welcome to hear their music with them. John Broadwood's marketing strategy, after all, was based on his customers' desire to maintain the social distinctions. Society was changing. It was complex and bewildering, and there was safety in like-minded exclusivity.

Hannah More, reflecting on her observations of London society in *Thoughts on the Importance of the Manners of the Great to General Society* (1788), noted the progressive refinement of manners, the art of polite conversation and the sociable sharing of ideas and cultural pastimes. Such civilized social intercourse found its natural home in the private subscription concert, convivial gatherings of like-minded connoisseurs who joined together for exclusive evenings of refined music-making. In a society where commerce and an ability to pay was a potential leveller, entrance to subscription concerts depended more on who you were and knew. Payment was for a series of concerts rather than one event, and although they were announced and reviewed in the *Morning Post*, entrance to these little communities of taste was confined to invited subscribers and their guests. People were elevated simply by being there.

Subscribers to the concerts given by Charles and Samuel Wesley, who lived with their father, the Reverend Charles Wesley, at Number One Chesterfield Street, Marylebone, came from the highest ranks of London society. They included members of the great and their guests, foreign diplomats, a sprinkling of the middling sort and a few of the capital's most celebrated artists. Many were customers of John Broadwood and a few, in 1778, were already buying his pianoforte. They paid three guineas for a series of seven concerts known collectively as 'A Concert' that took place at fortnightly intervals through the winter months. The Wesley subscription concerts were as far as may be imagined from the cacophony and discord, the drunkenness and violence in the streets on the seamier side of London.

In 1778 the Reverend Charles Wesley was seventy-one. He was the younger brother of John Wesley (1703–91), the founder of

Methodism. After Oxford and ordination in the Church of England, the brothers had sailed for Georgia in 1735 with General James Oglethorpe, who had founded the colony two years earlier. Filled with missionary zeal, John had preached to settlers and American Indians in Savannah and at Fort Frederica. Charles, his charismatic older brother's able lieutenant, went as General Oglethorpe's secretary with special responsibility for Indian affairs. But the brothers' idealism was short-lived. Charles was overwhelmed by the physical and spiritual obstacles of life in a new colony, and John's strict Methodism did not at first find favour with the local populace. Both brothers became objects of scandalous accusation and within two years they had returned to England. They maintained a lifelong reticence about their experience. Nonetheless they had sown the seeds of Methodism in the colony, and their deacon and friend, George Whitefield, stayed on to nurture the new faith. In time Methodism became a major religious denomination in the United States and the most dynamic missionary movement of the nineteenth century. The Wesleys took home with them a lifelong opposition to slavery, culminating in John Wesley's condemnatory 'Thoughts Upon Slavery'(1774).

After America, John and Charles Wesley continued their mission as leaders of the evangelical revival in England. Because of their evangelical style, they were denied access to the pulpit in many churches and so held their meetings in the open air and upper rooms. They remained close throughout their lives, despite their having extreme disagreements at times. Charles directly and dramatically interfered with John's wish to marry Grace Murray in 1749, and when Charles married Sarah Gwynne the same year, his brother refused him the annual stipend of £100 he requested. There were deeply felt religious differences as well. Charles always supported his brother's Societies, yet feared separation from the Church of England; his diaries and letters show his emphatic opposition and a desire to die within the communion of the established church.

Like his brother John, Charles Wesley was an inspiring preacher; but his great gift was as a writer of powerful hymns that are still the core of the English hymnal. He gave up itinerant preaching and in 1771 moved from Bristol to London with his wife and three surviving children, Charles (b. 1757), Sally (b. 1760) and Samuel (b. 1766) to live near the Foundery, the centre of Methodism in London. The parish rate-book for Marylebone shows him as the householder of Number One Chesterfield Street, a mansion on the edge of town with fields to the north across Marylebone Road, then called New Road. The house belonged to a wealthy adherent of Wesleyan Methodism, Mrs Gumley, who had given him the unexpired twenty years of a lease on the property.

Life there revolved around his sons, Charles and Samuel. Both boys were musical prodigies and had learned Latin, Greek and Hebrew from their father, a great believer in early rising who began his day at 4 a.m. and allowed his sons only an hour longer in bed. Daines Barrington, a frequent visitor to the house, described their remarkable abilities in *Miscellanies on Various Subjects* (1781), writing of Samuel, 'He was able to sing at sight from his first knowing his notes. The delicacy of his ear was likewise very remarkable.'

According to their father, they had been able to compose from an early age. As well as having a prodigious keyboard technique on both organ and harpsichord, they were able to extemporize freely. Charles, the older by nine years, could play the harpsichord by ear at the age of three; Samuel had written an oratorio when he was eight. They both went on to study with the masters: Samuel with the violinist and composer Wilhelm Cramer, who was the leader of the orchestra at the Bach-Abel concerts, and Charles with both William Boyce, organist at the Chapel Royal and Master of the King's Music, and Dr Joseph Kelway, composer and organist at St Martin-in-the-Fields, who traced his musical line back to Geminiani and Corelli; it was this tradition of English baroque out of the Italian that Charles passed on to his pupils.

Number One Chesterfield Street was large and well-furnished. It had a grand music room with two chamber organs, a harpsichord, ten music desks and space for four or five singers. In this room Charles and Samuel performed for visitors and held their fort-nightly subscription concerts between January and April each year from 1779 to 1785. It was here too that Charles taught his pupils, and in September 1778 when he was twenty-one, he accepted fifteen-year-old Jack Langshaw from Lancaster as his new pupil, or 'scholar.'

This was not the arrangement John Langshaw had had in mind when he sent his eldest son to London to further his musical edu-cation. Jack had quickly become dissatisfied with Dr Cooke of Westminster Abbey and wished to leave. After all the first organ-ist's carefully laid plans, his son seemed bent on throwing away the opportunity he had secured for him to study with the best of London's organist doctors under the patronage of the great Sir John Hawkins.

In the autumn of 1778 letters flew back and forth between London and Lancaster. Twenty-two letters from the Reverend Charles Wesley to John Langshaw, with three draft replies from the Lancaster organist, have survived from these years. The first few tell of Jack's unhappiness with Dr Cooke, of the anger of Sir John Hawkins and the kindness of the Wesley family. They continue with an account of Jack's life and musical progress in London between 1778 and 1784 during his three separate periods of study with Charles Wesley. No letter of Jack's has survived, although he was the reason for all the letters between the two fathers and many of his comments are reported in them.

As their correspondence developed into friendship, the letters between the two fathers range over many subjects, including Methodism, the American War of Independence and musical life in London, with many references to the established masters of the day, their tuition fees, their jealousies and rivalries. Those from Reverend Charles are sprinkled with lines from his own poetry and visionary hymns; John Langshaw's reflect his anxiety for his son's well-being and gratitude for the kindness of the Wesley family.

There is a letter from Charles Wesley junior to Jack in 1785, then, after a gap of many years, a second group of letters, one from Samuel and five from Charles to his former scholar, who by that time had succeeded his father as organist at the priory church in Lancaster.

The letters, exchanged over a period of fifty years between the Reverend Charles Wesley, his sons and the two Lancaster organists, were kept by descendants of John Langshaw for 210 years until they were sold in 1988. They began with Jack's first visit to London, which would last from autumn 1778 to summer 1779.

———

John Langshaw's organ duties at the priory were over for the day. He had two difficult letters to write. He sharpened his quill again, picked up three or four small pieces of paper from his desk and glanced at what was written on them in a youthful hand. He knew their contents well and they did not please him. A gasp of exasperation escaped his taut, closed lips. He was fifty-three; he was worried; he shook his head. Children!

He sat at his desk and opened a book of blank, laid paper. Holding his chin in one hand, he thought a moment longer, then dipped his pen in the ink and began to draft his first letter to the Reverend Charles Wesley. It was 28 September 1778.

Dear Sir,

I have received several agreeable letters from my Son, giving an account of the very kind reception he meets with at your house. The poor boy has been no little mortified at the method Dr. Cook first took with him . . . Your kindness to the lad comes at a very seasonable time . . .

Jack is the oldest of seven Children & he but fifteen last February. All my hopes are on him to support my Wife & little ones if I fall while they are helpless; therefore I must make haste to get the boy well, & speedily instructed; & I must make use of my friends; as a hundred a year (the utmost I get) will not both mentain [*sic*] my large family & pay the high fees some Masters demand . . .

He wrote the word 'agreeable' through gritted teeth, forcing himself to write with a calm, steady hand. He abbreviated the words 'received' and 'account,' for quickness; he would write them in full in the fair copy

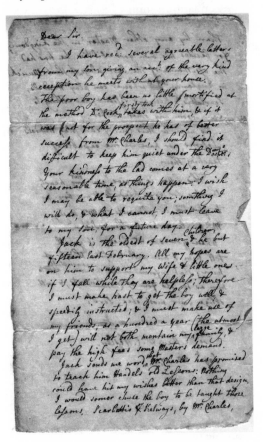

Letter from John Langshaw to the Reverend Charles Wesley, 28 September 1778. Reproduced by permission of the Manuscript, Archives, and Rare Book Library (MARBL), Robert R. Woodruff Library, Emory University, Atlanta, Georgia.

to send. Being careful how he expressed himself on this first page, he altered 'takes' to 'first took,' just in case Dr Cooke's method had improved. He inserted the word 'Children' after the word 'seven' and spelled 'mentain' the way he spoke, adding 'large' before 'family' for emphasis.

Halfway through the next paragraph he turned the page and began writing on the reverse. His thoughts accelerated and his writing became more agitated. He dipped his pen frequently into the ink, more often than was necessary. Blots fell from the overloaded quill. He crossed out and inserted words untidily. Some he amended as he went along; others he would correct when he read through the draft. By the time he reached his final paragraph he was dipping into the ink every four or five words. He pressed hard on the quill, the ink flowed fast; his writing slanted, it was messy, scratchy, black; it suited his mood.

John Langshaw wrote in a fever of apprehension. He had made good use of his friends. Jack was already in London, still with Dr Cooke, but pressing his father to let him leave to study instead with Charles Wesley.

How the two young men met is not clear. It may have been through Dr Cooke, whom Charles already knew; it is also possible that an introduction was made through William Langshaw, Jack's uncle, an early and prominent Wigan Methodist who knew John Wesley from the time of his preaching there in 1772. What is clear from this first letter is that Jack's wish to leave Dr Cooke had caused a row and that his father wanted to be sure of the Wesleys before letting his son change teachers.

John Langshaw knew of Charles Wesley's prodigious musical ability. In January that year he had bought a quartet composed by Charles and he had heard him play in London earlier that summer. But would he take Jack? At this rate the lad would be adrift in London without instruction. What was more, he was committed to Dr Cooke for half a year's lessons; he may also have wondered privately if there was good reason for his son's disinclination to study with Dr. Cooke.

The problem was that Dr Cooke would hear Jack play the

harpsichord but was not inclined to teach him anything; and he shouted at him. John Langshaw drafted a second letter, this time to Dr Cooke. It was brief, calm and restrained. Although deferential, it hinted at his doubts:

> Dear Sir,
>
> . . . you hear him play Harpsicord lessons . . . yet I could wish he would have something in his head as well as his fingers . . . The lad is desirous of learning, & of an open free temper, but hard words are too much for him; he will do his utmost for a word of approbation . . . I shall shortly have an opportunity of sending you half a years pay for Jack . . .
>
> I desire my kind respects to my good friend Sir John Hawkins.
>
> Your most obedient and obliged Servant,

Dr Cooke was friendly with Sir John Hawkins, whose intervention in the affair turned a little difficulty into a row.

Two years earlier Sir John had been one of the founders of the Concert of Antient Music, a group of prominent and noble men dedicated to resist modern trends and perpetuate the music of the English baroque, Handel in particular; Dr Cooke was the Director. Both men had been members of the older Academy of Ancient Music, one of whose aims was the education of young musicians. Sir John was highly critical of Jack's departure from the doctor and his keen, not to say outraged, attitude suggests that he had been instrumental in obtaining Jack's place as Dr Cooke's pupil.

Sir John Hawkins was also chairman of the lay justices in the criminal court of London's Middlesex Quarter Sessions, and something of a hard man. Among the other members of Dr Johnson's Literary Club he had a reputation for rough argument and Johnson, his best friend, famously described him as 'a most unclubbable man'; he also said of him that he had 'a degree of brutality and a tendency to savageness that cannot be defended.' Sir John was furious when Jack Langshaw pressed to leave Dr Cooke, and the irascible old knight never forgave him.

John Langshaw had need of his 'uncommon assiduity' to deal with the business. His letter to Reverend Charles continued:

> . . . if it was not for the prospect he has of better success from Mr Charles, I should find it difficult to keep him quiet under the Doctor . . . Jack sends me word, that Mr Charles has promised to teach him Handels old Lessons . . . I wish I may be able to requite you. This letter is to give hearty thanks for what you are doing for my boy.
>
> your most obedient Servant

By early October 1778 Jack had started lessons with Charles Wesley, but the row over his transfer was still simmering. The Reverend Charles Wesley also thought carefully before writing his first letter to the Lancaster organist on 21 October. Although he sympathized with Jack Langshaw and wanted to help him, he had a concern for his own son's standing with two great men on London's musical scene. When he began he wrote fluently, underlining for emphasis. Dr Cooke, it seems, was not much of a teacher.

> My dear Sir,
> . . . I know not what you pay the Doctor for his Instructions: but as a Friend, I must inform you. <u>He is generally thought to know a great deal of Music; but not to have the Talent of Communicating his knowledge.</u> Your Son's board, I hope, costs you little . . . He is already a Favourite of my whole Family, who love him for his Sense & Modesty.
>
> Your very affectionate Servant

John Langshaw's reply is lost, but the next letter from Reverend Charles, on 16 November, suggests that Langshaw did confide details of the financial arrangements for Jack, including a payment of £10 to Dr Cooke.

Dear Sir,
The Doctors think the Trade overstocked: therefore you must not expect They woud multiply Masters. D. W[organ] had half a guinea a Lesson from every future Organist. Dr. Boyce has the same . . . Dr.'s ——'s [Cooke's] Terms would be very reasonable indeed, if he had really <u>intended</u> to make your Son Master of his art. Ten pound is too much to pay for Nothing.

    Your affectionate Servant

The letters between the two fathers continued at the rate of one a month during the winter of 1778–79. All but two of John Langshaw's are lost, but their contents can in part be surmised from those written by Reverend Charles.

Another problem was that John Langshaw could not afford to pay much for his son's lessons, and, while it is never openly stated, it can be inferred from the early letters that Charles Wesley made no charge for teaching Jack. In Reverend Charles's October letter, for example, he wrote: 'My Son thinks himself happy, that it is in his power to assist a worthy Friend. You would be glad to shew the like kindness to me, or mine. Your Son I bear a Paternal Regard to . . .'

Jack spent Christmas 1778 with the Wesleys. The next letter from Reverend Charles, written on Christmas Eve, makes it clear that a gift (a pudding?) had been sent from Lancaster and that the new arrangement suited them all:

My dear Sir,
We thank you for your Present: which, we doubt not, will prove very good when we taste it . . .

. . . In your absence I look upon Jack as my adopted Son, & we all love him, as one of the Family.

Again his words and a quotation from Milton's *Paradise Lost* imply that the lessons were given without charge:

You know the Masters too well, to wonder at their Selfishness. My Sons are glad to supply their lack of service & assistance: And your Son is glad to receive instruction . . .
If Charles makes a good Musician of your Son (which there is no reason to doubt of) he has his reward . . . And as to You –
A grateful mind by owing pays, at once
Indebted & discharg'd.

The cost of Jack's lodgings is still of concern to Reverend Charles:

Ought you not to be at a certainty with the Friend he boards with? You will excuse the Question as I know you have no great Superfluities. But we know the way to provide all these other things, namely by seeking the kingdom First.

your very affectionate Servant

Five weeks later, on 1 February 1779, in response to a letter from John Langshaw, there is further suggestion that Charles made no charge for Jack's lessons:

Dear Sir,
. . . Charles sets out . . . to give his Scholars all the advantages he can. He will not be kind to teach a Dunce, or any person whom he despairs of making a Musician. Your Son is as willing to learn, as He to teach: & pays his Master by his Progress, & good Behaviour . . .

Yours most affectionately

And in a postscript he adds: 'My Father had 19 children; yet never turned away his face from a poor Man.'

Meanwhile, Sir John Hawkins's ill humour continued. In the same February letter Reverend Charles referred to a strongly worded letter that John Langshaw had reported receiving:

> Sir J's 'hard words' should give you no disturbance. They are the language of Passion not of Reason. Neither is he <u>much</u> to be blamed; as he has not his full Evidence. If he knew all (which it woud not be proper to inform him of) he woud commend Jack's prudent Behaviour.

Reverend Charles urged restraint on Jack's part and advised him not to say anything: 'I charge your Son to take it all patiently, & to hold his tongue, & to mind his business. It is not his business to write to, or expostulate with, a great man.' Many years later, when John Langshaw was putting his affairs in order at the end of his life, he wrote on the outside of this letter, which he had kept, 'Respecting the dispute with Sir John Hawkins,' and the row became Langshaw family lore.

The dispute did not subside until the summer, when the reason for Reverend Charles advising restraint becomes more clear. Dr Cooke was an eminent London organist and Sir John an influential figure in London musical circles, and young Charles Wesley was known to them both; any disfavour resulting from their displeasure with Jack could have proved injurious to Charles's career. On 2 June 1779 Reverend Charles wrote:

> My dear Sir,
> . . . Sir John: who, by the way, woud be perfectly reconciled, if he knew exactly how matters stand. Only Charles would not unnecessarily give offence to Dr. C.
>
> Your faithful Brother and Servant

By early summer 1779 Jack had made such good progress that the storm in the teacup ceased to matter. On 17 July Reverend Charles wrote:

Dear Sir,
Charles proposes to publish his Concertos next Winter. Jack will do them justice by his play . . . Sir John (between friends) over-rates his own Musical Abilities. The more Jack excels, the less he will be liked by some – whose judgement is not worth regarding . . .

Your truly affectionate Servant,

In ten months John Langshaw's son had become a first-class keyboard player. Charles Wesley had been an inspired choice as a replacement for Dr Cooke. Jack Langshaw became a fine musician who carried the keyboard culture back with him from London to Lancaster and north-west England, and the reports that the Reverend Charles Wesley sent to John Langshaw in Lancaster ensured that Jack's life in Georgian London was recorded for history.

How did Jack Langshaw learn so well so quickly? He had found a gifted young teacher and the two seem to have taken to one another. Charles Wesley was six years older; he was fun, good-natured and agreeable, despite having great vanity. He was quick-thinking and perceptive, but so immersed in music that: '. . . he knows no heaven beyond his harpsichord and when unemployed with that he passes his time in Dress, mimicking ridiculous characters . . . at the altar of good humour and buffoonery. Wesley has never thought deeply about any subject and no domestic misfortune can render him unhappy for more than twenty-four hours.' (Anonymous note in the Wesley Scrapbook, John Ryland's Library, Manchester).

Reverend Charles confides in his letters that Charles is not ambitious: he 'goes on well in a private way, not seeking great things'; and 'He has nothing mercenary about him.' John Langshaw also mentions Charles's kindness and specifically of having heard from Jack 'that his Master is for attempting to get a Ticket for Bach & Abel's Concert, & will then go with him, Jack's Master proves a Brother to him.'

As noted previously, the letters contain details of Jack's musical progress. Charles Wesley taught him in the tradition of his own training from Boyce and Kelway, and it met with John Langshaw's full approval. In the letter of 28 September 1778 he wrote to Reverend Charles:

> Jack sends me word, that Mr Charles has promised to teach him Handels old Lessons: Nothing could have hit my wishes better than that design. I would sooner chuse the boy to be taught those lessons, Scarlattis or Kelways, by Mr Charles, than by any other Master in the kingdom; for besides his own good abilities, he has had the assistance of the best player of that Musick in England [Kelway]. And whoever can play Handel's, Scarlatti's & Kelway's Lessons [suites]; has nothing to fear from any other author.

John Langshaw regarded such music as the foundation of keyboard competence, something seldom met with in his part of England. His letter continues: 'No man in this County [Lancashire] can play Handel's Lessons, nor have we one capable of teaching them.' Three weeks later Reverend Charles replied: 'Charles has begun teaching him Scarlatti's Music, which he catches with surprising Quickness. Handel[,] Kelway, Geminiani follow – as he is ready for them.'

Jack had made a good start and the teaching routine settled down. In his letter of 16 November, Reverend Charles wrote:

> Charles has appointed him [Jack] to come for instruction twice a Week; which will be sufficient to set him up for a Country

Organist in One year . . . On the Evening which he spends with
us every week, he may hear the most excellent Music: which will
be as useful to him, as playing himself . . . both my Sons will help
him forward:– if he continues sober[,] diligent and teachable.

Your Affectionate Servant & Friend

During the winter months Jack attended the Wesley's subscription concerts and experienced Georgian London's elite
musical life at first hand. In the letter from 1 February 1779
Reverend Charles wrote to John Langshaw:

Charles has taken him in to his Concert, which will be of real
advantage to him . . .
    Return my love to your Brother, who has some hand (tho' he
does not know it) in Jack's Instruction. At leaving town he made
me a present of a Guinea; (at a time I wanted it) which I have
lain it upon Charles, never to forget.

Yours most affectionately

This was exactly what John Langshaw back in Lancaster had hoped
to hear. His son was learning from the best in the land and asso-
ciating with people in high places, just as he himself had done
twenty years before. The brother referred to in this letter was John's
younger brother William Langshaw (1734–1825). William had experienced a dramatic conversion to Methodism after John Wesley
had first preached at 'Wicked Wigan' in 1768. Six years later he and
a charismatic young preacher, Samuel Bradburn, had ridden from
Wigan to London, raising funds as they went for a new Methodist
chapel in Wigan. Bradburn's diary speaks of 'this wonderful City'
and its 'remarkable places,' and records at least two occasions
during their ten-week stay in London when they met the elders of
the Methodist Conference and heard Charles Wesley preach.

John Langshaw drafted another letter to Reverend Charles on 15 February 1779. He wrote this one closely and evenly on both sides of the page. Crossings out and reconsidered words were fewer. Things had settled down and he felt free to confide in Reverend Charles the anxiety he had felt for Jack the previous autumn:

My dear Friend,

. . . When Jack pressed so to leave the Doctor, I told him you must first be secured, for I had my fears on more accounts than one, but one was, that Mr Charles might have objections, as it is natural for those Masters with uncommon capasities, to expect something of their own likeness in a Scholar; here I feared for Jack; but when I had your consent, & knowing Jack had been tried, I told my Wife I was sure Jack would do or Mr C would not be plauged with him. And from Your letters, & what Jack plays I have such hopes as give me pleasure . . . When I was last in London I was desirous of hearing your sons play, but from my own rustick tempers, I had no reason to expect it, but mentioning my <u>Wishes & Fears</u> to Dr. Worgan, he assured me you would let me hear them, – You did so, & moreover promised that they should help Jack, then I was quite amazed . . .

He refers to his brother William:

I have just wrote to my Brother, & given him as much of your letter as will make him happy. Will: always said you was good natured, I find it so to a great degree.

William Langshaw was also an organist and organ technician, but he had had a somewhat chequered career. After his time in London he had decided to try his luck in the cotton industry. He erected a mill at Eagley Bridge near Bolton that remains today, having illegally felled the local landowner's timber to build it.

Trouble beset the venture from the start and William did not remain long in that business either. He seems to have been an attractive, restless character whose generous gesture had clearly made a lasting impression on Reverend Charles, who often asks about him in his letters.

John Langshaw was content not only with the tuition Jack was getting but also with his son's evident happiness. In the same February letter he writes:

> By his letters he seems to be in good spirits, he tells me in this last that he has begun on Handel's 4th lesson, & has got four of Scarlattis, by some other letters I was informed he had got two of Handel's Concertos in the 3d set, & the 5th & 2d lessons, by this account I am satisfied he is not idle . . . Jack says not a word of his own improvement, nor how much time he spends in practice, I can only guess from what he plays, It is your letters give me the most positive information . . .
>
> From Your most obedient & obliged Servant

Two months later, on 6 April, Reverend Charles replied with encouraging information about Jack: he worked hard and seems to have learned remarkably swiftly:

> My dear Sir,
> Your Son goes on well . . . He seldom practices at home less than 5 hours a day. The Afternoon he spends in reading. He is a good deal of his time with us; & never idle . . . My Wife's Sisters, just by, like him as well as we do. Our Concerts, I believe, have been of use to him . . . his Master will lose no credit by him.
>
> Give my love to your Brother, & tell him to call on us whenever he visits London.
>
> Your affectionate Servant & Friend

Jack thrived in the kindly atmosphere of the Wesley household. His words home are quoted in one of his father's letters to Reverend Charles:

> With your last kind letter, I got one from Jack, which begins thus 'Mr. Wesleys are indeed the best friends I have got in town, and I hope I shall always continue to deserve it.' I hope he always will keep a grateful sence of your goodness to him in his mind.

Like his brother, Reverend Charles held strong views on bringing up the young. He believed that children of the same age were a bad influence on one another and that early rising was essential for their sound development. On 17 May 1779 he wrote to John Langshaw:

> My dear Brother,
> When young, I had, like Jack, an odd Notion, That one might learn more from old people than from young; which made me covet the company of the former. Jack has no desire for acquaintance of his own age; which is a distinguishing mercy.
> He talks of visiting you in a month. But his Master (to say nothing of the rest of my family) will not part with him so soon. He must stay here for as long as Charles does; which will be 2 or 3 months longer. He is one of our family . . .
>
> Your faithful friend and Servant

And in a postscript he adds:

> . . . No young man in health requires more than Seven hours sleep. Let him go to bed at Ten & rise at 5. – all the year round. – I had rather leave my Children such an Habit than an Estate – but alas! these mothers – put in their thwarting oar . . .

By July 1779, Jack, who was then sixteen, was ready to return home with his brother from Charterhouse. George Langshaw had continued to enjoy the patronage of Sir John Hawkins, despite his older brother's fall from grace. On 2 June Reverend Charles wrote to John Langshaw:

> My dear Sir,
> You have begun counting the days to Jack's Return. We shall be sorry to part with him . . . Your other Son seems a very promising Youth. By & by he may bring his Brother again into favor with Sir John . . .

The Langshaw brothers were still in London a month later and there was talk of George trying for a place at Oxford as a Servitor, or Poor Scholar, one who would perform menial tasks in return for his fees. Undeterred by the thought of such a humble start,

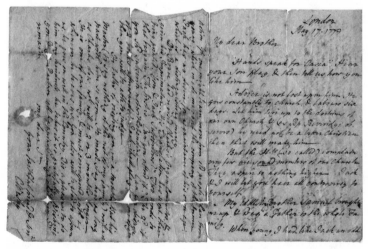

Letter from the Reverend Charles Wesley to John Langshaw, 17 May 1779. Reproduced by permission of the Manuscript, Archives, and Rare Book Library (MARBL), Robert R. Woodruff Library, Emory University, Atlanta, Georgia.

Reverend Charles foresees bishop's vestments for George Langshaw. On 17 July he wrote to John Langshaw:

> My dear Sir,
> . . . He [Jack] talks of leaving us soon. Whenever it is, we shall all miss him. George I shall try to reconcile to a Servitor's Gown; which several have worn; & afterward Lawn Sleeves.
>
> Your faithful Brother and Servant

In the summer of 1779 Jack and George Langshaw returned home to Lancaster.

9

JACK'S RETURN TO LONDON

BY THE AUTUMN of 1779 Reverend Charles was reflecting on Jack's progress and looking forward to his return. In a letter written to John Langshaw on 26 October he praised Jack's musical abilities and passed on a compliment made by a Mrs Luther, one of the subscribers to the Chesterfield Streets concerts, a lady whose name appears regularly in the earliest Broadwood books. (She had a tuning contract as early as 1772 for her Shudi harpsichord and made an early transition from harpsichord to pianoforte.)

> My dear Friend,
> He is certainly improved in more things than Music. Charles's First Scholar, Mrs Luther, a Lady of fashion, & of great discernment, told Charles That 'Jack was one of the best-bred Youths whom she had seen.' Dont tell this to Jack for young fellows, you know, are too apt to be vain. I allow his Father to be a little vain of such a Son . . .
> Another 6 months Visit would set him up A.M. [Master of Music] . . . had you not better send him to us, before Winter?

He recognized that Jack's musical abilities would soon exceed those of his elders:

Jack laughs at difficulties; & will soon be able to teach them [all]:
Dr. C[ooke,] Sir John, or – [you] his Father . . .

He ended on his favourite precept for the young, and included a quote from the poet Edward Young:

> My one Condition is That he keep early hours. He must rise at
> Six, if he woud attain his point
> 'By straining up the Steep of Excellent.' Early rising is good for
> soul, body, & estate.

> Your faithful Friend & loving Servant

However, Jack did not return to London for over a year. During his absence letters continued to be exchanged by the two fathers at approximately two-monthly intervals. Reverend Charles's letters reveal his practical Christian generosity, a genuine affection for Jack and a growing friendship with John Langshaw.

Although John Langshaw's letters of this period are lost, something of their contents can be deduced from those of Reverend Charles. The Langshaws, it seems, did not rise as early as the Wesleys:

> Does Jack rise as early as his health permits? Let early hours and
> Punctuality distinguish him [Jack] from the whole Tribe of
> Musicians.

> It is your fault if he does not rise early: for what is Precept without example?
> He must not look to you for an Example, but to us.

> He knows my single Postulatum, Early & constant rising. You
> know not the importance of this Habit. I do, & therefore recommend it earnestly to all my young friends . . .

They discuss practical matters. John Langshaw has gout, and Wesley comments: 'You have no right to the Gout, unless you <u>sit still.</u> Gentle, but constant, Exercise is the only palliative Cure.'

When John Langshaw's organist's salary of £100 a year is increased: 'We sincerely rejoice with you in the Augmentation of your salary.'

William Langshaw starts building his cotton mill at Eagley Bridge, with high hopes of prosperity. The next letter from London warns: 'Your Brother I shall be very glad to see – that I may remind him . . . Beware of Covetousness!'

Both fathers worry about their sons and Reverend Charles asks: 'Who brought <u>us</u> safe thro' the slippery Paths of youth?'

They also discuss music teaching and John Langshaw asks about lessons for one of his pupils whose mother is reluctant to pay Charles's entrance fee. Reverend Charles's reply, dated 15 July 1780, sets out the rates for music lessons in London:

> He would not dislike a Scholar of yours for she must know what she is about . . . Bach [J. C.] & the first Masters have 6 Guineas entrance, & half a guinea a Lesson of 20 minutes. Charles's price is 3 Guineas Entrance, & 3 Guineas a month. He never keeps a Scholar less than an hour . . . he spares no pains to make his Scholars Musicians. He takes but a few, that he may do them justice . . . for his own Credit [he] insists on Entrance . . . All are satisfied with him.

There is no mention in this letter of the terrifying events in London during the previous month. The Gordon Riots had erupted on 2 June as a result of the support of a London mob of more than 60,000 for Lord George Gordon's petition calling for the repeal of the 1778 Catholic Relief Act. A week of rioting followed; prisons were opened, and property burned. The riots had aspects of violent egalitarianism, of settling accounts with the rich. When the mob marched on Blackfriars, the Royal Exchange and the Bank of England, thousands of troops were called out and hundreds of lives were lost. Sally Wesley was in Bath for her health, and on 8 June, at the end of a week of the worst riots in the history of the capital, her father wrote to her: 'Everybody is well – yr Mother not yet frightened out of her wits. Last night she sheltered her sons at yr. Aunts' and sat up to guard them.' The image of Sarah Wesley guarding her two grown sons against the mob may seem extraordinary, but there were aspects of those few days in London in June 1780 that presaged events in Paris nine years' later.

By the autumn they were looking forward to Jack's next visit. On 25 September he wrote to John Langshaw:

> We rejoice to hear of your Family's Welfare: & expect Jack at Christmas, while my Son's Concerts will be rehearsing. His Concertos are in the press. Your Son will soon master them: and in Six months commence Master himself – if he takes time by the forelock . . .

And there is the usual advice about early rising:

> . . . I have constantly rose at Four, till weighed down by age I am compelled to rest till Five . . . Will he [Jack] take the trouble to rise at Charles's hour, which is Six, winter & summer? . . . On this only condition, my Sons are at his service.

> Your truly affectionate Servant

Jack Langshaw's second visit to London began in December 1780 and lasted until July 1781. He would have taken the stage coach from Lancaster. The 'Liverpool and Lancaster Flying Machine' left from The King's Arms on the corner of Meeting House Lane, and passengers for London travelled on by stages via Preston and Manchester. Coaches had started running from Manchester in 1754 when, according to

Shercliff's history of the city, an advertisement for a 'flying coach' announced that 'however incredible it may appear, the coach will actually arrive in London (barring accident) in four days and a half.' The fare was £2 5s (or forty-five good tavern dinners), the luggage allowance was 14lb and outside passengers and children went half price. By the turn of the nineteenth century the journey was down to thirty hours and there were eighteen coaches a day.

Jack arrived back in London in time for the Wesley's third winter series of subscription concerts.

The Concerts had started in an informal way some years earlier. A note left by Reverend Charles, 'Hearers of Chas. and Sam.,' contains details of a private performance at Chesterfield Street in 1775 in which Charles played music by Corelli, Scarlatti and Purcell. Two years later, when Samuel was eleven, the two brothers had performed again. Their audience was carefully listed by Reverend Charles, beginning with dukes, duchesses and the Archbishop of Canterbury and descending in order of rank through lords and ladies, several bishops, archdeacons and doctors, to Sir John Hawkins, Dr Johnson and Mr Garrick. The fortnightly winter concerts from 1779 to 1785 were more formal.

These private concerts at Chesterfield Street did not accord with Wesleyan Methodism's tenets of plain living and high thinking, and met with the disapproval of John Wesley and other leading Methodists. There was also a suspicion of spectacle about them. Some years earlier, the wunderkind Mozart had performed at Ranelagh Gardens, and Samuel Wesley, who became known as the London Mozart, came to resent what he considered the element of show about his own boyhood performances.

Jack had attended the concerts during the winter of his first visit. Now, as a young man of eighteen, he had returned to savour again some of the most exclusive musical evenings London had to offer. People of distinction who subscribed to this third concert series included the Earls of Exeter, Dartmouth and Mornington, several bishops, the fashionable Mrs Luther, and Sir Watkins William

Charles Wesley, Court Musician seated, 1780, by William Russell, RA, unsigned. Reproduced by permission of the Royal Academy of Music, London.

Wynn, one of the promoters of the Handel Commemoration (which in 1784 would mark the twenty-fifth anniversary of the death of the composer). For the son of a provincial organist with 'no great Superfluities,' these must have been heady evenings.

No letters have survived from the early months of 1781, and by the summer Jack was preparing to return home again. This time the reference to his brother George is ominous. On 1 July 1781 the Reverend Charles Wesley wrote to John Langshaw:

My dear Sir,

. . . With great care George may get over the evil which threatens him.

In his previous letter John Langshaw must have expressed worries about George's health, as well as his concern about how he was going to support him at Oxford, having written that there will be no 'getting money in' from him; for which Reverend Charles now admonishes him:

> Oxford is not a place for 'getting money in'. If he gets learning without losing his innocence, it is sufficient. He may do, 'without calling on you for help.' But then you shoud help him a little without his calling.

Having said that, he ends this July letter on a reassuring note:

> Again I say – Jack may, if he please, make a great Master.

The previous few months in London had not been without danger for Jack and Charles. Press gangs armed with cutlasses and clubs roved the streets recruiting men for military service. They were paid £1 for each new 'recruit' and carried off men with a random ruthlessness that amounted to kidnap. Reverend Charles is relieved that Jack is returning home again not only safe but 'uncorrupted.'

And in a letter from 23 July Reverend Charles refers once more to John Langshaw's gratitude for Jack's lessons and says it is recompense enough:

> I must refer you again to Milton – 'A grateful mind by owning pays, at once Indebted & discharged.' Jack well deserves more than all the kindness we coud shew him . . . he plays so well . . . I doubt whether the Country will be his Sphere of Action. My sons have not seen the last of him . . . He will make his way without Sir John's favor.
>
> Your affectionate Servant

Jack went home to Lancaster and did not return to London until early 1784. The six surviving letters from the intervening two and a half years, all written to John Langshaw by Reverend Charles, touched on many things.

They discuss politics. At home Reverend Charles's sympathies lie with the king and William Pitt the Younger in their struggle against the Fox-North Coalition. He refers to the continuing War of American Independence – Reverend Charles is opposed to the American rebels and their British supporters and writes of his fear of invasion by the French and Spanish who had formed an alliance with the American patriots.

A picture of the daily life of the Wesley family emerges. Reverend Charles's letters are scattered with biblical allusions and snatches from his own visionary hymns. Both fathers express views on life and the hereafter, about bringing up their children, about their fears and hopes for them. They discuss religion and the ways and purpose of God, the fleeting nature of life and the hope of heavenly reunion; and they speak of Jack. Reverend Charles writes on 28 September 1781:

> My dear Sir,
> We shall miss Jack in the Winter . . . but rejoice that you have him safe and sober . . . I dont doubt his Progress in Music. It is his business & shoud take up all his working time. He & Charles should be constant correspondents.
>
> . . . Your old useless Servant

And three months later he writes:

> Dear Sir,
> . . . You see my thoughts on the present Crisis [the American War of Independence] in the enclosed hymns written for this day which all my Brother's Societies observe as a Fast . . .

Your Son George . . . as well as Jack, will live to be both a Comfort & an Honour to you. Jack need not fear playing before any Doctor [of music] . . .

Farewell in Christ

The reference to George is in response to further anxiety expressed by John Langshaw over the health of his second son, which continued to decline during the winter. In February 1782 Sir John Hawkins, too, was moved to write a letter of concern about his protégé in terms that show the great man in a better light:

Your son George is highly favored by Dr Beardsmore [Headmaster at Charterhouse] . . . you know how greatly he has exerted his interest at Cambridge in his behalf: I see him often . . . you must be very attentive to his health when he comes to you, for I assure you both my wife and myself are in no little concern for him . . .

PS My eldest son was this day and my wife goes tomorrow to see George. He is very bad and you must get him to you as soon as possible.

George Langshaw was brought home to Lancaster in the spring of 1782. He was recorded as a member of Cambridge University (rather than Oxford) where he had won a place as a Sizar, or Poor Scholar, but he died in May before he could take it up. Reverend Charles had seen it coming too, but had not been able to bring himself to say anything. On 5 June he wrote to John Langshaw:

Dear Sir,
The Flower is cut down – but transplanted to paradise. I thought it cruel, Not to warn you of his danger: But I coud not find it in my heart to tell you <u>all</u> my fears. – He is at rest . . . safe and happy in the haven . . .

He offers practical comfort: 'God can make one Son as useful as Two, or as Twenty. He has given my friend Jack a Paternal heart'; and he reflects: 'We must wait, till all the waves & storms are gone over us also.' He comments on the fleeting nature of life and the folly of grasping at everything material, and he writes sadly of the earlier loss of some of his own children, ending: 'All here join in love with Your faithful and affectionate friend.'

The untimely death of the young scholar was felt by all. It was a tragedy in the Langshaw family, and Jack, who had travelled with him and shared time with him in London, would one day name his own second son after this brother. John Langshaw had exerted all his influence to educate George. The letters show how much he and Reverend Charles loved their children. They cared about their education, the fulfilment of their talents, and their corporal and spiritual well-being, and they sought to protect them from worldly dangers. George's death, the random intervention of nature, challenged the prevailing optimism of the Age of Reason. The clergyman and naturalist Gilbert White might well write in his study at Selborne that 'Reason resembles a celestial flame . . . it sparkles and spreads its luster every way,' but reason could not explain the tragedies of life. Reverend Charles found solace in his God, but John Langshaw, a man who had always depended on his human faculties to overcome adversity and make progress, must have had his belief in both human capability and in God shaken by the death of his promising younger son.

At a practical level the melancholy event must have pressed home still further the need for Jack to be able to support the family if his father fell ill. Keyboard skills would not be enough; like his father, Jack would have to be versatile. He started composing and sent his efforts to Charles in London, and he assisted his father in Lancaster throughout 1783. The chapel of St John the Evangelist, built in 1754, needed a new organ, and John Langshaw had been asked to build it.

The new organ followed closely an earlier design by John Snetzler, the master organ builder with whom John Langshaw had worked in the 1760s. Its elegant case, reflecting the influence of Robert Adam, was made of dark Honduras mahogany incorporating a circular, central compartment of dummy pipes. Unusually, the two-manual instrument had ivory slips both above and below each key. The music board, made of quartered oak, has never warped. John Langshaw and his son built a fine organ with an exquisitely warm tone that has been restored to its original working order. Jack's participation ensured that he was first in line for the job of sub-organist.

It was not until early 1784 that he was released for his final visit to London.

10

A SUBSCRIPTION CONCERT AT THE WESLEYS

'IT IS NOT yet settled, whither we shall have a Concert this year or not,' Reverend Charles had written in November 1783, but by the time Jack returned in the bitter winter of 1784, the first concert of the Wesley brothers' sixth concert series had already taken place.

They played music in the tradition of the Academy of Ancient Music, founded in 1726, and the more recent Concert of Antient Music, the conservative concert society started in 1776 by Sir John Hawkins and Sir Watkins William Wynn with the aim of keeping out the moderns and promoting music by the composers of the English baroque, especially Handel. Both Ancient and Antient music appealed to 'all those,' as Charles would one day write, 'who love good harmony.' It was an older rather than a modern taste. Distinctions between the Ancient (Antient) and modern schools mattered to some: no music less than twenty years old was admitted to the Antient concerts, and Sir John Hawkins dismissed the modern European music, with its diminuendos and crescendos, pianos and fortes, which reached its zenith with Mozart and Haydn, as 'noise without harmony . . . the frittering of passages into notes . . . trash.' But both traditions were popular in London, and musicians and audiences moved easily between the two.

Thomas Arne was happy to write light opera, and Charles Burney listened to the music of Handel and Haydn with equal enthusiasm. What both schools had in common by the 1780s was that people went to listen to the music rather than to talk.

The notebook kept by the Reverend Charles Wesley giving details of the Chesterfield Street concerts is held at the Royal Academy of Music in Marylebone Road. It measures 7" × 6" and has 'Concerts by Charles and Samuel Wesley 1779–1785' lettered in gilt on the leather spine. The first twenty-four pages record the names of the subscribers to every concert season from 1779. About 125 people paid a subscription of three guineas for 'A Concert' and many of the same people subscribed each year. The concerts took place on Thursday evenings. Reverend Charles recorded everything: the dates, those who were present and their guests, the programme, the musicians, their instruments and their pay. Refreshments were an important part of the evening and the notes say what they were and how much they cost. The Wesley family's domestic and business expenses in preparation are also noted:

Proposals [programmes] printed	8s 0
Tickets	2s 0
Tuning Harpsichord	5s 0
Porter Violono	1s 0
Mats	3s 0
Rehearsal Wine	6s 6d
D[itt]o Punch	2s 0

There are also numerous items for Sally Wesley. She was twenty-four and much loved by her father. After her father's death in 1788 she would lead an increasingly secluded life and remain unmarried. For this sixth concert series she had a new gown made for a guinea and a cap at seven shillings. Her hair was usually dressed for 1s, once as much as 10s 6d – the fashion was for hair to be worn high, arranged over frames, powdered and ornamented. Reverend

Charles noted briefly, 'Wife's gown 12s 6d.' Samuel's shirts cost 11s 6d and his watch was mended for 5s.

Subscribers that season included Lord Dartmouth, Lord Barrington and Lady Despenser, and the Earl and Countess of Traquair; the Wesleys did things in style. James the waiter was paid 1s for his services and his gloves cost 1s 4d. Constable Shade was hired at a cost of 1s to keep out the uninvited. Hire of a footman was 2s 6d and the charwoman was paid 1s. Candles were always the biggest expense, costing as much as 9s at one concert and 3s for a lamplighter to look after them, but modest compared to the 3,000 to 4,000 candles that illuminated one masked ball at the house of Mrs Cornelys. Teapots always cost far less to hire than the tea inside them.

Today Marylebone Road is a busy six-lane highway. Students from the Royal Academy of Music carrying oddly-shaped instrument cases cross quickly, and make their way into Marylebone High Street, past the Wesleyan school and the memorial to the Reverend Charles Wesley and his sons. Chesterfield Street is no more, but Wesley Street is nearby, and the spirit of the Wesleys still lingers hereabouts. It is easy to imagine another music student, long ago, hurrying towards the house of his music master, to a concert perhaps; perhaps to the concert that took place on the evening of 14 March 1784.

The young man wears a greatcoat; his hair is tied back and tucked into the collar. Bending forward against the wind and rain, he carries a bundle and hums as he turns into Chesterfield Street. He runs up the steps of the first house in the street, an old London mansion house. He stamps the water off his boots, speaking to Constable Shade as he does, and goes in. A powdered footman in three-quarter cutaway coat, knee breeches and light hose takes the bundle of candles and the greatcoat from the young man, who says something to an elderly woman mopping the mud and rainwater from the hall floor. She chuckles. The young man runs up the stairs and pauses outside closed doors; he smoothes his hair.

A buzz of polite conversation comes from inside the room. The sound of repeated notes played on a harpsichord is followed by the tuning of three or four fiddles. The young man opens the doors and goes into a large room lit by many candles. A crowd of people, more than fifty, is sitting with their backs to the door. They are facing towards a group of musicians arranged in a semi-circle in front of long curtains drawn over the street windows. The harpsichord's lid is raised, and the conversation fades; a concert is about to begin.

Reverend Charles Wesley, seated just inside the door, looks at Jack and writes the name 'Mr Langshaw' in his notebook at the bottom of a list of those present at this concert. As Jack sits next to him he adds his sons' initials, C.W. and S.W., and S.W. for their sister Sally.

Mr Charles Wesley conducts from the harpsichord in the middle of the players. His brother Samuel, who is eighteen, plays first violin; next to him stands Mr Huxtable, the second leader. Two second violinists, Mr Holmes and Mr Higgins, stand slightly to one side. This evening Mr Hill is playing violincello; sometimes it is Mr Sharp – he played a fortnight ago. The two horns are played by Mr Gilbert and Mr Ellaby as usual. The singers, Mr Saunders, Mr Wilcox and Mr Printer the tenor, and three other men whose names are not known to Reverend Charles, are all seated at the music desks during this performance of a symphony by Mr Charles Wesley.

The audience is fairly evenly divided between men and women. Mrs Luther, accompanied by Miss Lidiard and Miss Wilmott this evening, is in her usual place. She was Mr Charles's first scholar and has a Shudi from the master's best days. Three years ago she bought one of the new square pianofortes Shudi's son-in-law makes, and had it sent with her harpsichord to her house in Brighthelmstone for the season. When the symphony ends she glances round, sees Jack and bows her head slightly towards him. 'He is one of the best bred Youths I have seen,' she thinks, as she once remarked to Reverend Charles. The fashion is still for paint and patches and powder. Many of the gentlemen, being older, still wear wigs. Samuel has gone to one of the two chamber organs and is now playing extempore, modulating *through keys and harmonies in a way that everybody marvels at. Miss Carr, another of Mr Charles's scholars, sits with her two brothers. She looks round nervously at the unusually large audience. Then it is Mr Charles again, this time in the first performance of his own concerto grosso. 'His youth terrifies the mothers from trusting him with their daughters. So many masters have married their scholars,' thinks Reverend Charles, a problem he confided in a letter to Jack's father in Lancaster more than two years ago. Charles Wesley would never marry.*

The Reverend John Wesley is here this evening, despite having expressed his disapproval of the concerts, sitting next to Mr Attwood and Mr Cole. Now Miss Carr leaves her seat and goes forward to the harpsichord while Mr Charles moves to the other chamber organ. They play a double concerto for harpsichord and organ that he composed while Miss Carr was his scholar a few years earlier. Miss Carr, who also sings and plays the pianoforte, is a favourite of Mr Charles. After she had paid her entrance he presented her with two years' lessons. Ladies of course never perform in public: only here in a private concert can she demonstrate her skills. Captain Shepherd, in his scarlet uniform, watches intently and applauds vigorously when the concerto comes to an end. The final piece in this first half of the concert is a violin concerto by Giardini, and Samuel, as ever, does credit to himself and Wilhelm Cramer, his teacher. Now it is time for refreshments and the subscribers go into the next room where James, wearing new white gloves, attends their wants.

This room is well lit with the additional candles brought by Jack. Only he and Reverend Charles know they cost nine shillings this evening, more than ever before. The other expenses are already entered in the notebook: bread, 1s; and meat, 5s 6d; and cakes of course, flavoured with orgeat, a sweet barley and almond syrup, always expensive, 6s 6d tonight. Teapots at 8d are filled with tea at 3s, for which the cream cost 10d, sugar 4s and lemons 1s. Some guests prefer wine, 3s 10d, and others porter at 3s 4d. Reverend Charles looks approvingly at his wife's gown, only 12s 6d, and at Sally's elaborately arranged hair.

He looks too at Jack Langshaw. 'He will be a blessing to his family, and a credit to his master,' he thinks, and resolves to put that in the letter he is writing to Jack's father. He recalls the troubled fifteen-year-old boy who came to them six years earlier after the row with Dr Cooke and thinks with disapproval of the doctor, who is now organist at St Martin-in-the-Fields as well as Westminster Abbey: 'What signifies it his grasping at every thing, & carrying every thing, when he must leave everything?' He watches Jack moving easily in society and remembers how Jack had laughed at the most difficult lessons. In a week the Reverend will hear from his friend in Lancaster that Jack is in line for the sub-organist's job at St John's Chapel there. 'We are all as happy as you in Jack's prosperity,' he will write back to Jack's father.

The ladies finish their tea; wine glasses are emptied and the company moves back into the music room where Samuel and Mr Charles are already tuning for Julius Caesar, the overture to the concert's second half. A chorus by Handel follows, sung by the six men. Reverend Charles sits patiently. He is seventy-seven now and recently complained in a letter to John Langshaw, who is almost his only correspondent these days: 'I am quite weary of our Concerts, and have a right to spend my last days in peace and quiet.' The evenings are still popular: fifty-nine people tonight. Not as many of the nobility as five years ago. Reverend Charles recalls the Earl of Mornington, who sometimes performed with them; the German ambassador, Count Bruhl, another patron of Broadwood, that piano maker his sons talk about; the Archbishop of Canterbury, the bishops, the lords and the ladies, William Cowper, Mr Garrick. He sighs. He had never expected his sons to get 'much more than Reputation and increase of skill' from the concerts. Lord Dartmouth is here tonight and Lady Despencer – and that painter of miniatures, Cosway, is he here again?

Mr Printer rises for his solo. The strings begin: five slow notes, G$^\sharp$, G$^\sharp$, G$^\sharp$, G$^\sharp$, B; followed by five more, F$^\sharp$, F$^\sharp$, F$^\sharp$, F$^\sharp$, A, introduce the accompanied tenor recitative, 'Comfort Ye, Comfort Ye My People.' Mr Printer's voice sails effortlessly over the heads of the company.

Who can tell what thoughts entered the minds of those who listened that Lenten evening so long ago? For all their differences, their patches, paints and powders and high hair, they probably mused on much the same subjects as an audience listening to the same music today would. The state of the country perhaps, the latest novelty, family hopes and fears, the waves and storms of life, its brevity, the possibility of a heavenly reunion. Did some people think of the forthcoming Handel Commemoration? Did the composer's sublime setting of the Prophet's words bring comfort to some, as it still does?

Perhaps Miss Worgan privately resolved to learn a Clementi sonata on the Broadwood square pianoforte her father had bought the previous April. The thoughts of others may have turned to the struggle between the king and Parliament. The Fox-North Opposition's majority had been reduced and the dissolution of Parliament looked imminent; perhaps Reverend Charles thought, as he would soon write, 'The Lovers of his Majesty rejoice in the late Defeat of his Enemies.' Or perhaps, as he watched his two sons play the next piece, a 'Duet for Two Organs,' he inwardly composed the words he would next write to his friend in Lancaster: 'My little strength grows less daily. We must soon expect to leave our children behind us, with The World before, & Providence their Guide.'

The concert is coming to an end. For the final grand chorus all the gentlemen stand and sing 'Blessing and Honour' from the Messiah. *It is surprising how much sound a chorus of six men and nine musicians can achieve. They earned their 10s 6d.*

Then Misses Turner, Higgs and Alley drift away downstairs, and gather up their pelisses at the foot of the stairs. Outside, sedan chairmen cry: 'By your leave, Sir,' as they push and jostle in the muddy street for passengers who are people of the first consequence. Mrs Luther is taking her leave, still talking to Charles and Jack about the pianoforte; she is a lady of fashion and discernment and assures them that the charming small pianoforte is 'the thing.'

There is no mention of a piano in Reverend Charles's concert notes, but Samuel was already writing piano music and an entry in the Broadwood Journal in the Bodleian Library for the same month as this concert records: 'March 21 1784 – Mr Wesley – for a pianoforte.'

Was this a purchase or a tuning? The relevant sales ledger is missing, but the word 'for' in the journal suggests that it was a purchase, since tunings were usually indicated simply by the possessive apostrophe, as in 'Mr Wesley's pianoforte.' If Charles went to Great Pulteney Street to Broadwood's to try the piano, as became his practice whenever he bought one on commission for someone in the future, did Jack Langshaw, his music scholar and friend, go with him? It is tempting to think so. Jack undoubtedly knew Broadwoods in 1784; in October that year, by which time he was back in Lancaster, the Langshaw name appears in the Broadwood Journal for the first time, when a Mr John Langshaw ordered a 21-guinea square pianoforte for Thomas Scott of Wigan. It was John Broadwood's first year of serious commercial piano production and a turning point in the history of the piano, and the Langshaws were among their first business customers. Jack continued to buy from them for the next fifty years.

11

PIANOS, CULTURE AND COMMERCE

AFTER THE LAST concert of the season, on 29 April 1784, Jack's time with the Wesley family was almost over. Parliament had been dissolved at the end of March and London treated to scenes of frenzied electioneering. William Pitt was returned with a substantial majority, the Opposition lost 160 seats and Parliament reassembled on 18 May. Reverend Charles wrote to John Langshaw on 20 May 1784:

> Your Son will be soon forthcoming, and return, we hope a Comfort to you and a Credit to Charles. His future Proficiency will depend on his own diligence, and sobriety.

Jack delayed his departure from London to attend the Handel Commemoration at the end of the month. Sir Watkins William Wynn, a regular Wesley concert subscriber, had promoted the festival. It was to be the greatest musical event of the decade:

> Expect from Jack a full and true Account of the Jubilee . . . We must soon expect to leave our children behind us with The World before, & Providence their Guide,
>
> I remain, dear Sir, your faithful & affectionate Servant

A week of Handel's sacred music ended with a performance of the *Messiah* in Westminster Abbey. People flocked to hear all the concerts. Several were repeated; even rehearsals, for which there was a charge of half a guinea, were sold out. Charles Burney, who had 'long been watching the operations of good Music on the sensibility of mankind,' could not remember ever having seen a more enraptured audience. Handel's music, the core of the Antient Music, became at once a focus for patriotic sentiment not only against threats of musical innovation from the Continent but from invasion of all kinds.

The bitter winter was followed by a hot summer. Charles was now twenty-seven, and Samuel eighteen. Jack was midway between them, and the three were good friends. Just before Jack's final departure Samuel wrote a Sonata per il Organo for Jack, who noted on the first page:

> This charming voluntary was composed for me by S. Wesley, the first two pages were composed while I was taking my lesson from his Brother, & in so short a time that a good copyist could not have written the first page. This being the composing copy shews the corrections with which he wrote.
>
> John Langshaw (Junior)
> Sonata per il organo.
> S.Wesley   May 24th 1784. Soli Deo Gloria

The sonata, in three movements, is Samuel Wesley's first extended piece for the organ. According to his biographer, Philip Olleson, it is quite unlike anything else in his output for the organ: 'The style is thoroughly pianistic, although unlike Wesley's own writing for the piano at the time, and were it not for the title, there would be nothing to indicate that it was for the organ rather than the harpsichord or the piano.' Jack returned to Lancaster with the sonata and it remained in the Langshaw family for 204 years.

The three friends wrote to one another on and off for the rest of their lives. Charles Wesley never secured a royal appointment or quite fulfilled his early promise, and his reputation was overshadowed by his brother's. Samuel shocked his father by converting to Catholicism. He was a free spirit and, like William Crotch (who went on to become the first principal of the Royal Academy of Music), he would look back on his childhood performances with pain, although, as Philip Olleson has suggested, the Wesley concerts introduced the brothers to the best aspects of professional music-making while shielding them from commercial excess.

Jack began life in Lancaster. He was appointed organist at St John's Chapel and on 2 January 1785 the organ that he had helped his father to build was officially declared ready for use. The Reverend Robert Houseman, a friend from Lancaster Grammar School days, was the curate. Later that year, on 4 September, his father wrote again to Reverend Charles:

Rev'd Sir, – I have now the advantage of giving you a line in a franked cover. High postage, and the scarcity of franks, has been one cause of my long neglect in writing to you.

Today my son got a very agreeable letter from his friend Mr S Wesley, and I have great pleasure in the prospect that their present friendship may be a lasting one. I hope my son Jack will always strive to keep the affections of his Master and Mr Samul; he owes much to them. Jack improves in his playing, but I cannot get him to compose, he wants to write well without the trouble of it. I wish he thought a little better of his abilities that way, or was less afraid of spoiling his paper.

Jack is now organist of our chapel – about eleven guineas p. ann.: but he has a promise to succeed me, near 100 p. ann.: which is much better.

I shall be much obliged to you for another letter, it is now long since any have passed between us. I understand you have had my brother lately, he would give you a better acct. how he gets on than I can.

When Jack will be able to visit London is uncertain, we have now two organs to attend, I have a son [Joseph] ten years old, in training up for the organ, if he and I live. Jack may be at liberty in a year or two . . .

I am Rev'd Sir, your most obedt. and servant
John Langshaw

The reply from Reverend Charles took the form of a postscript to a letter from his son Charles to Jack on 20 September 1785:

I thank you my dear Friend for your letters . . . It makes me very happy to hear you give satisfaction. I believe few organists in your parts understand the true music better than yourself . . . I find I am not to despair yet of seeing you again in Town . . .

with much esteem

[PS from Reverend Charles to John Langshaw]

To Mr Langshaw snr.

Dear Sir,
. . . Jack's Master has been thrown away upon him, if he can be content with being a Player only. He must be a Composer or a Dunce: therefore let him begin today & never suffer a day to pass, without composing something.

Jack did become a composer and his output was prolific. Most of it remained unpublished in manuscript form, and, according to Grove, 'is said to be extant,' but has yet to be discovered. Jack remained in Lancaster after 1784 and never lived in London again. Soon after his return a Captain Dewhurst of Blackburn who knew his uncle, William Langshaw, recorded in his diary on

27 June 1784: 'To Heaton; [William] Langshaw's brother's son mending his organ. His father would be there next week and stay two days.'

Other, less fortunate events also required Jack's presence in Lancaster. At the end of 1784 his young brother James died four days before his eleventh birthday and within twelve months another brother, Joseph, the boy his father was training up for the organ, also died, aged ten. John Langshaw senior was now sixty. His eyesight was failing and Jack was increasingly responsible for his father's duties at the priory as well as his own at St John's. There were two organs to attend to and he was still the only one who could take care of the family if his father fell ill. It is unlikely that he would have been 'at liberty' to return to London in 'a year or two.'

Then there was the Langshaw business with Broadwoods. The first recorded order is in the Bodleian Broadwood Journal.

1784 – October 4th

Thomas Scott Esq. for a Piano-forte sent			
Wigan Lancashire, ordered by Mr. John Langshaw	21	0	0
Packing Case	21	10	6

A month later '21' was noted in the journal against 'John Langshaw,' probably payment for Thomas Scott's piano. But why not 'Mr John Langshaw' as before? Broadwoods were scrupulous about titles. The use of the first name might suggest a younger man, possibly one who was already known to them; was it to distinguish son from father? These archival minutiae suggest that possibly both organists were ordering pianos from Broadwood. Whether it was the first organist or Jack, then twenty-one, who had ordered the piano for the Wigan merchant Thomas Scott in 1784, it was the first time the word 'ordered' was used in the journal in connection with an individual piano agent, the first unequivocal record of a provincial organist, rather than a music seller or an established harpsichord agent, ordering a piano on behalf of someone else.

The following April another square piano was booked out to 'Mr Langshaw, Lancaster' and paid for in May. Tantalizingly the journal ends there in 1785.

Records continue nine years later with sales ledger C in the Broadwood Archive (ledgers A and B are missing). Ledger C begins in 1794 and an early entry in 1795 shows that 'Mr Langshaw' had been doing business with them in the previous trading period:

Ledger C, 1794–6

Folio 212

Mr Langshaw, Lancaster.
1795

Sept 29			
To Ledr. B 151, transferred from	19	0	0
To Ledr. B 113, transferred from his Brother Wm's account	35	4	6
Nov. 28			
A piano Forte and Case to Mr Burrows	16	5	6
1796			
May 11 A do.	16	8	0

It is possible that the 'Mr John Langshaw' in the Broadwood Journal is the first organist, but this first Langshaw entry in Ledger C almost certainly refers to Jack. He was now thirty-two; his father was seventy and blind and increasingly reliant on his son. The two earlier folios listed under 'Sept 29,' 151 and 113, have been brought forward from Ledger B, the sales ledger preceding 1794. The amounts shown are commensurate with the cost of square pianos at that time. Had Jack, 'Mr Langshaw, Lancaster,' also bought pianos in ledger period A and in the nine years since the last entry in the Broadwood Journal in 1785? The Broadwood records show that he bought on average two pianos a year throughout his life.

Forty years after his time in London when Jack (by then Mr Langshaw) sent his autobiographical note to John Sainsbury, he recorded his lifelong gratitude for the 'unremitting kindness' shown him as a young scholar in London by Charles and Samuel Wesley. He never mentioned his Broadwood agency, which had begun at the same time. Yet it placed him in the vanguard of the democratization of music whereby millions of people eventually bought pianos and came to enjoy something of the musical life he had experienced as a young man in London with the Wesleys.

Seldom is any human activity capable of only one interpretation. While the Langshaws, father and son, may have been catalysts for the democratization of music, so John Broadwood and his sons may appear to be the beneficiaries of its commercialization; yet they were all promoting pianos. John Broadwood made a business and a fortune out of them; Jack Langshaw was a musician who taught people how to play them and supplemented his income by distributing them. Yet both were part of the piano culture.

The interrelationship between business enterprise, urban wealth and socio-cultural development is exemplified by the story of the piano in Britain at the end of the eighteenth century, although the boundaries between these various aspects of the same activity are often difficult to discern.

By the 1790s there were about twenty-eight piano makers in London. Broadwood pianos were no longer the product of master, journeyman and apprentice working in a craft workshop, as Shudi's harpsichords had been. The pianoforte was ideally suited to division of labour and there were pairs of hands enough in London to continue Broadwood's hand-made ethos, after a fashion. Parts were made by hand, numbered and assembled into pianos. Only planking was done by steam engine. An early-nineteenth-century Broadwood inventory shows that wages for both skilled and unskilled men were the highest outlay in their labour-intensive industry and that they employed additional outworkers, such as fret-makers and keymakers. In premises that were twice their original size, a steadily increasing workforce made the separate components and assembled pianos in increasing commercial numbers.

From the beginning, piano-making and celebrity concert per-formance had gone hand in hand. Zumpe had J. C. Bach launch his square piano, and John Broadwood engaged the rising star Muzio Clementi to promote his. Clementi's life was contemporaneous with the nascent piano industry and he probably did more to pro-mote the piano than anyone else. His life story was the stuff of fic-tion. Born in Rome in 1752 and brought to England in 1766 by a wealthy English patron, he spent seven years in Dorset where he perfected a dazzling keyboard technique. By 1775 he was in London making his name as a keyboard performer. He was different from the boy Mozart or 'Little Billy' Crotch. Their uncanny gifts com-bined with the insouciance of childhood were novelties, something slightly other, to be marvelled at rather than copied. Clementi was an energetic man of the world and a musical polymath and his abilities were, as he pointed out, the result of eight hours' practice a day. He was gifted, but he showed what could be done with the piano if one worked at it.

He performed in Paris in 1781 on both harpsichord and piano, sent from London by John Broadwood, and established a collab-oration between piano makers and concert pianists that still continues. In the same month that young Mr Charles Wesley bought a piano from Broadwood's, Clementi introduced his pro-tégé John Baptist Cramer to London in duet performance. When European musicians came to London rather than Paris during the years of the French Revolution, the rise of the virtuoso concert pianist began in earnest. Jan Ladislaw Dussek – 'Le Beau Dussek' – sat sideways to give his audience the benefit of his profile. Josef Haydn, brought to London by the impresario Peter Salomon, was astounded at the money he made while English composers

struggled. His late keyboard sonatas, with their tuneful slow movements, 'electrified the audience,' according to Charles Burney
and 'excited . . . an attention and pleasure superior to any that had
ever . . . been caused by instrumental music in England.' His performances on a Broadwood piano in London's Hanover Square
Rooms in 1791 established a taste for the Viennese-German school
of music that eclipsed English composition for almost a hundred
years.

By the end of the century Clementi, Cramer and Dussek were
London's three leading piano virtuosi. They were stars whose
ascent coincided with the bigger sound and impressive presence of
the grand piano. Their technical wizardry and bravura public style
reached its apogee in Franz Liszt, fifty years later. From the begin-

The Piano Lesson, late eighteenth century; Victorian oleograph.
Reproduced by permission of David Winston, The Period Piano
Company, Biddenden, Kent.

ning they were courted by piano makers and they all performed in the Hanover Square Rooms on Broadwood grand pianos. Lesser keyboard musicians, many of whom became Broadwood agents, performed in provincial assembly rooms such as the one in Lancaster. Fans who swooned over Dussek could go to Corri and Dussek's music shop in the Haymarket and order a Broadwood, or order one from an increasing number of provincial agents like John Langshaw who would also teach them how to play. Anyone who could afford twenty guineas for a new square piano, or seven for a second-hand one, could become a domestic virtuoso on his, or more often her, own instrument.

Clementi promoted every aspect of the piano. His fame as a performer enabled him to launch his own pianos, made for him first by John Longman then by Collard. He went on tour, even in the thick of the Napoleonic Wars, to promote them. Clementi knew his market: his pianos, with their floriated cases, were some of the prettiest ever made. They still turn up, as delightful to look at as to play, and must have charmed all the young women who were increasingly the main recipients, if not the purchasers, of pianos.

Although keyboard music at this time was often written for either piano or harpsichord, Clementi had been one of the first to write specifically for the piano. His impressive technique was the result of hours of practice at the harpsichord and his early compositions owe a debt to Scarlatti. Of his Sonatas Op. 2, published in 1779, the three solo sonatas are not easy; and his tour de force 'Octave' Sonata is fiendishly difficult. The three easier sonatas for flute or violin with keyboard accompaniment published with them gave aspiring amateurs something to get their baby teeth into while contemplating the challenge of the three tougher keyboard solos.

After he met Mozart in 1781 Clementi's music changed. It became less mechanical and showy; instead he gave the aspiring pianist pieces that retained the bravura of his public performances but were technically less demanding. His sonatinas are joyful little exercises in the sonata form that call for sensitive phrasing and yet are well within reach of the parlour virtuoso. They are full of pianistic instructions like *legato* – smoothly, *leggiero* – lightly, and expressive markings such as *dolce, con espressione, crescendo*. They are also fun to play and sound captivating on a late-eighteenth-century square piano. His more difficult *Gradus ad Parnassum*, one hundred studies written many years later, is still used as a foundation for piano technique.

He went into music publishing. Clementi's *Introduction to the Art of Playing on the Piano Forte* (1802), a tutorial that took beginners through fifty fingered lessons, contained pieces by 'Composers of the First Rank' such as Bach, Mozart and Beethoven as well as his own compositions. His arrangements of chamber music and popular oratorio were designed to demonstrate the piano's versatility and to inculcate a correct technique by encouraging pupils to 'cultivate the highest musical taste as they develop their skills at the piano.' He thus established himself as the arbiter of keyboard taste from the start and laid the foundation of the classical piano canon. Two years later, Cramer produced the first book of graduated piano studies. In 1767 Henry Fougt had patented a process for printing music from type and at the end of the century the lithographic process made music-printing quicker and cheaper than ever. There was a huge expansion of music publishers, and specialist music magazines appeared, some with music printed inside them. In 1797 *The Pianoforte*, a weekly magazine, promised a pianoforte in exchange for 250 issue vouchers.

Clementi had thrown in his lot with the piano from the beginning, and every aspect of his enterprise sustained and promoted the others. He had more influence on piano composition and performance than even the great masters, and his music and the composers he published became a cornerstone of piano technique. He was a great co-ordinator, a fine pianist and a man of business who understood the value of publicity. For the last twenty years of his life he gave up playing in public, taught less and less and devoted himself to business. In a society concerned with maintaining social distinctions at a time of bewildering social change, it was difficult for a performing musician to qualify as an English gentleman and questionable whether a gentleman could engage in commerce, unless it was at the highest level.

Serious money became a route to gentility and both Clementi and John Broadwood took it. Both men made a fortune and acquired a country estate, indispensable for a true gentleman. By the time Clementi died in Evesham in 1832 the small wooden-framed square pianofortes on which his career had been founded were no longer made. By then pianos had become a modern, iron-framed commodity at the centre of a global culture. Clementi had used his fame to direct musical taste and shape the market in his own interest. His epitaph in Westminster Abbey reads: 'Father of the piano'; it could as easily be 'Father of the music industry.'

John Broadwood continued to make harpsichords until 1794. By then taste had changed. Charles Burney wrote disparagingly of 'crouded and complicated harmony . . . and elaborate Music,' continuing: 'There is no instrument so favourable to frothy and unmeaning Music as the Harpsichord . . . neither the tone nor the tuning depends on the player.' He castigated the old order of counterpoint as the 'glare and glitter of this kind of tinsel . . . *notes, rien que des notes,*' and stated:

> . . . on the arrival of the late Mr Bach [J. C.], and construction of pianofortes in this country, the performers on keyboard instruments were obliged wholly to change their ground; and instead of surprising by the *seeming* labour and dexterity of execution, had the real and more useful difficulties of taste, expression, and light and shade, to encounter.

In 1793 a grand pianoforte was used for the king's birthday ode, and with that royal seal of approval the piano's ascendancy was established once and for all. Broadwood's last harpsichord, a 'Double key'd, with Swell and five stops. Solid mahogany,' was sent to China a year later. It cost seventy-three guineas, the same as his six-octave grand.

Harpsichords were built by craftsmen, requiring individual attention from a diminishing pool of expertise. During the ten years or so of their decline as demand for the pianoforte increased, John Broadwood's pricing kept them at the top end of the market where an older, wealthier, more conservative clientele retained a taste for the Ancient Music. At the same time he was turning out simple square pianos produced by division of specialized labour and assembled in his workshops at a rising rate of about 250 a year. These were aimed at a wider market and priced to appeal to new customers of the middling sort. He had embraced innovation but kept his backstop, the harpsichord.

By then he had positioned his grand pianoforte at the top of the market. When he stopped making the harpsichord, his grand pianoforte, so similar in shape, structure, and price, was already there to inherit the harpsichord's mantle. It had all the modish appeal of the piano without the loss of the harpsichord's status. With a more advanced action than the square piano, a compass of six and a half octaves and costly cabinetwork, the grand pianoforte remained high in price and perception. Two hundred years later its aura of superiority is undiminished: the shiny black ten-foot concert grand at centre stage announces an impressive performance by a supreme artist before a note is played.

While continuing to serve the great in London and in the Shires with fashionable grands and superior squares, John Broadwood continued to respond to new consumer markets in Britain's provincial and industrial centres and expanding overseas territories. He offered pianos to suit many incomes, from a plain square at twenty-one guineas to a decorated, six-and-a-half-octave grand at eighty-four, and a wide range of people bought them. Professional and military men, bluestockings and an emerging intelligentsia, the musicians of the Cathedral Close, political and mercantile administrators at home and abroad and self-made businessmen such as John Broadwood himself could all find a piano to suit them.

Zumpe retired and was succeeded by dozens of other small piano makers: Christopher Ganer, Abraham Kirkman, William Rolfe, Thomas Culliford, John Geib, Schoene, Longman, Clementi and a host of others whose pianos still come to light. In 1798 William Southwell made a lavishly inlaid upright square; Tomkison made pianofortes that were elegant pieces of furniture. But Broadwoods were the biggest and, advised by Thomas Sheraton, even their plainest instruments were attractive pieces. They retained the house style of the Shudi-Broadwood days, using fine woods and veneers. Their pianos remained unpainted, conservative, English. So great was the demand for the plain Broadwood square piano that in 1798 James Shudi Broadwood had to write apologetically to an irate customer whose square piano was delayed: 'Would to God we could make them like muffins! . . . many others have been waiting as long, or longer than you have.' Six years later, writing to Leiber of Berlin to order wire for strings, he could say, 'we use a greater quantity of wire than any other manufacturers in the Kingdom.'

Improved production. Clever promotion. The third constituent in the Broadwood success story was global distribution. The young James Shudi in his list 'Wagons Set Out' had identified early on the movement of pianos outward from London; in the key year of 1784 Corri and Sutherland of Edinburgh alone had ordered more than twenty pianos. As the piano culture spread from London to the old wealth of the Shires, to the new wealth of provincial towns and manufacturing centres and to the overseas colonies of the Empire, it was served and stimulated by the presence of local musicians and agents. Building on their original harpsichord contacts, Broadwoods expanded their network, using sales intermediaries of all kinds until what had begun as a fashion became, by the end of the century, the wholesale transportation of a culture from the capital.

War with France had not had the disastrous effects on the English economy envisaged at the start. The French navy was defeated at the Battle of the Nile in 1798; the Baltic trade routes remained open, supplying timber for boat-building and flax for sailcloth; canal transport counteracted the hazards of coastal shipping; and, most important of all, British naval supremacy in the West Indies protected the North Atlantic trade. Sugar, cotton, mahogany and other raw materials such as those that brought prosperity to Lancaster continued to be imported. Mahogany from Jamaica and Honduras had become available at a decisive time for the piano industry. The wood was close grained and the planks were long. Pianos made of mahogany were stronger and more stable, more resistant to the warping effects of string tension and climate change. No other piano had the strength or power of a Broadwood, particularly in the notes of the lower register, and they stood well in the warmer climates to which they were increasingly exported.

Despite the early appearance of pianos in America (as mentioned, German-born John Behrent had made one in 1775, in Philadelphia), the American piano industry advanced slowly until the end of the eighteenth century. Immigrant makers from Germany and England tended to settle in Philadelphia, a centre of furniture and cabinet-making, where in 1789 Charles Albrecht, another German immigrant, opened America's first piano factory. His custom-made pianos resembled those imported from London, as a comparison between a fine Albrecht square piano from c. 1790 at Vassar College with a Broadwood square of 1796, also at Vassar, shows. And while Charles Taws, another Philadelphia piano maker and importer, inveighed in the *Philadelphia Aurora* in 1799 against the discounts and commissions offered to American importers of pianos, and American piano producers invoked the post-revolutionary mantra 'equal to anything imported,' London still had the strongest cultural influence in East Coast cities such as Charleston, Philadelphia, New York and Boston. Until the American piano industry gained momentum in the early years of the nineteenth century, 'London made' continued to mean superior instruments. Possession of a Broadwood or a Clementi piano signified the owner's good taste and elevated status in the United States just as in England, and for a time Broadwood and Clementi had a clear market.

When John Jacob Astor arrived in America in 1784 with seven flutes and a suit, he also had the Broadwood piano agency for New York in his pocket. Astutely reading the new market, Astor began importing 'from London . . . an elegant assortment of musical instruments such as pianofortes, spinets etc.' In 1789 he founded the Bacon Piano Company for the purpose of importing 'Piano Forte's of the Newest Construction made by the best makers in London' through its 'wareroom.' The Broadwood square at Vassar College is probably one of a consignment of six, dispatched to New York on 16 July 1796, for which Broadwoods charged Astor £129 4s 1d. Six years later, in order to concentrate on real estate, he sold his piano interest to John and Michael Paff, who continued the agency and built up the business.

In May 1799 Broadwood dispatched square piano number 4702, three sets of strings, a ream of paper and 200 pens to a M. Barraud of Virginia, and Robert Crew, also of Virginia, bought one of their new grands, number 1431. The same year also saw the start of serious piano business in Charleston, South Carolina, where agent Mr L De Villiers bought nine pianos – six squares, two ornamented squares and a grand.

With William Pitt at the helm of Britain's economy and Nelson at the helm of the navy, the country prospered as never before, despite a series of bad harvests in the 1790s, a naval mutiny in 1797 and rebellion in Ireland. Exports neared £34 million in 1798, an increase of more than 20 percent in one year. 'Our trade,' announced Pitt in the House of Commons, 'has never been in a more flourishing situation.' His genius for the country's financial management, the demographic explosion of the previous fifty years and robust trading due to control of the sea and 'the invention and application of machinery' created an economic climate in which new industries could flourish.

It was a time of extremes. People lived in fear of revolution, yet social and religious change was already happening in this intense phase of the Industrial Revolution. Britain was poised to become the richest and most powerful nation in the world, yet the pursuit of money brought fears of bankruptcy and insolvency to many. Debtors prisons began to fill; sponging houses proliferated. The basis of wealth began to shift from land to money and what it could buy: not only the essentials, but leisure, pleasure, social status, culture and philanthropy. The aspirations of wage earners caused unrest and violence. The gulf between rich and poor was wide, yet the accumulation of money at many levels in between promoted a sense that life could be enjoyable. The enlarged market for leisure and pleasure favoured pianos. Since Shudi's day, industry and technology had been stimulated and encouraged by royal patronage. The Plume of Feathers remained over the doorway in Great Pulteney Street and Broadwoods continued to expand and innovate, constantly improving their pianos, making them bigger, stronger, louder, and leaving the sound and mores of the eighteenth century behind.

The piano gave many people more than music – it gave them jobs and money. Men of business, composers, professional and amateur pianists, those who arranged concerts both in public rooms and private houses; publishers of music, music magazines and tuition manuals, printers, engravers; teachers, tuners, repairers and carriers – all owed their livelihoods to the piano. As piano-making became an industry it gave rise to a plethora of smaller, interdependent enterprises. Pianos were hired out for public and private subscription concerts, for soirées and receptions, for every imaginable social event. Every aspect of the piano industry supported and promoted the rest. The industry fed into itself. Mahogany was shipped in, and finished pianos were shipped out. Metal parts, wrest pins and hitch pins, fretwork, ivories, keys and felts were produced in the hundreds of thousands. Legs were turned, decorative brasses cast, dust covers or baffles shaped and painted. Bellymen made soundboards, keymen cut keys, cabinet-makers veneered and polished pianos and innumerable clerks in counting houses and porters' lodges recorded every transaction. Porterage of pianos was an industry in itself; at any one time there might be a dozen pianos on the streets of London. It was the com-mercialization of a culture.

Britain led the world in piano-making. At the turn of the nine-teenth century serial numbers of Broadwood square pianos had reached five thousand. Seven years later they were making a thou-sand squares a year and serial numbers of grand pianos had reached three thousand. The social distinction of a costly and elab-orate grand piano was not diluted by the increased output of squares at twenty-four guineas. In this broad market-place the piano completely eclipsed the harpsichord, whose demise, apart from a few rarefied examples, would continue for 150 years until the early music revival of the mid-twentieth century.

For a few years Broadwood took harpsichords in part exchange for pianos and managed to sell them on: in May 1791 a Mr Freeman of Chelsea bought a second-hand, double-keyed Kirkman harpsi-chord, 'late [the property] of Hodges,' from Broadwood for £40, but at the end of the century they were writing to Marchioness Howard offering apologies for not being able to take her harpsi-chord in part exchange for a new grand piano because of 'the little chance we have of ever selling it.'

With the demise of the harpsichord an era of music-making ended. Belief in material progress made people look forward rather than back. A society entering the Industrial Age had little taste for music associated with the elite coteries of the eighteenth century; they preferred the waltz to the minuet. John Stanley had died in 1786, the Reverend Charles Wesley in 1788, followed a year later by Sir John Hawkins, and in the north of England another harpsichord-playing member of the Ancient Music brotherhood was coming to the end of his days.

————

On 3 March 1798 John Langshaw senior died in Lancaster. His obituary in *Gore's Advertiser* speaks of his 'unaffected manners . . . a man who endeared himself to a numerous and respectable acquaintance.' He had lived in interesting times and met a good many people from all walks of life. Despite his humble birth and disability and a constant struggle for money, he had, through his 'uncommon assiduity,' improved his lot by using his curious and inventive mind, and his skills had taken him to high places.

He described himself as 'Organ Maker' on the barrel organ in the Judge's House Museum in Lancaster. Although a professional organist in the Established Church, he had possessed the eighteenth-century spirit of enquiry. He was an Enlightenment man: curious, inventive, with a bookish interest in religious debate and the zeal to enlighten others. His pamphlets defended his faith, but unlike Reverend Charles, who could afford to 'seek the Kingdom first,' John Langshaw took the precaution of making additional arrangements of his own. Life was no easier then than now for an uneducated man of humble origin and 'no great Superfluities.' Few men knew better than he that enquiry and education could influence a man's life for the better.

He had lived in an era when professional musicians were regarded as menials; Mozart had been required to sit below the valets in the service of the Archbishop of Salzburg. In England musicians ranked as tradesmen; Lord Chesterfield, writing to the godson he adopted in 1755, advised: 'Nothing degrades a man more than performing upon any instrument whatsoever.' Sir John Hawkins in his *General History of the Science and Practice of Music* had been at pains to prove that music was respectable, but only when studied as a science; even William Crotch had studied academic music rather than become 'a mere ignorant orchestral musician who could never be received in genteel company.' In such a climate John Langshaw had taken a narrow route to respectability by becoming an organist of the Established Church. Such 'favour in the sight of our Fellow creatures,' as he found, came with a struggle. He had acquired a high level of musicianship through his own efforts and used his nimble mind and talents to obtain 'every good Gift and Blessing' for his sons; and he remained true to his musician's calling.

Regarded as something of an expert in history and divinity, he also made himself a good judge of men. From his northern organ loft he had observed the events of musical life in the capital 250 miles to the south together with the manouevres of London's masters of music. On seeing the death of William Boyce 'in the News Papers,' he had contemplated the unseemly spectacle of rival organists jockeying for the vacant post, and had written to Reverend Charles: 'Now for the whipping between Dr. Worgan & Dr. Cooke, for the King's Plate.' (Boyce's job as Master of the King's Music went to John Stanley.)

He was also a good judge of a keyboard player, citing Handel's Second and Fourth Suites, 'as hard as any in the book,' as a good test; 'and whoever can play Kelway's Lessons: has nothing to fear from any other author.'

Despite his 'few advantages from education,' he had become the regular, eventually almost the only, correspondent of the Reverend Charles Wesley, a master of the poetic word and ringing phrase who used the English language to powerful and lasting effect in works that are still the core of the English Hymnal. The letters he wrote to John Langshaw contain some of his most vivid expressions of humanity and they called forth the best from the man to whom they were written. In February 1779 John Langshaw had written to Reverend Charles:

> Ever since I was young I have received good for ill. I could write such things as would to many appear all Romance, or Enthusiasm . . . with one Eye I looke to the second <u>Causes</u> &

wish to be grateful, but with another Eye I see the moving first <u>Cause</u> of all, but cannot say I am truly thankful.

This enigmatic expression may have referred to the accident that shaped his life. John Langshaw always chose his words carefully. In his day religious conflict was sharp and Methodism was seen as something of a threat to a quiet and somewhat lazy established church. The 'enthusiasm' or fervent emotion associated with Methodism was abhorrent to many people, particularly in the upper classes. He may have used the word to keep favour with Reverend Charles on whose goodwill his son Jack had depended. He learned quickly from those whose advantages in life had been greater than his own. His pamphlets and letters have mostly disappeared, but his last letter to Reverend Charles is far more confident than his first written only seven years earlier. He always played the subservient role in their correspondence. When he signed himself 'your most obedient and humble Servant,' he meant it. Without loss of dignity, his letters are filled with deference and gratitude to a man in a higher place who was a true friend. He knew that great men and men of stature are not necessarily the same.

His passion for learning made a lasting impression on his children, particularly Jack, and it has endured through eight generations of his descendants. Many of them, doctors, surgeons, lawyers, inventors and teachers, professional men and women, joined the English intelligentsia and continue to improve the lives of everyone within their sphere. How he would have enjoyed disputing with his great-great-great-grandson John Langshaw Austin, White's Professor of Moral Philosophy at Oxford, one of the most influential British philosophers of the twentieth century, whose avowed aims were 'the fun of discovery, the pleasures of co-operation and the satisfaction of agreement.' How intrigued old John Langshaw would have been with his great-great-great-great-grandson Tim Austin's Nuclear Incident Criticality Detector.

When young George Langshaw had died many years earlier in 1782, Reverend Charles had confided in his letter of consolation, 'I have five children waiting for me in one grave. The days of our mourning will soon be ended.' With the death of his youngest son Benjamin in 1797, John Langshaw had lost six of his nine children. By then he was old, lame and totally blind. He had sold his books and perhaps as he waited to discover 'the moving first <u>Cause</u> of all,' he thought of other words that Reverend Charles had written to him many years before:

> Partner of the Heavenly Hope
> Travel on and meet me there.

Why else have we met on earth, but that we may spend an happy Eternity together?

After his death the promise he had secured for Jack to succeed him as organist at Lancaster Priory was honoured. A vestry minute for 29 March 1798 signed by the vicar records:

That he hereby appointed John Langshaw to be Organist of the Parish Church of Lancaster. He will take possession of his place on Easter Sunday next the eighth of April.

Jack Langshaw entered into his inheritance. Thereafter he was known as Mr John Langshaw.

12

MR JOHN LANGSHAW

MR JOHN LANGSHAW was forty-four in the summer of 1807 when the square piano he had ordered from Broadwood in June arrived in Lancaster. Described variously in the Broadwood records as 'Mr John Langshaw Organist,' occasionally as 'Music Master,' once as 'Professor,' he was by then also a family man with four children. On 2 January 1800 he had married Sarah Grundy in the parish church at Bolton, near Manchester, where she and her three sisters had been brought up by their uncle. John had met her through his sister Elizabeth, a woman of striking beauty who was married to Thomas Green, a widower whose first wife had been an aunt of the four orphaned Grundy sisters. 'A more attached affectionate family could not be met with than these four sisters,' wrote a grandchild from Australia many years later. The four sisters remained devoted to one another and their offspring. Sarah managed, remarkably in an age of high infant mortality, to rear all her nine children through infancy. She lived to be ninety and during a long life her loving nature and practical good sense complemented the respect for learning handed down by John's father.

Piano 10651 was not the only arrival in Lancaster in August 1807. The *Lancaster Gazette* reported that one hundred hogsheads of Fine Pusey Hall Sugars had arrived on the *Will* from Jamaica. The following week the *Friends* from the Baltic and the *Betsy* from Riga brought cargos of deal and flax for Lancaster's shipbuilding and sailcloth industries. But the arrivals and sailings of West Indiamen were no longer the most important announcements in the weekly *Gazette*; those days had passed.

In 1807 Lancaster was no longer the flourishing town it had been when the Langshaws had first arrived thirty-five years earlier. Its layout was much the same and many of the proposed buildings shown on Stephen Mackreth's 1778 map had been built. There was a new town hall with a recent full-length portrait of Lord Nelson by James Lonsdale. Common Garden and Spring Garden, streets with fine Georgian houses, had been built; so had a high street, where the Langshaws would eventually live. There was the Grand Theatre, where touring companies performed in repertory, and a poorhouse subsidized by a poor rate of 2s 8d. Mail coaches arrived regularly in Market Square, and a new bridge designed by Thomas Harrison crossed the river. But Pitt was no longer at the helm of the country's economy and the Napoleonic Wars had begun to affect Lancaster's maritime trade adversely. Merchants became cautious; building slowed.

The development of Dalton Square did not match up to the original grand vision. A number of proposed streets on the Skerton side, with names like Antigua, Jamaica and Barbados reflecting the basis of Lancaster's former prosperity, were never built. Immediately after the trading peak of 1800 came a sharp depression and Lancaster's maritime decline set in; when Charles Clark, a Lancaster printer, published his 'History and State of Lancaster,' in the second week of August 1807 he referred to the town's 'present stagnation.' French privateers preyed upon shipping, and convoys that operated mainly out of Liverpool had become obligatory. The price of goods fell when the convoy ships all arrived at once, and additional produce from former French colonies caused them to fall even further. Lancaster's boom in West Indian imports collapsed, and several merchants who traded at their own risk went out of business.

St Mary's Priory Church, Lancaster.
Author's photograph.

The depression in the town's maritime trade had as much to do with local problems as the French wars and the ending of the legal slave trade in 1807. The Lune estuary was shallow, and shifting sandbanks required pilot navigation; ships above 250 tons had to anchor off Glasson Docks four miles south of the town and transfer cargo to lighter vessels.

For some years, commerce dependent on the plantation economy continued. John Brockbank still built boats on the Skerton side for Liverpool's 'Guinea Trade.' He bought the Old Bridge and took down the first arch in order to launch the *Demerara*, the biggest Lancaster ship then seen. According to Clark, the bridge was 'verging on decay' and a major event in the summer of 1807 was the collapse of another arch after heavy floods. Mahogany furniture was still made at Gillows, and candles, clay pipes and shoes 'suitable for the West Indian climate' continued to be made in the town, but Lancaster merchants transferred their interests and registered their ships in Liverpool and cotton mills had already appeared along the banks of the Lune.

There was increasing dependence on canal transport. The Lune Aqueduct designed by John Rennie and built at the enormous cost of £48,000 was opened in 1798. It was a wonder of engineering with five arches, each fifty-three feet high with a seventy-foot span. Foundation piers sunk twenty feet below ground supported battlements seventy-nine feet above. The aqueduct carried the Lancaster Canal for 664 feet over the River Lune before a level run of forty-three miles to Preston. But it was built too late to avail Lancaster's failing maritime trade. The economic depression that followed the Napoleonic Wars and the reduction in maritime trade bit deep and slow, and by the time a canal arm to Glasson Docks was opened the West Indian trade had almost ceased.

One place that did not suffer from the decline was the castle. By 1807 it had been substantially rebuilt. There was a modern assize court and a county gaol that could hold over 400 prisoners; these included captives from the Napoleonic Wars, male and female felons from Manchester, as well as local debtors. Clark noted in his directory that the prison was clean and no fetters were used, 'except for the refractory.' He praised the keeper, Mr Higgins 'for promoting a system of industry by which every prisoner capable of labour is engaged in some useful employment.' That summer Joshua Newsome was pilloried in the Market Square and three highway robbers were sentenced to death by public hanging.

The Langshaw family moved from Skerton, 'still inhabited principally by labouring people,' to Upper King Street on the castle (or south) side of the river. According to Clark there were just over 9,000 people living in Lancaster in 1807 in 'about sixteen hundred houses.' Not yet being a freeman of the borough, John Langshaw would not have voted for either of the town's members of Parliament, John Dent and John Fenton Cawthorne. He would have known John Taylor Wilson, the mayor, and other members of the corporation, the seven aldermen, twelve burgesses and twelve common council men; they paid part of his organist's salary.

On a mid-August morning in 1807, did John Langshaw walk the few hundred yards from Upper King Street into town with Sarah to the Wednesday market to buy fruit, butter, eggs or poultry? As they walked, did they discuss the town's latest scandal? Gideon Yates, a local artist, was in court again for non-payment of rent to Mrs Bentham, who kept a lodging house on Castle Hill. Did they pause while Sarah looked at printed calicos, dimities and muslinets in Mary Caton's draper's shop window? If she decided to go inside to try on one of Agnes Caton's chip or willow hats, did John walk on to Church Street to visit his banker, Thomas Worswick? Was that the morning he arranged for a bill for 24 guineas in payment for square piano 10651 to be paid to the London piano maker, John Broadwood and Son? The bill was entered in Broadwood's Letter Book on 22 August. It was his only piano purchase that year.

Did he stop at Merchant's Coffee Rooms on his way back for a quick look at the previous Saturday's *Gazette* and read that the Four Misses Adams were performing 'New and Elegant Dances' that week at the Grand Theatre? Was he tempted to take Sarah to see their 'celebrated and much admired Skipping-Rope-Pas-de-Trois'? Did he smile as he imagined Miss E. Adams performing her 'Fox Hunter's Jig'? Was he bemused at the thought of 'Parisot's Hornpipe'? When he went on his way, did he linger to talk to Miss Parrin, his father's first organ pupil, now secretary of the Amicable Society's Circulating Library, whose members paid twelve shillings a year for access to over 4,000 books? Was he really putting off a visit to Mr Whitlock the travelling dentist, who visited Mr Savages every year 'to perform all operations on the TEETH'?

Or was he not in Lancaster at all, but teaching in Preston, some thirty miles south of Lancaster, having left at eight o'clock that morning on the daily canal packet?

By his own account John Langshaw, 'after visiting London three times . . . commenced his career as a teacher of music,' and 'In discharging the professional duties of Organist & Teacher, occasionally varied by presiding at the P. Forte, at local concerts, his life has since been chiefly spent' (from his letter to John Sainsbury, 3 January 1824). Other than this letter, written towards the end of his life, he left no record of his work. His piano business with Broadwood is recorded in their ledgers; an idea of his life as a north-country music master is contained in a letter written by Martha Sharpe of Lancaster to her nephew William Whittaker, a curate in Manchester.

Martha was the widow of Francis Sharpe, who had been a music master and organist in Knutsford. In his youth he had lived in London and like John Langshaw, his slightly younger contemporary, he had became an early agent, or 'Country Friend,' of Broadwoods. He left a small fortune of more than £13,000, an astonishing amount for a provincial organist and music teacher, and Martha had moved to Lancaster to be near her sister. Her son Edmund would found the Austin Paley architectural practice, and her daughter Emily, then at school in Bath, would marry Pearson Langshaw, John and Sarah's youngest son, many years later; Emily's sketchbooks are the ones in Lancaster's Maritime Museum.

'Aunt Sharpe' wrote regularly to William, her favourite nephew. Much of their correspondence is family talk, but one long letter dated 11 February 1828 in reply to William's request for advice for a friend, 'who proposes setting up as a Music Master,' contains a detailed account of the life of an organist and music master in the first decades of the nineteenth century and goes a long way to explaining her husband's success.

> . . . His clear gains for the last few years were at least eight
> Hundred a yr . . . but then in spite of the high charge, he was . . .
> so kindly welcom'd everywhere, that he dined Slept or Lunch'd
> with the Families he visited . . . & never frequented an Inn . . .

I think his terms were never less than half a Guinea for the very shortest distance – (an hour's Lesson, or ¾th) at some places where there were sisters 5 Lessons for 3 Guineas – at others a Guinea a Lesson one Pupil – at the schools I know it was – 8 Guineas a yr & 6, for singing (in addition) – half hour Lessons, one a week only . . . Pupils in the town 7s/ a Lesson (three quarters each) or 3s/ the half hour, – or, School terms, giving half hour Lessons and the same Holidays as at the Schools – this Mr Sharpe considered more certain than the 7s/ Lessons – because so many excuses were often made of head aches, or engagements, or not having had time to practise, to put off private lessons – but when a certain sum must be paid yearly, Parents take care to make the most of it . . .

Her letter, full of advice to her nephew for his friend Mr Harris, continues:

In this place [Lancaster] there is little musical taste – but we have three Teachers – Mr Langshaw the oldest. . . 8 Guineas a yr 2 Lessons a week half hour – both at Schools & in town – of his Country teaching I do not hear . . . I should think Mr H would gain useful hints from Preston where Mr Langshaw in his best days did teach, & perhaps does now – but I have no acquaintance with him & cannot tell . . .

The social position of a music master during John Langshaw's lifetime was still an ambiguous one. In his father's day, organists had been largely working class. Their existence had been insecure and they had had to diversify into repairing, teaching, performing and composing – composing being more highly regarded than the rest. Music played for leisure or pleasure was acceptable in a man and to be encouraged in a woman. The science of music was a subject fit for manly study; but music as work smacked of servitude and was no occupation for a gentleman.

A music master was a professional, though not on the same level as a lawyer or surgeon. His exact social status was ill defined in an era that liked to be sure of the social distinctions. As late as 1825, when Edward Baines published a list of Lancaster inhabitants 'according to Trade Lists, Gentry, Clergy and Manufacturers,' Mr Langshaw's name was not on it. He was not a gentleman of private means; he had to work. Lips could curl at a whiff of the effeminate associated with performing, at music that gratified the senses rather than the intellect, at someone who served others, at teachers who abused their position of trust with wives and daughters, at the proximity of artisan forebears. Foreign music (Italian) hinted at 'popery' and passion. Unease about music masters, déclassé and vaguely suspect or worse, risqué and predatory, had lingered since the previous century when the Earl of Chesterfield had advised his son: 'piping and fiddling puts a gentleman in a very frivolous and contemptible light . . . and takes up a great deal of time that might be better employed.' Male attitudes were particularly wary. Mr Langshaw's profession may have been one that no gentleman would wish for his son, but he was also an organist and he derived status by association with the Established Church; nevertheless he had to tread carefully.

Lancastrian society was still dominated by the old merchant elite, the Rawlinsons, the Worswicks, the Burrows and the Masons, and their daughters would have been among his pupils; music was not high on the list of suitable diversions for young men. It was the practice for music masters to visit their pupils at home, and it was this arrangement that made them an easy subject of caricature or, worse, led to a reputation as a ladies' man and a fortune hunter. A music master could be either a gentleman or a knave. There being no code of practice other than his own conduct, his standing in his locality was very much what he made it, as Martha Sharpe's letter to her nephew explains:

[He] must <u>not</u> on <u>any</u> account compromise his own consequence – his manners should be very Gentlemanly, & <u>quiet</u> – &

he must begin by exacting <u>proper</u> respect from Servants etc. – by requiring his Horse or Gig to be brought to the door, etc etc – for all this goes a great way with high, or, <u>Purse Proud People.</u> – It was, I dare say a wonder to many <u>little People</u>, why Mr Sharpe was call'd upon to sit next to Lady Warburton, or Mrs Leycester, or Mrs Grey in a Party of the proudest Cheshire Gents. While Mr Hollins – & Mr Wright, our most leading law-Men were dining in the Steward's room – . . . & Mr S would <u>order</u> his Gig to the door, whilst they <u>went</u> to the <u>Stable</u> . . . some are <u>born</u> <u>Gentlemen</u> & have <u>tact</u> – others can never learn either . . .

Thirty years later Martha's niece, Elizabeth Gaskell, encapsulated these sentiments of 'very much acknowledged gentility,' in her novel *Cranford*, based on the society she observed in Knutsford and Lancaster.

In 1807 the music that Mr John Langshaw's pupils played would have been light, popular and contemporary; it was only in the second half of the nineteenth century that people started playing the music of earlier generations. Serious English music was largely overlooked in favour of the works of German-Viennese composers. There was a demand for simple piano arrangements of orchestral works by Mozart and Haydn. As a result, pianos started to get louder and bigger. By 1807 additional keys were standard, even on square pianos. Many people, however, found Mozart and Beethoven too difficult and played lighter music at home on their square pianos. The vogue was for piano duets where two people sat in sociable harmony, as in so many prints of the time, making music in the manner prescribed by refined sensibility.

As a musician trained in the Ancient tradition, Mr Langshaw may have preferred his own *Sonatas in the style of Geminiani (Corelli's as they are known)* or one of his *Adaptations of choruses from the works of Handel and the Creation of Haydn arranged as duets*. His pupils may have determined on something more modern. A collection of early-nineteenth-century printed sheet music in the Broadwood Archive gives an idea of the sort of music he might have taught and played with them. *A Collection of German Waltzes* by J. Moscheles and *Six Waltzes for the Pianoforte* by Ferdinand Reis reflect the waltz craze that swept the country. The more serious-minded young ladies may have preferred a sonata by Steibelt, while their lighter-headed sisters could see only as far as *The Bridesmaid's Chorus, carillon rondo, composed and dedicated to Miss Davenport* by Augustus Meves. Bold girls may have been tempted to try *Dramatic Airs from English, Italian, German & French Operas*, and the really daring ones might have flaunted *L'amour est un Enfant Trompeur*, by Dussek. In addition there were plenty of single-line melodies for those who struggled.

Scotch airs were all the rage, and pianos were used to accompany the voice and other instruments in such pieces as the evergreen 'Bonnie Wee Thing and I Hae Laid a Herring in Salt,' from *Caledonian airs for pianoforte and flute*; or gems for voice and piano such as the Dibdin family's 'Beautiful Maid' and 'Lovely Kitty.' Who can now guess the appeal of John Davy's 'The Tight Little Fellow that wears the Blue Jacket' or the wisely anonymous glee 'Palala, sum, nootka gunza,' otherwise known as 'Do Thy Duty and the Rest to Heaven'?

Mr Langshaw's own lighter publications included 'The Farewell,' which he described as 'an anonymous ballad much sung by the late Mr Meredith,' and the more serious 'Can Joy that Wretched Bosom Cheer?', 'thought to convey much of the spirit and pathos of the words.' His adaptation of Pleyel's 'The Flow'r that's Unvalu'd' and his own ballad with harp or pianoforte accompaniment 'Dear Boy Throw that Icicle Down,' must surely have moved the coolest listener. These parlour pieces, however diverse in style and mood, all depended on the piano, already the heart of popular domestic music-making.

Title page 'Dear Boy Throw that Icicle Down,' c. 1802, by John Langshaw. Reproduced by permission of Lancaster Library.

In the evening he might have given his own daughter a piano lesson. Elizabeth, known as Bessy, was John and Sarah's oldest child, and almost seven in the summer of 1807 when piano 10651 arrived. She might have played pieces from *The Fairing*, a collection of early-nineteenth-century children's songs now in the Broadwood Archive that included 'Dickory Dickory Dock,' 'Pat a Cake' and 'The Miller He Grinds his Corn.' Her brothers John and George and her sister Sarah may have joined in 'The Cock a Doodle Song' until the music-making ended and their father played 'Bye Baby Bunting' before bedtime, ignoring their pleas for the frightening 'Dr Faustus' song instead.

His day may not then have been over. Assizes in Lancaster were a time of social activity, of balls, parties and concerts. It is likely that with Mr Langshaw 'presiding at the piano' at Assembly Room concerts, there would have been an Ancient music element, a Corelli concerto, an Aria or Chorus from the *Messiah*, perhaps a Haydn overture. As the leading local professional, John Langshaw would have been invited to private concerts to support the gentlemen amateurs and see them through the shoals and rapids of Mozart and Beethoven. He obtained printed music from his own publishers, Preston in the Strand, and Broadwoods dispatched music to him with his piano orders. As in his father's day, amateur performers were 'stiffened' by professional musicians. In addition to Mr Langshaw these would have been Messrs Winder and McGregor, Lancaster's dancing masters, and military musicians from the Lancashire Yeomanry. There was still resistance, however, usually on the part of the wives of gentlemen amateurs, to any further social contact.

At the end of the evening, John Langshaw might have discussed family affairs with Sarah – the fragility of their younger daughter Sarah's health, perhaps, or the expected arrival of their fifth child. Possibly he spent some time reading by the light of tallow candles before retiring to bed; something perhaps bought from Mr Clark the bookseller's sale three years earlier, which had included books 'good as new,' on travel, West's *Guide to the Lakes*, novels by Fielding and Defoe, a life of Sir Walter Raleigh and a *Dictionary of the Wonders of Nature*. John was also fond of poetry, a legacy from William Cockin, his old writing master. His ballad 'Dear Boy Throw that Icicle Down' was a setting of words by Robert Bloomfield whose anthology, *A Farmer's Boy,* was a best-seller in 1800, running to 26,000 copies. He also subscribed to the less well-known *Poetical Effusions* of Miss Isabella Lickbarrow, an early Lake poet. Or, perhaps, instead he worked by candlelight on his music master's memorandum book and his Broadwood accounts.

At last, lying in bed before going to sleep, he might have thought about the priory organ. It was still at the centre of his life, as it had always been and it was more troublesome than ever.

The question of music in church had been debated since the Reformation. Martin Luther saw music as a gift of God that reflected the harmony of Creation. In England, after the austerity of the Commonwealth and the uncertainty of the Restoration, organs were regarded by some as a dangerous innovation, and there were many in the aftermath of the Jacobite uprisings who felt that music in church smacked of 'Rome' and unnecessary ritual, diverting attention from worship and rousing passions akin to the abhorred 'enthusiasm.' There were practical concerns too about raising the money to build organs and pay the ongoing costs of repair and maintenance and the organist's salary. Few churches had an organ at the beginning of the eighteenth century; their reappearance after the austerity of Cromwell's Commonwealth in the mid-seventeenth century was gradual. A hundred years later an organ and someone to play it were still missing from many English parish churches.

In Lancaster, as elsewhere, the organist's finances were always obscure. Twenty-four laymen known as the Twenty Fourtie managed the affairs of the priory church, appointed sextons, paid the bellows blower and rewarded the extermination of foxes, sparrows and vermin from the churchyard. Some of the Twenty Fourtie, together with the commissary of the Archdeaconry of Richmond and the mayor, recorder and vicar of Lancaster, were also trustees for the organ and the organist's salary. In his letter of 1779 to Reverend Charles the first organist had mentioned: '100 a year, the utmost I get.' In addition the organist was entitled to rents from seats in the church up to a fixed maximum, beyond which he was required to 'Balance the Account on the other side,' from any surplus. Pew rents could be sold like property. A handbill of 1801 announces a sale 'To the Highest Bidder . . . of seats in St. Mary's Church [the Priory] . . . belonging to John Langshaw, the Organist . . . situate in the Chancel . . . and the Organ Galleries.' On the whole the pay was not good; there were, as Reverend Charles had long ago identified, 'no great Superfluities.'

Provincial organists were often only a generation removed from their artisan forebears and still ranked as servants. People of the middling sort, anxious about their own social standing and often not far removed from the people they shunned, could take an exaggerated view of the social niceties. The fact that John Langshaw had mingled with the mighty in London would have carried little weight. His livelihood depended not only on his talents and skills; he had to navigate the unsettled social waters of provincial Lancaster with great care.

It helped that he worked in the House of God, which raised him above other professional musicians in the town. In becoming an organist of the Established Church he had earned the right to be called 'Mr.' Nonetheless his reputation could be easily compromised. An organist's choice of music – complex or obscure hymn tunes, evangelical chants of stultifying simplicity, 'modern' organ voluntaries played with bravura tour de force, could excite swift comment from the congregation, then as now. An organist was not expected to be a virtuoso performer showing off the latest style. The evangelicals preferred plain music or none at all; John Wesley approved of a congregation singing lustily in unison but detested choral church music. London organists had to satisfy the taste of their sophisticated congregations: the moderns found psalmody dull; elaborate arrangements aroused passion. Organists had to be sensitive to turbulent religious views. When Mr John Langshaw set Psalm 9, 'Sing Praises therefore to the Lord,' he needed to write music that was an adjunct and support to worship, that reflected current religious thinking yet maintained harmony. He would have needed more diplomacy than he ever thought he possessed when as a boy he had faced up to Sir John Hawkins all those years earlier.

Like his father, he was a High Church organist; unlike him he seems to have taken a liberal view of church politics. He played traditional services in the priory church; he also inaugurated the organ in Lancaster's new Church of St Anne founded by his old school friend, the controversial 'Lancaster Evangelical,' Robert Houseman.

Part of the priory organist's contract had always been to tune and repair the organ. Mr John Langshaw had grown up in attendance on the temperamental old instrument, learned its secrets, helped his father to keep it going, and no doubt pumped the bellows when necessary in the four-foot space behind the pipes while his father played. Before his appointment he had fulfilled his ailing father's duties to it and as organist he continued to coax music out of it for several more years.

In 1809 the priory organ wheezed its last. It was, according to a vestry minute, 'in a ruinous state.' A new one was to be built by public subscription under the management of another committee. Two years later, £816 10s 3d had been raised from local notables whose names were duly minuted. News travels fast in the close world of organs and organists, and John heard from his old friend Samuel Wesley in London in a letter of 2 December 1809:

My Dear Old Friend
. . . the present Occasion of my immediate Application to you,

relates to an <u>Organ</u>, which it seems is to be constructed for your Quarter of the World, & I understand that several Estimates have been, or are about to be delivered etc.

He goes on to urge the case of Thomas Elliot, saying there was 'no Organ Builder in England whose Work could do him more credit,' and that if he did build the new organ at Lancaster, 'you will not be disappointed in your Choice, nor I in Danger of Disgrace for my Recommendation.' Whatever John Langshaw's reply, the job did not go to Elliot but to the organ builder George Pike England. The old organ that had occupied John Langshaw and his father daily for forty years, on which he and his brothers had learned to play and on which he was already teaching his daughter Bessy, was removed. The church floor was strengthened and a new three manual organ was installed at a cost of £770 10s with an allowance of £70 on the old one.

This was not the end of the old organ. George Pike England offered it to Whalley Abbey, near Preston, 'with Improvements,' for £300. After some negotiation for the cost of packing cases and travelling expenses for two fitters, a deal was done at 300 guineas. The old organ on which the two Lancaster organists had spent so much of their lives was rebuilt and installed at Whalley Abbey, 'with two notes added to each sett of keys & five notes to the lower part of Swell to make it down to Fiddle G . . . Varnish the case and entirely new gilded with best gold the front pipes.' When the job was completed the organist at Whalley wrote to Mr John Langshaw, inviting him to visit the abbey and play the improved organ.

The instrument's former organist composed his reply from his own recollections and information from 'an old book in the Vicarage.' He wrote to the Whalley organist, Adam Cottam, on 5 May 1813:

My Dear Sir,
. . . I am happy that you have got our old organ . . . a very excellent instrument.

His faded writing on fragile paper recounts the history of the organ and its previous organists, ending with his own father: 'of course it has been with us ever since, and I can with truth say I do not yet wish to part with it.'

It was a generous letter from a busy man. By then he had seven children, a life filled with work as a professional organist, teacher, composer and performer and agent for Broadwood pianos; he had sold three pianos in the previous year, three more in this one. Unlike his contemporary John Marsh, a gentleman amateur musician of Chichester who left thirty-seven volumes filled with details of his musical life and who seems somehow to belong to an earlier, more leisured age, Mr John Langshaw did not leave a diary. With his work, his family, the constant pressures on his time, he comes across as a modern man making a living where he can in an uncertain world. He had to decline the Whalley organist's invitation: 'It would give me great pleasure to play upon my old organ again and to see Mr England's improvements, but I am afraid the time is far distant, my engagements are of that nature that I have little leisure for pleasure.'

13

BROADWOOD'S GLOBAL
NETWORK

THANKS TO THE Wesleys, Mr Langshaw had been part of London's fashionable music scene as a young man when pianos arrived and John Broadwood began producing them in commercial numbers. He had been in the perfect place to learn to play the new instrument and when he went home he became a conduit for the piano from London to the north of England. In his 'rough and hasty account of my life' for John Sainsbury's *New Biographical Dictionary of Musicians* he made no mention of his business with Broadwoods, although it had been part of his life since the time he had left London in 1784.

Broadwood's sales ledgers and porters' books contain the details of his piano business with them from the first recorded Langshaw order in 1784 to the last in 1831. During those many years he obtained at least one hundred Broadwood pianos, if the nine missing ledger years before 1794 are included. Of that number, twelve were grand pianos, there was one cabinet piano, one cottage upright and eleven 'Best Squares.' The rest were plain square pianos at the lowest end of Broadwood's range. The first was bought for twenty-one guineas, and he sold his last in 1831 for only £19 more. Judging by the number of second-hand cases he ordered from Broadwoods he probably operated in the used-piano market too, where a square could be bought for as little as four guineas. So although he supplied a few expensive pianos to the upper end of the market, the majority of Mr Langshaw's customers were less-well-off people who were playing pianos in their own home for the first time.

The Langshaw account was Broadwood's first piano business conducted through an individual organist musician outside London. It was a new kind of business, not simply the continuation of a harpsichord agency. Mr Langshaw was not a music warehouseman who bought at a reduced price and added a profit, nor was he an occasional agent who received a commission on sale. He was a distributor. He ordered pianos, sold them to his customers at Broadwood's retail price and deducted his discount when he settled his account with them.

His dealings with Broadwood were complex. He often paid for more than one piano at a time, as well as for accessories such as covers, cases and spare strings. He bought what he needed to repair and tune pianos, his orders including 'plyers' and brass and steel wire to make strings. He had hammers re-leathered or ordered leather to do the job himself. Sometimes he sent part of a piano's action in for repair; sometimes he bought sets of piano keys. He was versatile, a technician like his father, and repaired harpsichords too – there was an entry for a new set of harpsichord jacks. And he was one of the last to obtain used harpsichords from Broadwood, in 1799 and 1800. Occasional small payments from his Broadwood account to his brother William were too small to be consistent with a business partnership. William was nine years younger, also an organist, who worked with a barrel-organ maker in London and probably tried out a piano at Broadwood's from time to time for his brother in Lancaster. There were many bigger accounts than Mr John Langshaw's, but none more complex.

His payments in settlement of his account were also difficult to unravel. Cash payments and bills drawn on his bankers, Messrs Worswicks of Lancaster, seldom corresponded to the cost of the

Mr John Langshaw's folio page, Broadwood Wholesale Sales Ledger I, 1811–1815. Reproduced by permission of Surrey History Service.

pianos and accessories he had ordered. But he always paid promptly, either on demand or by a forward-dated bill to earn maximum discount. The amount of his discount was difficult to calculate. The word 'Disc.' appears in small letters next to his payments, showing that it had already been deducted at source. He clearly used all his old writing master's skills to work out what amounted to about a 10 percent commission on sales, or £2 4s on a square piano. On an average of two or three pianos a year it would not have made a great contribution to his income, but it helped.

The Broadwood porters' books always identify the customer to whom a piano is dispatched. Mr Langshaw almost always bought in his own name and pianos were sent to him in Lancaster without identifying his customer. But in fourteen instances his customers were named because their pianos were delivered directly to them somewhere outside Lancaster. Mr Burrows, Mr John Dalton, the Duke of Hamilton, Mr Thomas Green, Mr Chippindale and others were all, as might be expected, Mr Langshaw's pupils, family and friends, the people he knew in his everyday life in and around Lancaster.

Edward Burrows, for example, for whom Mr Langshaw bought a square piano in 1795, was godfather to his son Edmund; Elizabeth, Mary and Alicia Burrows were baptismal sponsors to three of his other children. The Duke of Hamilton, of Ashcroft Hall near Lancaster, who bought a best square piano through him in February 1810, was one of the subscribers to the new priory organ fund. John Dalton, the developer of Dalton Square, was the head of Lancaster's leading Catholic family. His piano was sent directly to the family seat at Thurnham Hall, Cockerham. Thomas Green, who taught at Winnwick Grammar School, was married to Mr Langshaw's beautiful sister Elizabeth. Then there was Mr Chippindale, who performed in repertory at the Grand Theatre Lancaster. On 15 August 1807, after the Four Misses Adams had performed their final 'Pas-de-Quatre,' Mr Chippindale rounded off the evening with 'A Favourite Comic Song called Nothing at All.' His six-octave 'Upright Grand Pianoforte,' ordered by Mr Langshaw, was sent directly to his home in Yorkshire.

The five years between 1799 and 1804 were some of Mr Langshaw's busiest with Broadwood. Newly married and with a growing family the increased commission on the sixteen pianos he sold during that period would have been welcome. Six of them were grands that included one of the most significant sales of his career, on 5 March 1800:

> A GPF com. No. 1784 & cover
> A Do. [ditto] No. 1785 & cover

'for Mr Langshaw at Lancaster,' meaning they were ordered by him. But the two grands, valued at £136 10s, packed in their deal and tin cases, were delivered to Farlow, Broadwood's overseas shipping agent, 'to clear and ship on the *Galin*. Consigned Mr John Baynes, merchant, Boston New England.' With shipping costs, insurance etc. the transaction totaled £181 10s.

This is the first record of a shipment of pianos to Boston in the Broadwood Archive, another first for Mr Langshaw (whose commission on this transaction was £37). Ten weeks later, on 24 May, the *Columbian Centinel* newspaper of Boston carried an advertisement for John Baynes's emporium at 50 State Street, announcing the sale of an assortment of goods received 'per ship *Galin*,' consisting of all manner of printed fabrics, calicoes, parasols, hats, telescopes, carpets, Two Grand Piano fortes and one elegant patent barrel organ (the organ was possibly made by Mr Langshaw's brother William).

The Broadwood Letter Book (1801–1810) also contained entries for John Langshaw, recording his orders for pianos, occasional harpsichord spares and tools. It was steady business amounting to £152 0s 6d in 1803 and £106 in 1804. In spring 1805 he was invoiced £57 and sent a list of prices. Every few months there was another order, followed by an invoice and a record of his payment.

Although an organist music master's socially uncertain position had its difficulties, it also gave him access to a wide range of people. When Mr Langshaw introduced the piano to the local gentry whose daughters he taught, to maritime merchants on both sides of the Atlantic, to friends who were godparents to his children, to teachers and performing artists visiting Lancaster, he was not consciously playing a part in a piano culture that would spread through the world and last for more than 200 years. He was simply a professional musician who supplied people with pianos where and whenever he could to earn some extra money for his family.

And he was not alone. By the time he bought piano 10651 in 1807 there was a network of Broadwood distributors throughout Britain that included many other organists. At first there were no established business practices. Commerce took time to evolve and people played it off the cuff as they went along. In the hurly-burly of a developing new industry, arrangements between principal, distributor and agent were almost as varied as the pianos Broadwood manufactured. Their 'Country Friends,' as they called their sales intermediaries, were of three kinds: some of the earliest were organist music-masters such as Mr Langshaw; there were also music warehousemen and ad hoc agents.

The early nineteenth century was an era of organ-building. In the cathedral towns, the old ecclesiastical foundations and wherever a new organ was built, organists such as Mr Langshaw of Lancaster, Mr Mutlow of Gloucester, Mr Ambrose of Chelmsford, Marshall of Warwick, Anderson of Montrose, Nicholson of Norwich, Benn of Plympton, Sharpe of Knutsford, Hull of Winchester and many, many others, distributed Broadwood pianos to the parlours and drawing-rooms, the parsonages and schoolrooms of Georgian provincial England.

Their relations with Broadwood varied like their discounts. A letter to organist John Boult of Preston Middleton in September 1807 set out the standard terms: 'Our usual credit is six months, should you think it proper to remit us cash we allow a discount of 5% on the amount of the instrument.' Sometimes Broadwood allowed more, as they did to Mr Langshaw, but they were quick to remind even their 'Oldest and Best Friends' about any discrepancies. At a time when some of their more illustrious

London customers kept pianos for as long as six years nominally on hire, they wrote to Mr Langshaw on 4 October 1802 acknowledging receipt of his discounted payment of 27 September and reminding him that he had forgotten to include payment for some harpsichord jacks: 'this article we believe we must debit you a Guinea for.'

A provincial organist, glad of the piano business, was easy to reprimand. For example, on 5 September 1807 Broadwood wrote to Mr Hill, organist in Pontefract:

> . . . from your description we are satisfied the instrument must have received a violent fall through the carelessness of the carrier – and we think he ought to make good the damage sustained . . . we are sorry it has happened but you are under a wrong idea in supposing it not to be a new instrument as it has not been made three months.

Not all organists allowed themselves to be pushed around, however. The organist at Hereford Cathedral had not been so easy to lean on, as Broadwood's reply of 17 September 1808 shows:

> We should not have supposed that our letter of the 12th would have produced a reply so angry as in your letter of 15th inst. We have been very explicit and liberal to your utmost wishes. We have never taken more pains to conciliate or concede more to any correspondent than you and we regret to perceive with so little success. In future orders must be paid for according to our statement . . . deduct only 5pc if you pay us in 2 months and submit to your deducting 5pc from your commission when we allow the like disc. to a customer paying us recommended by you . . . we are little pleased with the correspondence between us.

These organist music-masters played a vital part from the start in establishing the piano in provincial England. Those like Mr

Langshaw who had trained in London carried their knowledge of the new keyboard instrument back with them when they returned home to the provinces, and Broadwoods were glad to give them a discount on any piano they sold for them. The nascent piano industry depended on them; they were the obvious first means of distribution. The organists and music masters and a few music mistresses who ordered pianos regularly, who performed on them and taught others how to play them, were crucial to the expansion of the social and cultural phenomenon of the piano throughout Britain and the world. After about 1815 Broadwoods relied increasingly on distribution by businesses dedicated to selling pianos and less on individuals, but for thirty years before then it was the steady stream of business from musicians such as Mr Langshaw that led the way.

The part played by these early organist distributors in spreading the piano culture is recorded only in the Broadwood Archive, their existence remembered only in the rolls of church organists. Yet they brought about a quiet revolution. In bringing the piano out of London at the end of the eighteenth century, they bridged the era from the time keyboard music was the preserve of a wealthy London coterie, to the 1820s when pianos were supplied throughout the kingdom and the world. The pianos promoted by these long-forgotten musicians had a profound effect on the music, culture and society of the new century and the modern world.

Music sellers and warehousemen also distributed Broadwood pianos for discount. They increased in number as the industry gained momentum. Corri and Sutherland in Edinburgh, capital of the Scottish Enlightenment, had bought seventeen pianos, two harpsichords and two dozen tuning forks as early as 1784 and their substantial business continued. In 1795 Corri and Dussek in the Haymarket, London, bought over £1,000 worth of pianos. In the same year Messrs Linterns of Bath had ordered nine grands, thirteen squares and sundry cases, strings and music. 'Merchants ordering one or two', were allowed 10 percent; the bigger distributors got anything up to 25 percent.

The trend from personal to commercial distribution continued. By 1815 there was a network of piano businesses covering most of Britain. Charles Clarke of Worcester, McFadyen of Glasgow, Hodges of Bristol, Rudge of Wolverhampton, Crosbie of Birmingham and Wellman of Southampton were but a few who sold pianos from their music warehouses. Organized business was taking over. Five years later, in 1820, Beales of Manchester ordered pianos worth £3,000 in one year, and individual distributors and agents on 5 percent were playing a lesser part in what had become a global industry.

Ad hoc agents were paid commission on personal introductions. The use of 'pr' or 'per' in Broadwood's retail sales ledgers denotes that someone had bought a piano through an occasional agent rather than a regular distributor. Such agents, acting on behalf of country customers, were often based in London and were allowed 5 percent commission from Broadwoods on sale. For an additional fee from the customer they would go to Broadwood's 'Dining Room' to play and select the instrument, as Mr Langshaw's brother William probably did.

In Jane Austen's novel *Emma* (1816) concern is expressed lest Colonel Campbell, the supposed donor of Jane Fairfax's new piano, 'should have employed a careless friend [agent] and if it should have a deficient tone,' a nice instance of Georgian reticence about what was essentially a business arrangement for cash. Charles Wesley acted as a London agent from time to time, 'By Comm' for occasional purchasers, including once for his old scholar John Langshaw. He wrote to John on 24 November 1824:

> . . . I am surprised that the Instrument did not come from Broadwood . . . I chose a Piano Forte at Broadwood's lately but I had no idea that you had not the one you commissioned me to get you a long while ago.

As mentioned, this rather gentlemanly manner of doing business had always included a few music mistresses. Between 1801 and 1806 several customers bought pianos 'per recommendation' of a Miss Wedderburn of Hanover Square. Mr Crouch, an innkeeper, bought a grand piano 'per Miss Woodall of Mrs Larching's School at Pentonville.' Miss Parrin of Lancaster was another occasional agent. The doyenne of these ladies during the early years of the nineteenth century was Miss Sharpe of Bath, another rare female professional musician. Her name had first appeared in the journal in 1778 in connection with harpsichord tunings, and after teaching in fashionable Bath for a number of years and introducing a number of piano customers to Broadwoods, she felt she should have been paid more than 5 percent. James Shudi Broadwood responded to her on 21 October 1807:

> . . . I should have been able, by showing you the account of several eminent Professors, to prove to your satisfaction that you were treated by us on our most favourable terms . . . we agreed to put you on the same footing as one of our Oldest and Best Friends, Mr F Sharpe.

Perhaps Miss Sharpe got wind of the much larger discount allowed to Messrs Linterns in the same city and had consulted her brother, the Knutsford organist and music master Francis Sharpe.

What were they all buying? Pianos in the early years were not the polished instruments we are used to. They were highly idiosyncratic individuals, sometimes given to unwanted noise, as the following urbane letter from Broadwood's to Miss Hutchinson of Guildford, 29 September 1807, shows:

> . . . all instruments have certain defects such as rattling, jangling and noises of the mechanism which are not defects [but] . . . when observed by the ears being continually watching, therefore appear intolerable and peculiar to the instrument observed.

In the early 1800s the plain square piano at twenty-four guineas was Broadwood's most popular model. Best squares at thirty-two guineas had ormolu mounts and a music shelf, but even the plainest had the Broadwood name elaborately set in a cartouche on the satinwood nameboard. The Sheraton-influenced tapered legs of the late eighteenth century had been replaced by turned legs that became more bulbous as pianos got bigger: '6 legs are so much in vogue here that we cannot scarce sell any instrument without them . . . the bottom seldom warps,' wrote James Shudi Broadwood to Mr Harmon of Philadelphia in January 1807.

Covers made of leather or cloth were extra; green roan was Broadwood's best at £1 8s; red cost £1 2s 6d and purple was 19s. A cover for a large square 'hung deep all round' was £1 4s. There were mid-range vertical grand pianos and cabinet pianos 'fitted up with drawers' at forty-five guineas. At the top end of the price range were the six-octave grand pianos starting at eighty-four guineas.

There was a piano for farmhouse and a piano for palace at a price to suit the pockets of a broad middle and upper band of society, as John Broadwood had foreseen. In the first ten years of the nineteenth century the king, the princesses, lords and ladies, military and professional men, society ladies and schoolteachers, parsons and colliery owners, West Indian planters and Bombay quartermasters, country organists and their pupils bought Broadwood pianos. By keeping the two ends of his range wide apart, John Broadwood ensured that the piano did not become devalued because of the ever-increasing popularity of the square. The Prince of Wales's 'Ornamental Grand' cost a princely £92 12s, and was entered in the sales ledger in copperplate letters twice the size of any others, while Miss Polly Flinders of Lincoln's second-hand square cost her £13. Square pianos were technically less advanced than grands and the cases were plainer, but prince and country girl were playing essentially the same instrument. In February 1803, when James Shudi Broadwood wrote and complained to his Edinburgh distributor who was supplying city customers with Tomkison's pianos and country ones with Broadwood's, he was nettled because, as he wrote, his pianos were 'as fit for the delicate Citizens of Edinboro' as for the fists and dreary abodes of Clodhoppers.'

When John Broadwood died in 1812 he left £125,000, a business worth much more, employing over a hundred men, and substantial London properties. He had seen the piano change from fashionable craze to a serious musical instrument and his far-sighted business skills had ensured its successful commercial production. He had revolutionized piano-making and was the biggest manufacturer of pianos in Britain, arguably in the world. In his lifetime the piano became a symbol of gentility and it remained a measure of social standing until the advent of the motor car. John Broadwood's glory was the grand pianoforte, but square pianos had been the mainstay of his enterprise for twenty-five years. He had taken the business route to gentility and accumulated enough money to buy a country estate. He continued to refer to himself as a harpsichord maker until the day he died.

He left what was in many ways a modern business. His firm, then under the direction of his two sons James Shudi and Thomas, laid out risk capital on expensive materials: mahogany and rare veneers, ivory and limewood for keys. They made and marketed a non-essential consumer product, they responded to demand, constantly developing their product and pricing strategy, and sold through a global network of distributors with a profit at each turn.

In other ways they were not so modern. They continued to call themselves harpsichord makers; they paid more for coals and coke than they did in tax; their pianos were carried around London by men pulling carts, delivered to the country by horse-drawn barges, sent overseas on sailing ships. They bought ink in quarts and quill pens by the hundred. Their insurance cost them £202 a year, less than the annual wage of their best craftsman, and they protected their premises with three dogs and a bear! (The bear's official food allowance was £12 10s a year.) Their increasingly large workforce continued to make pianos by hand; half a century after John Broadwood's death it was the firm's proud boast that their pianos, each consisting of 3,800 separate pieces, were hand-made by one of the biggest workforces in London.

———

In March 1800 the ship *Maria*, under Captain Inglis, sailed from London to Charleston, South Carolina, carrying fourteen Broadwood pianos: seven for Mr L De Villiers (six squares and a grand) and seven for Mr Thomas Bradford (six more squares and a grand), who was another Charleston agent. Thirty-seven pianos in all would be sent to Charleston that year, nine to Virginia, one square to Savannah, a grand to Philadelphia, two squares to Quebec as well as Mr Langshaw's two grands to Boston.

After returning to London Captain Inglis prepared to set sail again in August. This time there were ten pianos and a second-hand harpsichord (with a Venetian swell and spare strings) for Mr De Villiers, whose consignment, with shipping costs, came to £327 6s 1d. They were all squares: some plain, some ornamented, some with and some without additional keys and loud pedal. Clearly the social distinctions operated to a nicety in Charleston as in London. With an additional piano for a M. Depeau, a private customer who had ordered through a London agent, they were taken to Broadwood's overseas shipping agent in London, Mr Farlow, then transferred to the *Maria*. Three days later Broadwoods sent a further six square pianos, all with additional keys and a loud pedal, to Farlow, also for shipping on the *Maria*, to go to Thomas Bradford. The *Maria* was not the last ship to sail to Charleston that year. In October the *Birmingham*, under Captain Cochran, carried three more pianos to Mr De Villiers, a grand and two squares, and some music books.

Broadwoods had been selling overseas since Shudi's day. In April 1772 they had sent Harpsichord No. 674 to Mr Brooks of Oporto.

Mr Brooks bought a piano a year later. He continued importing harpsichords for the port-producing English grandees of the region – in 1783 he bought a double manual for Mr Offley – but from then on his purchases follow the same pattern of transition from harpsichord to piano as in England. After the end of the American War of Independence the number of overseas distributors increased rapidly: Brooks of Oporto and Ware of Belfast were joined by Harmon of Philadelphia, Obert of Boulogne, Delamain in Cork. Following Clementi's appearance in Paris in 1781, Pascal Taskin bought two Broadwood pianos. Other overseas distributors were based in London. In 1783 Mr Packreotti sent pianos to Spain; Mr Garrett sent one to Lisbon the same year. Napier also sent pianos to Oporto; Manning and Vaughan sent them to Copenhagen.

War with France did not prevent Broadwood's overseas piano network from continuing to expand. In the 1790s, wherever the British navy established a presence in support of English interests, Broadwood distributors appeared. Delonguemare imported pianos into Port-au-Prince. At the end of the century three Broadwood grands were shipped to Chevalier Gizzi in Naples, where the English ambassador Sir William Hamilton and Lady Emma entertained the king and queen whose regime was supported by Lord Nelson and the presence of the Mediterranean Fleet. Within ten years, by the time square piano 10651 was dispatched to Lancaster, Broadwoods were sending pianos to most of the known world. Their global network extended from Copenhagen to Cadiz, Moscow to Madras, Hamburg to Palermo, Rotterdam to New York: on 1 February 1803 Broadwood had dispatched Gpf. No. 1753, fifty guineas, to Colonel Barclay, the British consul general in New York.

Their Letter Book (1801–1810) reveals the spirit of enterprise that characterized their business and the new age. They established overseas agents wherever they could, issuing letters and instructions from the hub of a global business based in Great

Pulteney Street. The regular use of words such as 'solid' and 'solid materials' by this time indicates the increasing numbers of pianos sent overseas, pianos 'peculiarly adapted to every climate.' Undeterred by the most hazardous voyages into uncharted seas, they packed their pianos, grand and square, in their deal and tin cases and sent them off to far-flung places. Their letters emanate urbanity and confidence in their ability to deal with any problem. They threatened, cajoled, made their arrangements, withdrew their favour; they ruled their world as surely as their most illustrious London customer in Buckingham House ruled his.

For example, they wrote to a Mrs Christmas in Copenhagen on 11 June 1802:

> [We] are extremely sorry you are displeased with the piano we sent you, it may have got damp or wet on the way but when we selected it we thought it a very good instrument or would not have sent it . . . when we hoped to procure more orders . . .
>
> Sell it for any price you can get & we will send another . . . in handsome ornamented case with pedal such as we retail at 32 Guineas . . . we send many to Petersburg and Mosco but we believe none have found their way to Copenhagen if you will permit us . . . we will send such an one as <u>shall</u> please.

Five years later they had established a distributor there, Black, Erickson & Co, to whom they wrote on 7 January 1807 with instructions to procure stronger wire from Berlin: 'please particularly recommend to Deitz that the steel wire be made particularly tough.'

They had eyes and ears everywhere: on 8 October 1802 they wrote to Edmund Phelps in Trinidad, requesting settlement of a bill for £79 1s 6d for a grand piano. They knew that 'despite a lengthy visit to London' he had left without paying. The letter ends with a threat to 'report [him] and put the matter into the hands of a friend high in the Law in Trinidad.'

International politics affected piano shipments as much as hazards of voyage, as Broadwood's relations with some of their agents in the United States shows. By 1803 their Charleston agent Thomas Bradford had moved to Norfolk, Virginia. He was replaced by Jacob Eckhardt, a German immigrant who was a Charleston organist, first at Saint John's Lutheran church, then at Saint Michael's Episcopal church. Like Mr Langshaw, he obtained pianos from Broadwood and taught people how to play them, at his home at 103 Tradd Street in Charleston.

Eckhardt began importing pianos from Broadwood in 1803: four squares that year, six the year after, and his business grew steadily until he was selling almost £500 worth of pianos a year – all without credit. Broadwoods wrote: 'In England we give a year's credit, which we do not feel ourselves inclined to abroad.'

In 1807 the United States government imposed embargo laws and Broadwood's American business diminished temporarily. In April 1809 James Shudi's brother-in-law Daniel Stewart of Petersburg, Virginia, who also acted as local agent, wrote that the American president would soon end the laws. In anticipation that 'everything will go on pleasantly for the future' he ordered 'two of your very best Square pianos with additional Keys, and send them by the first vessel for Norfolk or City Point.' He stipulated that with one of the squares, for Miss Harrison of Brandon, should be sent 'some of the newest Songs and Pieces of Musick for the piano,' and asked that Broadwood should be particular about choosing the squares, 'putting them as low as you can afford' as it might lead to 'more extensive orders.' He concluded by saying that he was going north and would try to establish agencies in the principal towns and 'carve you out some business' with anyone trustworthy. On 30 August Broadwoods were writing to Eckhardt in Charleston:

> ... we have sent a piano of the largest size fitted up with Drawer,
> a mode now much in use ... at Forty-five Guineas retail. We

meant to have sent you more Square Pianofortes but the great influx of orders in consequence of the raising of the embargo on your side of the water prevented us. We shall seize, however, the first opportunity to send out the other two on the 12th.

Five days later Daniel Stewart wrote again, this time from New York, recommending a Mr Thomas Western of Maiden Lane in Manhattan, instrument maker and seller, 'a respectable old Englishman,' who had long been settled in New York. Mr Western 'wishes to import a number of pianos yearly,' and he was prepared to send cash forward with his order. Daniel Stewart went on to mention others in New York who could be agents, but 'some . . . think your instruments rather high but they all acknowledge their superiority.'

You have also the Character of being rather hard in your bargains, obliging them to pay the money down in England upon receipt of the Instruments – You would probably extend your business here by Crediting responsible people . . . Clementi & Co have sold a good many instruments to people in this Country but they do not stand in the climate like yours. Astor sells a good many but they, like Pindar's Racer, 'made to sell.'

After the re-imposition of the embargo in 1811 the American piano industry grew apace. Instrument makers in the United States were less concerned about tradition then in England. In 1801 John Isaac Hawkins of Philadelphia had made a portable upright piano that he called a 'small grand.' It was remarkable – not so much for its size but for the use of iron bars behind the soundboard. While Broadwoods remained committed to the sacrosanct wooden frame, the great American makers Chickering and Steinway felt no such constraints. Charles Babcock patented a full iron frame in 1825, which held the increased tension of heavier, powerful strings without going out of tune, and by the middle of the nineteenth century the American piano industry was in the ascendant.

Broadwoods seldom gave lost pianos up for hopeless: in November 1804 three pianos, a grand and two squares ordered by a Major Fitzgerald, the proprietor of a riding school in Ireland, went missing, never having reached one Mr Josh White, the Dublin merchant to whom they had been shipped two years earlier. When news reached Broadwoods that Major Fitzgerald, acting as agent for a Mr Sandys, had sold the pianos at auction, they wrote to a Mr Galbraith of Dublin, who had offered his services: 'we still think Sandys has got them,' ending: '[We need] . . . some intelligent person of Dublin to sort it out . . . for the mode of doing all of this we rely on your ingenuity.'

Inevitably pianos went astray or languished on distant docksides. On 2 February 1810 Broadwoods wrote to Alexander & Co of Calcutta, instructing them to sell any pianos they could find from a missing shipment. But despite such setbacks, their overseas trade continued to grow.

When the newly appointed Governor Macquarie of New South Wales set sail for Australia on 17 April 1809, Mrs Macquarie went with him; so did her three-pedal Broadwood grand pianoforte. Wherever the British went, and they went almost everywhere, they took with them a way of life in which the piano was fast becoming the domestic centre. Colonial and imperial expansion favoured the spread of the piano, and the piano had a reciprocal effect on colonial culture and society. The same sonatas, arrangements, duets, waltzes and parlour songs that reverberated around the homes of Mr Langshaw's pupils in Lancaster carried on the breeze across the bungalows of Ootacumund and echoed from coralstone plantation house walls into the chattel houses of West Indian slaves.

After naval and military conquest, imperial territory was maintained by the presence of a militia and administered by colonial bureaucrats. Settlement and commercial exploitation were accompanied by belief in the British way of life and its perceived benefits. It was unthinkable for the British that there could be anything better or that it would have anything but a civilizing effect on the indigenous subject peoples. There were also fortunes to be made.

The masculinity of colonial culture – the navy, military and colonial administration, the mercantile officials, planters, and fortune seekers – was no bar to the piano. Broadwoods shipped pianos to senior military men such as Captain Eyles, the Commissary of Stores in Bombay, and Colonel Charles Ford, who commanded the Royal Engineers at St Anne's Garrison, Barbados, as well as to colonial wives and daughters. The colonial experience in lands forcibly settled by enslaved Africans differed from countries such as India where there was already a large population. In the former, a new society was in the making; in the latter, imperial intentions had to compete with local rulers and customs. At the end of the eighteenth century, after the loss of the American colonies, the West Indies played an increasingly important part in the British trading economy. Sugar planting in Jamaica and Barbados produced unheard-of riches, and the merchants of Lancaster were only a few of many in England whose prosperity depended on the fabulous wealth generated by the islands' plantation economies.

Unlike Jamaica, the largest sugar-producing West Indian island where two-thirds of the planters were absentee owners, most Barbadian planters lived on their estates. The white plantocracy there was of a higher social status than the manager class left to oversee Jamaican interests. This is not to say that the basis of occupation was any less cruel, but that more whites on Barbados lived a recognizably middle- and upper-class English life. By the first decades of the nineteenth century some planter families had already been in Barbados for several generations. White Creole culture was inevitably a modified form of the English way of life, constantly being reinforced by government and military officials and clergy and their families sent from England, as well as by visitors and fortune seekers. White Barbadians spoke a variant of the English language as they still do; not surprisingly, the island became known as 'Little England.'

The Barbadian plantocracy could afford to enjoy every sophisticated element of the British way of life and they entertained visitors royally. The journal of Sir Henry Fitzherbert, who visited the island in 1825, contains several references to musical evenings and accompanied singing. He describes Mrs Cumberbatch playing her harp during elegant evenings when the worst that could happen was strings breaking in the humidity.

Eighteenth-century prints of paintings by Agostino Brunias (1730–96) show men and women of mixed race wearing fashionable European clothes and being served by their own black slaves. They give a romanticized picture of what was a volatile and violent society, but they also show that English dress was adopted not only by the established white plantocracy and white settlers but by free blacks. Whatever the locally adapted variants, English customs and cultural diversions were measures of status that influenced every level of society.

The cultural crossover was not one way, and music was but one area of activity that absorbed and reinterpreted the island's many cultural influences. The beat of African drums and the snare drums and fifes of a military garrison mingled to produce the Barbadian tuk music that English diarists of the day found so uninhibited. Within living memory such bands could have included a violin, more recently the saxophone.

Dr Nicholas Ford in his 'Case Study of Barbadian Antique Furniture' has pointed out that the few ships' manifestos that have survived provide evidence of the opulent taste of eighteenth-century Barbadians. They enjoyed their desks, their mahogany furniture imported from Gillows of Lancaster, their clocks and musical instruments. The music of the English drawing-room was not new there. The will of Sarah Osborne who died in 1750 contains reference to her elegant and well-tuned harpsichord in complete order with a double row of keys by Kirkman. Another 'Harp'd for Barbados' was shipped out by Broadwoods in 1783. As elsewhere, harpsichords were followed by the piano.

The Broadwood sales ledgers show that on the same December day in 1821 as Broadwoods sent a new, decorated grand piano for King George IV to the Pavilion in Brighton, they sent a similar grand and a square piano to the West India Export Dock for shipment on the *Fortitude,* under Captain Butcher, to a Miss Andrews of Hindsbury House, Barbados. When the *Fortitude* anchored in Carlisle Bay in early spring 1822, Miss Andrews would have been forty-two or -three. She seems to have been a companion to the much younger Miss Hinds, of Hindsbury, the daughter of Benjamin Hinds, a former speaker of the Barbadian Parliament. Over the course of the next ten years she imported at least eleven Broadwood pianos into Barbados. Her folio page for the middle five years is missing, so the number may be nearer twenty. There is no record of Miss Elizabeth Georgiana Andrews's birth in Barbados, only of her death on 5 June 1855 at Maynard's, a plantation house owned by Miss Hinds's second husband, Joseph Lyder Briggs.

During her life on the island Miss Andrews would have seen the slow evolution of Barbadian society after the abolition of the legal slave trade in 1807 and emancipation in 1833. She also lived long enough to see Barbadian craftsmen from the former slave population copy the instruments she had imported. In the 14th Industrial Exhibition in Bridgetown in 1860 it was a piano made by a local man that stole the show. A public auction a month later included a 'fine-toned cottage piano by Broadwood'; and in May one of their full-sized grand pianos imported for Colonel Ford, Commander of the Royal Engineers, was sold from his residence at Shott Hall.

Pianos became the focal point of British colonial drawing-rooms and whether taken or sent out, British cultural perceptions went with them. The ideal of a harmonious Christian household was at the heart of the British way of life. This ideal was represented by the image of a woman seated at her piano, as shown in so many paintings and writings of the time, and pianos themselves became symbols of felicitous social harmony, wherever they were in the world. Pianos brought people together. This was as true in Barbados, a nation emerging slowly from the divisions and degradations of slavery, as it was in England. Miss Andrews and her pianos promoted harmony just as Mr Langshaw and his pianos did some 4,000 miles away in Lancaster.

14

PIANOS IN DRAWING-ROOM
AND PARLOUR

JOHN AND SARAH Langshaw's eighth child, Pearson, named after James Pearson who had brought up the orphaned Sarah, was born in July 1814. Although Mr Langshaw did not permit himself 'leisure for pleasure,' his efforts could not keep his family together. His eldest son, also named John, then aged twelve, was sent away to live in Bolton with his aunt Jane Fletcher and her husband, Colonel Ralph. The Fletchers were well-to-do colliery owners and Jane had managed her husband's business books so that, should the need arise, she could pass the job to her sister's son. Jane Austen might exclaim through the character of Mrs John Knightley, 'There is something so shocking in a child's being taken away from his parents and natural home!' – but for people in straitened circumstances like the Langshaws it was not unusual, well into the twentieth century, for children to be sent to better-placed relatives to be brought up.

The boy's departure in 1814 marked the start of several years of sadness for the Langshaw family. Although Sarah had managed to see all her babies through infancy, in 1816 their daughter Sarah died at the age of twelve. Her entry in the family Bible reads:

She said in her last illness, with her usual simple mindedness,
Mother, shall I die? When her mother told her so she said, Well,
if I do die I think I shall be happy, – God is so good.

Twelve months later another daughter, Jane, aged seven, also
died and their youngest child, Catherine, was born. Mr Langshaw
had to work on and diversify. His Broadwood agency continued,
with three squares in 1814, three in 1816 and two in 1817. As Charles
Wesley wrote to an organist friend, 'it is a profession that often wit-
nesses competition for the loaves and fishes.'

In 1823 Mr Langshaw was sixty. He had been organist at the
priory for twenty-five years and was as busy as ever. Like his father,
he believed in educating his children. With six of them at home he
still had little leisure for pleasure. His affairs were made increasingly difficult by matters at the priory. The church was in a ruinous
state. There had been no serious money spent on it for many years
and the necessary repairs listed in the vestry minutes would have
daunted anyone with responsibility for them. The floor of the
church was dangerously uneven after centuries of in-church burials, the building was damp because of earth shored up around the
outside, and vestry minutes speak of a vermin-infested churchyard
and rewards for fox heads and dead sparrows. Above all else, lit-
erally, the church roof was a major cause for concern. The
churchwarden was directed to procure a report.

The report called for a new roof, and the Bishop of Chester
directed that the work be carried out. The report also said, con-
fusingly, that the Corporation of Lancaster was obliged to repair
the roof, walls and windows of the chancel. It was not clear where
responsibility lay and no one wanted it. The members of
Lancaster Corporation and the priory's Twenty Fourtie Council
looked around to spread the financial load. The bishop paid a
visit and ordered the work to be done. The corporation
appointed a committee. The committee was asked 'to confer with
the Vicar and Organist to ascertain their sentiments as to the

repairs of the Chancel and as to the liability of the Corporation to take the Rents of the Seats or Pews now received by the Organist to reimburse the amount to be expended in the repairs of the Chancel for which the Corporation may be held liable.'

After threatening to take their proposal to 'some eminent Common Law Barrister,' the committee suggested that the vicar and organist should each pay £100 towards the cost of repairing the chancel roof. The Reverend John Manby refused outright. The vestry minutes record, however, that the organist 'was disposed to accede to the proposal.' Whether his response was freely given or made under duress, it was a decision Mr Langshaw and his family would bitterly regret. His meticulous accounts at Broadwoods show that he was a man who worried about money, but he appears to have had little choice in the matter and he was an easier target than the vicar of Lancaster. The committee resolved 'to wait until, the subject assumes a more distinct form.'

Matters dragged on unresolved. The opinions of learned counsel, Mr Espinesse and Dr Lushington, were sought. Their opinions, not surprisingly, 'differed very materially.' More money was spent on more advice from 'some other Counsel,' who could not agree either. From this saga worthy of the pen of Charles Dickens, there emerged one loser: he who was most vulnerable. Lancaster Corporation voted for £100 to be paid to the organist, who was instructed to have the chancel roof repaired and to find the difference out of 'the rents of the Pews in the Chancel' – seat rents that had been the church organist's as of right since they were voted as part of his salary back in 1731 when the first organ was built. It was also directed that Mr Langshaw should raise an additional £109 10s 3d from the 4 percent Annuities held in the name of the corporation, that sum 'having arisen from the Rents or other funds applicable to the salary of the Organist.'

At the beginning of 1823, desperate to supplement his salary, he wrote to Sir Robert Peel, applying for the minor government office of Collector of Stamps for the Hundred (a local area) of Lonsdale.

He hoped, he wrote, that his 'honest name and respectable connections,' would shield him from presumption, ending 'with
apologies for the trouble I am causing you.' The reply stated briefly:
'this appointment has already been taken.' The following year the
chancel was re-roofed. Henry Hogarth's carpentry estimate alone
was £330. The corporation duly paid its promised £100.

Against this background of family responsibility and financial
worry Mr Langshaw continued composing, mainly to help his
pupils. Few of his works were published. 'My publications which
are not numerous,' he wrote in his autobiographical letter to John
Sainsbury in 1824. They included 'The Farewell', 'Can Joy that
Wretched Bosom Cheer?' and the 'Icicle' ballad, as well as choruses
from Handel and Haydn arranged for duet, and a Theme and
Variations 'for P. forte or Harp.' composed for the Countess of
Dunmore, whose brother Lord Hamilton was another of his piano
customers. There was a brief renewal of correspondence with
Charles Wesley when Mr Langshaw had tried to find a London
publisher for his more serious compositions. Charles responded on
17 October 1822: 'I am highly pleased with your intended
Publication from Corelli, and the elegant and elaborate
Geminiani . . .' Charles had shown them to Dr Carnaby, organist
at the Hanover Chapel in Regent Street, who:

> . . . rejoiced that any one, in these degenerate days, would ven-
> ture such a work, and the Doctor promised me to use all his
> influence to promote Publication . . . you ought to be well remu-
> nerated . . . It does you real Credit . . . none but a real Master
> could do it . . . I doubt not all the amateurs of good harmony,
> and the judicious Professors will give due encouragement.

He regrets, though, that 'were it not for the obstinacy of the noble
Directors of the Antient Concert, the old Style would be entirely
forgotten.'

Despite Charles Wesley's enthusiasm, Mr Langshaw's keyboard

sonatas and piano concerti were never published. They came too late and John Langshaw knew it. In the biographical sketch he sent to John Sainsbury two years later, he listed his unpublished work and commented: 'the ancient style of Music is not so generally admired as to warrant either a Printer or a Professor to run the risk of publication, so that probably this work will never be printed.' He was right. By then, music in the Italianate tradition of Geminiani and Corelli was not wanted. Harpsichords, for which such music had been written, were no longer made and the pianos were no longer the small square pianofortes they had known in their youth. Charles, in his next letter, informed him that the printer 'Mr Goulding said Antient Authors would not do now.'

In the latter half of the eighteenth and first quarter of the nineteenth centuries a new middle class had come to importance and influence in Britain. It ranged from the smallholder to the professional man, but the most dynamic part, which changed the face of Britain, consisted of former craftsmen and inventors who became factory owners by the score. The enterprise of many lesser Broadwoods gave rise to other small businesses and to new middle-class professions such as insurance, engineering, banking and accountancy. Together with the tradesmen and shopkeepers who distributed their goods, they formed an expanding middle band of society that made money in the technical and economic revolution. At the same time the commercial production and promotion of pianos made access to keyboard music affordable and culturally thinkable for many more people than in Mr Langshaw's youthful days in London. The new middle classes could and did buy pianos, and each had a reciprocal effect on the way the other developed.

Broadwoods continued to improve their grand pianos, and 'improve' in the London school of pianoforte meant more volume. Pianos made in Vienna of the kind that Mozart and Beethoven would have known were lighter in tone with a more responsive action that suited the small chamber orchestras of German and Viennese courts. Grand pianos made in London had to speak to audiences who filled the concert rooms to hear concert virtuosi. They increased in size, with additional keys, thicker strings and bigger hammers. But it was the small square piano that remained the mainstay of the piano business for the first twenty-five years of the nineteenth century. As the middle classes expanded and stratified, so James Shudi and Thomas Broadwood continued their father's policy of making pianos to suit both parlour and drawing-room. Of nineteen pianos in their 1813 price list, five were grands (varying in price from seventy-eight guineas upwards), four were cabinet pianos and the remaining ten were squares:

<u>Square Pianos</u>

Square Piano forte; with add keys	31	10	-
Ditto with G.P touch	33	12	-
Ditto Ditto Extra size, elegant case	38	17	-
Ditto " " " " " with circular covers	42	-	-
Square p. f. extra size, elegant case, drawers	43	1	-
Ditto, largest size, ditto, drawers	49	7	-
Square P. F. with 6 Octaves from cc to CC	44	2	-
Ditto " " " " " with drawers	48	6	-
Ditto " " " " " 6½ Oct. cc to FF	47	5	-
Ditto " " " " " with drawers & ornamented	51	-	-

If there was not enough choice here to satisfy the social distinctions, a piano could be customized to order with brass ornament and superior veneers. Extras included decorative fabric covers in a range of colours of which the favourite and most expensive was Regency Red at £4 10s for a grand and £2 12s for a square. Square pianos were affordable but not cheap. Even the plainest, like 10651, was an elegant piece of furniture, probably the most important piece in all but the grandest households.

Broadwood's customers did not include farm labourers on 8s a week: at 24 guineas a square piano in 1807 had represented 25 percent of a skilled working man's annual wage. In Mr Langshaw's day it is doubtful if many men and women of the industrialized working class could afford one. For them the reality was that women and children worked as well as men. Many prospered by ignoring the miseries of a cheap labour market. But only through industrial production could living standards improve and threats of famine and revolution be averted. Carpets appeared in ordinary sitting rooms, walls were hung with paintings and prints and the presence of a piano showed that the occupants cultivated the accomplishments that sweetened domestic life. The piano revolution was not quick. Before it reached the working-class front rooms of the twentieth century, the piano had to pass through the middle-class parlours of the nineteenth.

Throughout the nineteenth century the piano reflected the changing social aspirations of a broad middle band of society as well as changes in musical taste; it became a measure of social status. Many who played the pianoforte were, for all their assumed sensibilities, purse-proud snobs who sought to maintain their social position by artifice and exclusion. An example is the piano-playing Emma Woodhouse, the heroine of Jane Austen's last novel written in 1816, who declares: 'A young farmer, whether on horseback or on foot, is the last person to raise my curiosity. The yeomanry are precisely the order of people with whom I feel I can have nothing to do.' At that time Broadwoods were selling pianos to the yeomanry and many others whom Emma would have shunned. By 1815 they had increased their range of square pianos to fifteen in their efforts to keep pace with the nuances of the middle market; five years later they had sold over 25,000. In a society inching its way towards democracy, the piano gave more people access to music than ever before; then it classified them, according to which model they owned.

The increasing availability of a wide range of pianos disturbed the social order as girls sat at their practice in both parlour and drawing-room, and so people created new rules and regulations to redefine the social distinctions. 'Are they musical . . . that is the first question you know . . . which every woman who plays herself is sure to ask about another,' says Mary Crawford in Jane Austen's *Mansfield Park,* written in 1814, and in *Emma* the 'entirely unexpected' arrival of a new Broadwood square piano for Jane Fairfax, who is staying at Miss Bates's house, was the latest topic of gossip in the village of Highbury. It is made clear that this piano for Jane, a woman in reduced circumstances, is 'not a Grand, but a large-sized square pianoforte,' and besides, a grand would have been too large for Miss Bates's small house.

The majority of people who played pianos were women, and an ability to play one became the defining attribute of a lady. Arthur Loesser has written: 'women and the piano were made for each other.' The ideal of feminine beauty was small in size, sweet, delicate and uncomplicated – more like a square than a grand. The stance and movements required to play the piano accorded more with ideas of female decorum than any other instrument; the cello and transverse flute were out of the question and the harpsichord was out of fashion. As sitting rooms with sand floors were carpeted and called parlours, the daughters of the lower middling sort began to emulate the accomplishments of their supposed betters. They might have 'the clumsy fists of clodhoppers,' but Broadwoods were glad to sell to them.

Farmer Giles's daughter at practice on her square piano rather than churning butter in the dairy became an object of ridicule and a popular target for cartoonists, but whether she played well or ill was not the point. What mattered was that a piano was a yardstick by which people could judge others and at the same time support their own possibly uncertain position. With a square piano, a fashionable teacher and one of dozens of printed piano tutors to put her through her paces, a girl could acquire the essential social grace of a Jane Austen heroine. A piano by Broadwood retained something of the courtly cachet of its harpsichord provenance. Hundreds of parlours were decorated with lesser conversation pieces depicting young ladies seated at the piano. They revealed far more about the girl's parents, particularly her father's standing and her mother's aspirations, than about the ostensible subject of the portrait.

Many of Mr Langshaw's pupils would have been young unmarried women with time on their hands, who filled hours of genteel idleness with trifling, time-consuming activities that were elevated to the level of 'accomplishments.' Accomplishments occupied women at home and prevented them from exercising any real power anywhere else. Playing the piano was an innocent, girlish pastime that kept young women under the watchful parental eye and away from predatory males (although the peripatetic male music teacher could be the Trojan Horse of this arrangement). Once married, many girls gave up the piano, either from domestic pressures or disinclination, and passed the obligation to their daughters.

An ability to play the piano, whether in drawing-room or parlour, ranked high in the marriage stakes, together with a degree of skill at watercolour, some French and a fortune if possible. Elizabeth Bennet's piano-playing, plain sister Mary in *Pride and Prejudice* (1813) 'was always impatient for display.' Printed pianoforte tutors held out impossible promises of proficiency for minimum effort, and young women learned to play the piano with varying degrees of success. What was important was not so much how they played, but the ideal that was represented by playing. The family was considered the natural, God-given basis of society, and the proper domestic woman at her square piano was its centre.

Women's increasingly home-centred and dependent role prevented them from doing anything serious if they did become proficient pianists. A lady could work at the piano, but she could not be seen to work for money: the men in the family took care of that. However many hours of solitary confinement at the piano a young woman endured, however well she played, there could be no question of her performing professionally in public. Public performance, always on grand pianos, was the preserve of male virtuosi. Clementi, Dussek and Cramer were followed by Kalkbrenner, Chopin and Liszt. Display was their forte and a woman like Thackeray's Becky Sharpe who played with similar bravura, even in private, was suspect; a woman in straitened circumstances like Jane Fairfax who played well might become a governess and teach piano, but she was an object of condescension.

By 1820 things were changing. Money and what it could buy had become a social determinant, and many people bought a piano simply for show. A grand piano distinguished the rich from the rest. 'It always has quite hurt me,' remarks Mrs Cole, a woman described by Jane Austen in *Emma* as of low origin, in trade and only moderately genteel, 'that Jane Fairfax, who plays so delightfully, should not have an instrument . . . especially considering how many houses there are whose fine instruments are absolutely thrown away,' and she admits that she does not know one note from another on the grand pianoforte in her own drawing-room. There was worse. Lady Catherine de Bourgh in *Pride and Prejudice*, one of 'the Great,' had a grand piano in her drawing-room and a square for her housekeeper, Mrs Jenkinson. After dinner one evening, when Lady Catherine has urged the virtues of pianoforte study on the young ladies, she invites Mrs Collins, the poor parson's wife, 'to come to Rosings every day and play on the pianoforte in Mrs Jenkinson's room,' whereas Elizabeth Bennet, who is the daughter of a gentleman, is commanded then and there to play her Ladyship's grand piano in the drawing-room for the assembled company, whereupon its owner promptly loses interest and continues to talk.

In *Practical Education* (1798), Maria and Richard Edgeworth in writing of the 'higher classes' had forecast: 'it is in vain that they entrench themselves, they are pursued by the intrusive vulgar. In a wealthy mercantile nation there is nothing which can be bought for money, that will long continue to be an envied distinction.' Thirty years later the square piano was being replaced by the upright cottage piano, which took up even less room and became the favourite domestic instrument of the Victorian household. For the remainder of the nineteenth century the middle-class home was seen as a utopian retreat from the hurly-burly of the male work-place, a haven where harmony reigned. For this, piano music was indispensable, whether the men or the women truly liked it or not.

With all its multifarious roles and social significances, all the glees and parlour songs, Scotch ditties, Battles of Prague, Beautiful Maids and Bridesmaids' Choruses, with the price of a new square piano at thirty guineas and a world-wide distribution, did the piano become devalued and diverted into a cultural cul-de-sac? Strangely, no; playing the piano continued and continues to be an envied distinction. One reason was that the grand piano retained its high price and elevated aura. Another was that square pianos, though widely available, were serious musical instruments. Musically speaking, as long as a piano worked well, and Broadwood squares did, it did not matter whether it had a plain case or one with knobs on. People like the Langshaws and their circle who cared about music, both men and women, actually wanted to play the piano well and make music both for their own pleasure and sociably together.

All over Britain, and in many parts of the world, musicians like Mr Langshaw obtained pianos and taught people how to play them. There were many, no doubt, who did not make the best of what they had to offer; but those who did learned to value music that made demands on them and rewarded them accordingly. The sons and daughters of clergymen, schoolmasters, lawyers and organists alike learned to play well and they passed on their love of music and the piano to their children and grandchildren and so down the generations. For these people, who were neither wealthy nor gentry, the piano was not just a social mounting-block, it was a key to a cultured intelligent life. It retained its dignity, and even the destruction of square pianos in the twentieth century did not destroy the seeds that Mr Langshaw and others like him had sown.

Although his compositions in the Antient style did not find a publisher in London, Mr Langshaw continued to write for his pupils. His unpublished works, 'much more numerous and perhaps more worthy of notice,' according to his letter to Sainsbury, 'consist for the most part of Voluntaries original, and arranged from modern and ancient composers – Concertos, Songs, Hymns, Chants & Duets and of an arrangement of the Concertos of Geminiani Corelli's (as they are called) for the P. Forte, Violin and Violoncello.' Only three of his psalm settings have survived; most of the rest of his music, including the Geminiani Corelli dedicated to his old master, have disappeared. But a copy of his dedication on the title page of his Trios does exist:

> Three Trios for Pianoforte, Violin & Violoncello, arranged from the Concertos of Geminiani – Corelli. Dedicated to Charles Wesley . . . undertaken to contribute to the amusement of a respected friend who seldom had an opportunity of hearing music, except in a family party. To those Amateurs who may be placed in a similar situation this work is respectfully offered.

The arrangement, he wrote, 'is to give access to music . . . which could otherwise only be enjoyed by having access to a Concert Room' and he particularly recommends the opening movements and fugues 'to the attention of young Organ players.'

He continued to send his compositions to Charles Wesley, who responded with encouragement; there was no further mention of a publisher. On 1 November 1825 Charles wote:

My Dear Friend,

. . . Your Voluntary is admirable, and the modulation, I think masterly. You have not studied the old Masters in vain. I think you would do well, to Publish it, not being too hard for the generality of Players. Mr Mather an admirable organist is charm'd with it.

Mr Langshaw's work, like that of many English composers of the period, was little known in his lifetime and forgotten after his death. German-born Handel had dominated English music for much of the eighteenth century. Composers of the English baroque, such as Maurice Greene, Boyce, Kelway, John Stanley and the Wesleys, were overshadowed by the late-eighteenth-century fashion for Viennese and German composers that continued throughout the nineteenth century. It would be a hundred years before an identifiable English school began to flower again, and late in the twentieth century before musicians began to search out and play the forgotten English music of the two Lancaster organists' era.

Charles's guileless letter is full of news about his own somewhat disappointing musical life after so promising a start, and about his brother Samuel, who fared rather better; and they are full of organists' gossip:

My Brother will take Dr. Crotch's Station this year to Lecture at the Royal Institution . . . your Anecdote of the Bates Family amused me. [Joah Bates (1740–99) conducted the Handel Commemoration and the concerts of the Concert of Antient Music in Freemasons' Hall thereafter.] He was a good Conductor but no great Performer.

My Dear Friend, Yours most truly

There are the usual references by the now elderly musician to an earlier age, regretting that the Ancient Music of their youth was no longer in vogue. He criticizes slovenly composing and recounts his own performances in different parts of the country.

Two months after this letter, Mr Langshaw lost his life's savings when the two local Lancaster banks crashed. A letter written on 10 February 1826 to his eldest son, who was then twenty-four, gives an insight into his feelings. Young John had been more or less adopted by his Aunt Fletcher in 1812, and Colonel Ralph later made him an

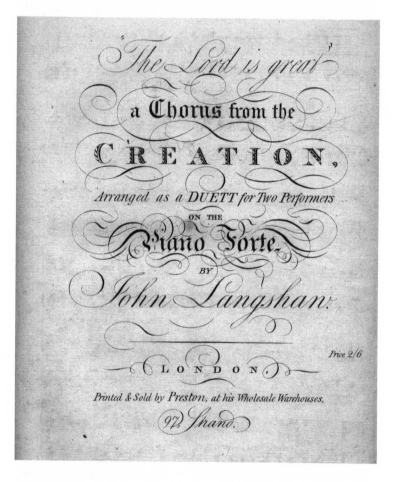

Title page, 'The Lord is great,' a Chorus from The Creation *by Haydn. Arranged as a Duett by John Langshaw, c. 1802. Author's collection.*

equal partner with his own sons in the Atherton Colliery near Bolton. It is clear from the letter that father and son had remained in regular, affectionate contact and that young John had become a man of business to whom his father could turn:

My Dear John,

... as you conjectured £2000 which I had ordered to be sold from the 4pr cents, with my running Account is now all locked up ... I think our Bankers have acted worse by me than Highwaymen, those you have some chance of escaping, here none ...

From the letter it is clear that he had ordered the sale of enough stock – £1,700 – to absolve him from the ongoing priory roof costs and to assist two younger sons with their studies: 'knowing that George and Edmund would want money for some time to come, I gave an order for the whole [£2,000] to be sold.'

Instead of paying him outright, his bankers had transferred the money to his current account, which required three weeks' notice of withdrawal. They went out of business the following weekend.

What the consequences may be I cannot tell to myself they are very unpleasant and grating to my feelings. I never cared much for money on my own account I only wish to make those comfortable whom I may leave behind ... half a century's savings are gone at a snap and without any chance of saving it ... I shall be glad of your opinion. I shall be in Preston on Tuesday evening. You will be glad to hear that I sent George £60 about ten days since. I think everything considered I have written with a tolerably steady hand.

Best love to all,

Yours affectionately,

John Langshaw

There was a postscript to this letter from Sarah Langshaw:

> Your Father (thank God) . . . bearing his loss with great firm-
> ness, trials we must have & we ought to be thankful that we are
> not again called upon to part with any of our family, a much
> greater affliction than the loss of property.

Eighteen months earlier the name of their daughter Frances, aged
twelve, had been added to the family Bible. Their son George was
at Cambridge, and Edmund was articled to a law firm in Bolton.
The youngest two, Pearson and Catherine, were still at home, as
was Bessy, their first child, who at twenty-six was almost a generation older.

Charles Wesley's last letter to his old scholar, on 11 January 1827,
recounts a visit by young George Langshaw and is reminiscent of
one written by the Reverend Charles Wesley to the first organist
half a century earlier:

> My Dear old Friend,
> . . . your Son kindly call'd on us, which gave us real Pleasure . . .
>   I am glad he has chosen the Clerical Profession and doubt not
> he will be a worthy member of the Church of England . . . He
> informed me you had heard of my Brother's Publication from
> Lord Fitzwilliam's Library at Cambridge, the words Handel Set
> from my Father's Poems are charming in the true Church
> German style . . . Do you never intend to come to Town again?
>   I am Dear Mr Langshaw your affectionate and obliged
>   old Friend

John Langshaw did not come to Town again. For six years the
obligation of re-roofing the priory had hung over him. The churchwarden's accounts remain strangely silent until an ominous entry in
November 1830 resolved to investigate the outstanding amount and
'to report generally on the arrangements made with Mr Langshaw.'

There was a direction that any outstanding amounts be paid by three instalments in 1830, 1831 and 1832.

He continued to distribute Broadwood pianos. Between 1820 and 1825 he bought thirteen squares and one grand. In the year of the bank crash his ledger account is blank, but it picked up again the following year with two more squares. After selling only one square piano in 1828, he made his most impressive sale – a grand at £128 10s – the following year. Broadwoods were now the biggest piano manufacturer in the world. They had been using solid iron resistance bars in their pianos since 1822, and steel rather than soft iron wire for strings, which were secured to metal plates. The sound of the square piano had changed for ever. Mr Langshaw's last piano, a 'Best 6 Octave Square' with a string plate, was dispatched in December 1831 directly to the home of Colonel Ralph Fletcher, the man who had brought up his son John.

There is little doubt that the 'very unpleasant and grating' feelings of his financial worries, of the public pressure and implied mismanagement, all hastened his end. John Langshaw was not Bach: the continuing wrangles with church and civic authorities did not call forth extra powers from him. Instead, reduced by the threat of a lawsuit, his health broke. When he could no longer play the organ, his son Pearson took over his duties at the priory. He died on 5 December 1832.

He had lived through tumultuous times when a society and its music had been in transition. At last, when the leisure for which he had always had so little time was finally forced upon him, perhaps he heard, as the best musicians do, the inner music of his life: the music of the English baroque on harpsichord and organ, and the faraway sound of the wooden-framed square piano, which had played in a new world.

After his death, eighteen-year-old Pearson continued to discharge his father's obligation for eighteen months, 'solely in consideration of the circumstances in which it is represented the late Organist Mr John Langshaw has left his Family.' In April 1835 a new organist was appointed.

Mr. Langshaw's outstanding balance at Broadwood was cleared with a final entry in Wholesale Sales Ledger N:

> Mr. John Langshaw Organist Lancaster
> Folio 473
> 1833
> Sept. 2 By Cash pr. Exors.   3s 10d

His will was as scrupulous as his dealings with Broadwood and, perhaps because of his calling, it did not reflect the conventional thinking of his day. He directed that his estate be shared equally by his sons and daughters, 'without any preference whatsoever.' To this end he deposited a memorandum book setting out the sums he had advanced to educate his sons that were to be deducted from their shares, although he left very few, in North East Railway stock. 'It will wear well, Sarah,' she would recall him saying, 'and it is honestly come by.'

Did he have some idea before he died that history might take an interest in him? Possibly. His autobiographical letter to Sainsbury in 1824 had assured a place in the *New Biographical Dictionary of Musicians* for himself and his father. The entry was the basis of everything known until recently about the two Lancaster organists. His original draft letter shows many alterations, crossings through, rephrasings; he was anxious to get it right. He composed very carefully what he thought worth recording, and made no reference to his piano business with Broadwood. His will refers to him as 'gentleman.'

15

THE WIFE OF THE CLERGYMAN

IT WAS CHRISTMAS Eve when Mr Langshaw's restored square piano came back home to me. This time its journey north took about three hours. How many other decorated Christmas trees had it seen, I wondered as it was carried in. It stood firmly now on its six legs; apart from that, it did not look very different from when David Winston had taken it away almost two years earlier. The catch of the lid was still broken; I opened it. Dust lay in the corners as before and there were the same odds and ends in the toolbox; the red felts under the strings looked even more faded and moth-eaten.

But the cracked soundboard, a common problem in old square pianos, had been fixed. Most of the strings had been replaced and the old ones returned in marked envelopes. There was a new set of hitch pins and the wrest pins had been cleaned. The keys responded to the lightest touch. The pitch was set only a tone below the modern standard, A=440, that is 440 vibrations of the string per second. Systems of tuning, known as temperament, adjust the slightly uneven intervals between the notes of the octave. Mr Langshaw's restored square piano was tuned to the equal temperament of modern pianos, with slightly narrower thirds.

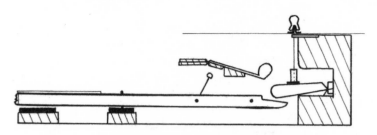

Single key action, square piano 10651. Author's drawing.

When I played his piano for the first time I felt an immediate connection with Mr Langshaw. It was the voice of history; I heard the sound that he and all the people I had been reading about had known. I had never heard a piano like it. The first thing that struck me was how quiet it was, like hearing a piano played in the next room. It was an unfamiliar combination of the sweet and the mechanical; not the sound of a modern piano. The middle notes were dry, soft and silvery. The bass was surprisingly powerful, rich and reverberative, yet the soundboard is hardly bigger than an acoustic guitar. I did not find the treble notes thin and wiry, as James Shudi had said, but edgy.

It needed a delicate touch. The keys are slightly shorter than those of a modern piano, fingers need to be more curved and more vertical to the keys so that the tips touch and feel the keys more directly, more like the way a harpsichord is played. As with a harpsichord, it was no good thumping it to play louder. Unlike the harpsichord, the dynamic range is there, but it is close and subtle. To make the most of it I had to touch lightly and listen carefully.

Prime costs of making a 24 guinea Broadwood square piano in 1807 were £14 11s 7d. It was a fairly rudimentary instrument. Each key is in effect a lever about ten inches long. Part-way along the key shank an angled metal rod tipped with a leather-covered knob, known as the old man's head, pushes the hammer up to the string when the key is pressed down. At the same time a stick damper with a leather hinge known as a dolly is raised by the action of the key.

The hammer strikes the string from below and falls back, leaving the string to sound. When the key comes to rest again the damper, known as a mopstick because of a cloth pinched into the wooden head, drops back into position over the string. Critics say that in rapid passages this simple mechanism means that the hammer can bounce back and strike the string again. With a heavy touch this can happen, but as Charles Burney wrote of Zumpe's square piano, 'the touch, with a little use, is equal to any degree of rapidity.' The repeated notes and musical ornaments in Haydn's Variations Hob. XVII written in 1789, for example, present no difficulty.

Although the contraptions for effecting dynamic change on harpsichords were not necessary on pianos, the use of devices to alter sound lingered. Square piano 10651 has a pedal to raise the dampers, and the dust cover that rests over the strings can also act as a baffle to reduce any mechanical noise inside the piano and enhance the tone. Because the serial number on the wrest plank had been partly obscured, I had originally assumed that the number on the back of this dust cover was the piano's correct serial number. I now knew that dust covers were fragile things, awkward to lift in and out, and few survived. Could dust cover 10651 have been a replacement from a different piano?

With a magnifying glass I examined every part of the case, the lid, the sides, inside and out. I lay underneath and shone a torch on the mahogany base planks. There was nothing, no number scratched discreetly into the woodwork anywhere, no initials to say who had once owned it. I shone the torch to the back of the tool-box: nothing; under the soundboard: nothing; only the flimsy evidence of the dust cover. I propped a mirror against the raised lid to reflect light from the torch back into the piano. There was something on the inside of the nameboard, a number, cut quite roughly into the back where it would never have been seen. I moved the light to the side and read the number in relief. It was 10651!

In theory the sound of a square piano made in 1807, being constructed from similar materials, has similar characteristics to a grand of the same vintage, yet the 1807 Broadwood grand in the Benton Fletcher Collection in London sounds more modern than Mr Langshaw's square piano. The difference may be accounted for by the bigger soundboard, the relative size of the hammer-heads and the sheer amount of volume, and the fact that Broadwoods were putting more detail into the grand's development. The edgy quality and direct response of Mr Langshaw's square piano reveals the revolutionary character of Beethoven's early sonatas, the 'Tempest' (1802) for example, in a way that a more modern piano does not. At the same time its light, legato touch perfectly displays the charms of his first set of Bagatelles. Many square pianos warped beyond repair, but those that have survived demonstrate that they were as right for the most serious music of their day as they were for lighter parlour pieces.

The number roughly cut on the inside of the nameboard, 10651, confirmed that this was the square piano Mr Langshaw had bought in 1807. The order and invoice were noted in the Broadwood Letter Book (1801–1810). Nine other pianos were sent out on the same day in July 1807, all to music masters, organists and warehousemen, in other words, wholesale customers like Mr Langshaw. Dispatch for his square was duly recorded in Broadwood's porters' book, and payment in their Letter Book a month later. It was his only piano purchase that year. (The transaction had gone through smoothly, with no special remarks in the margins.) The sales ledgers for that period in the Broadwood Archive are the most badly water-damaged, and while the retail ledger for 1807 has survived, the wholesale ledger for that year has perished. Without it there is no way of discovering the details of Mr Langshaw's purchase.

It is unlikely that Mr Langshaw had bought square piano 10651 for himself. By 1807 he had been a 'Country Friend' of Broadwoods for twenty years, buying on average two pianos a year. This means that he had already bought at least forty pianos from them, if the missing ledger years before 1794 are included. He was forty-four and had been a professional musician for more than twenty years. It would be surprising if he did not already have a piano of his own.

Without the missing wholesale ledger it is almost impossible to identify who he had bought the piano for. Neither the Letter Book nor the porters' book gives the name of his customer. However, his many other ledger entries show that he almost always bought in his own name except in the few cases where his customer lived outside Lancaster; then their pianos would be dispatched directly to them. There is no name and no special delivery instruction for square piano 10651 in the 1807 porters' book, nothing to identify the customer. It was simply dispatched to Mr John Langshaw, Organist, Lancaster. It is most likely then, that it was intended for someone there.

After arriving at the White Cross canal wharf about a mile north of the town, the piano would have been unloaded and carried by cart directly to the house of the unknown customer. Records of short journeys by local carriers for this period have not survived, if they were ever kept for small jobs of this kind. On arrival the deal case would have been opened and the piano lifted out, unwrapped from its cloth cover and assembled with its pedal and six legs, an operation no doubt supervised by Mr Langshaw, who would have tuned and played the piano for its new owner. The absence of his own private records and those of his bankers, Worswick's, make it impossible to know with certainty who that new owner was. It may have been the daughter of a local Lancaster worthy, a farmer or a merchant; or it may have been, like most of Mr Langshaw's customers who were named, either family or friend. In a letter sent from London more than seventy years later, on 3 June 1883, his son Pearson, who had taken over his father's piano distributorship, wrote to his daughter, Fanny:

> Our time here is half over . . . Yesterday I went to Broadwood's to choose a 'Cottage Grand' for Aunt Kate [Pearson's younger

sister, Catherine Merriman]. I sent in my card and directly had a most cordial shake of the hand from Mr Rose, [then Managing Director of Broadwoods] . . . he remembered me as one of the oldest friends of the firm and added, 'What a number of pleasant people you have sent us, mostly relations – and all so nice.'

If square piano 10651 had been bought by Mr Langshaw for a friend or family member in 1807, something in the family papers, the sketchbooks, scrapbooks, letters and old photographs in archives scattered around Lancaster and the north of England might yet reveal the identity of the unknown recipient.

———•••••———

Within a few years of Mr Langshaw's death his family began to disperse. Sarah, his widow, moved to Knutsford in Cheshire in 1848 when she was seventy-three, to live out the rest of her ninety years with her youngest daughter, Catherine, who had married Dr Charles Merriman eight years earlier. Sarah took with her some of Mr Langshaw's music and the Wesley-Langshaw letters. It is unlikely that she would have taken the square piano with her as well, if it had ever been hers, as Catherine had her own Broadwood, supplied by her brother Pearson.

Pearson had not been born until 1814, seven years after the arrival of square piano 10651. After his two-year stint as priory organist when his father died, he qualified as a surgeon and married Emily Sharpe in 1843. He became Lancaster's most distinguished physician. He and Emily and their daughter Fanny were leading lights in musical life there for fifty years, taking part in concerts by the choral society founded by Emily's brother. They lived until the 1890s in a villa on the outskirts of Lancaster. The family's Broadwood grand was listed in the sale at 'Elmside' after his death in 1896; there was no mention of a square piano.

Of Pearson and Emily's three sons, the eldest, John, died in India when he was twenty-one. The other two, George and Pearson

Sarah Langshaw in old age, c. 1865; James Pearson Langshaw,
c. 1870. Reproduced by permission of Tim Austin.

Charles, lived in Surrey and when they died unmarried in middle age old John Langshaw's direct line came to an end. Their effects reverted to Pearson's daughter Fanny, and there is no mention of a square piano in their letters and papers. (Of Mr Langshaw's nine children, only these two youngest, Pearson and Catherine, had children.)

Fanny lived across the road from her parents in Lancaster, in a house built by her husband, the architect Hubert Austin: 'The Knoll,' a handsome Arts and Crafts house where amber lights from stained-glass windows once danced to the music of her Broadwood grand piano. The house and piano were sold in 1915. Fanny's daughters, Ethel, Mabel and Sybil, went to live at the family's country house at Heversham and spent their time transcribing letters and family trees, copying Bible entries and preserving papers. 'Being descendants of these old Langshaw organists,' Ethel wrote in 1925, 'we are the possessors of various old records.' When Heversham House and its contents were finally sold in 1968, there was no mention of a square piano in the particulars of sale.

Mr Langshaw's oldest son, John, was five in 1807 when the piano had arrived. After he left home in 1812 he had been absorbed into the Fletcher family. He became a colliery owner and a prosperous man in the mid-nineteenth century, when business was regarded with respect. In one of his letters to Pearson he regrets their father's financial worries, in view of how well they had all done. He married his cousin Jane Fletcher late in life. There were no children and after her death he returned to Lancaster, where he saw out his days with Pearson and Emily.

George, Mr Langshaw's second son, had been a baby in 1807 and it is unlikely that the piano was bought for him. He became a Cambridge scholar and a clergyman and like his father's brother, after whom he was named, he too went into a decline and died young, in 1843. His graduation portrait shows a handsome young man whose expression is full of the kindness for which he would be remembered by his 'sorrowing parishioners' in a memorial they erected in St John's College to 'the faultless, indefatigable and self-denying Incumbent of this parish.' The third son, Edmund, was not born until the year after the piano had arrived. He became a lawyer and died unmarried in middle age.

Could the square piano itself yet reveal for whom Mr Langshaw had bought it? Although neglected and unplayed for many years, it had never been mistreated. Judging by the indented soft leather hammers, the dished ivory keys around middle C and the rubbed boxwood of the F sharp above, where the fourth finger of a pianist's right hand had continually reached up to touch it, the piano had once been played a lot. There was no damage to the working parts, no careless dents in the case, no initials scratched into the woodwork. The fragile dust cover was, remarkably, still in one piece and the tuning lever was still in the toolbox. Also in the toolbox was the little nickel instrument, Eardley's Patent. James Eardley had patented his improved pitch pipe in 1862 – thirty years after Mr Langshaw's death. This particular pitch pipe must, therefore, have belonged to a later organist choirmaster or other serious musician.

While separately none of these things might mean much, together they suggest that the piano was once well played by someone who had treated it with respect, possibly a musician, possibly a woman.

By 1862 square piano 10651 was more than fifty years out of date. There had been many changes since 1807 in the design and construction of pianos. The search for greater power had continued and after the introduction of metal in the 1820s, the sound of pianos changed and continued to change throughout the nineteenth century. As cottage or upright pianos became the popular domestic instrument, squares gradually became grander and more expensive. By the time Broadwoods made their last in 1866 they were more like oblong grand pianos, a far cry from their early wooden-framed antecedents. In 1862 the sound of a small, wooden-framed early-nineteenth-century square like 10651, with its intimate, edgy tone, would have belonged to a much earlier era.

Throughout the nineteenth century, developments in piano design and construction were always seen as improvements. The best piano was the most up-to-date piano. There was not then the appreciation there is now for period instruments. Early square pianos like 10651 fell into disuse, both musically and as a social indicator. No one wanted them.

Why then would a serious musician, possibly an organist and choirmaster, have played a square piano in the 1860s that was so out of date? Perhaps poverty was the answer; but pianos were made in huge numbers by the middle of the nineteenth century. There were inexpensive cottage pianos, and second-hand pianos were plentiful. A serious musician in the 1860s, however poor, would not have needed to use an old piano like 10651, unless by then it had been relegated to a poor school, possibly a Sunday school, perhaps for choir practice.

Or could it have been kept out of sentiment, perhaps by someone who had owned it a long time, someone who was attached to it and liked playing it; someone who loved it? If the piano's original owner had been a child in 1807 it could still have been in his or her hands more than fifty years later and he or she could still have been playing it. Could it have belonged to John and Sarah Langshaw's first child, Elizabeth (Bessy)? She had been almost seven when the piano had arrived in Lancaster in July 1807. When she grew up she became an organist and choir mistress.

If the square piano had been bought, even nominally, for Elizabeth Langshaw it would have been the only reminder of her childhood years before the family fell on hard times. Her mother brought her and all her younger brothers and sisters through the hazards of infancy and her father, judging by his letters and the Lonsdale portrait, was a kind man. But by the time Bessy was sixteen her brother John had gone to live with Aunt Fletcher and her two closest sisters had died. In later life, after her brothers George and Edmund had also died and her mother had gone to live in Knutsford, the piano would have been her only link to those early untroubled days and to the father who had taught her to play the organ and played duets with her on the square piano in the little house in Upper King Street. If it had been bought for her in 1807 it would be surprising if she had not retained an attachment to it.

When Master Lonsdale drew a portrait of Bessy Langshaw in 1820 he caught her intelligence as well as her beauty, and the carefully observed details of her dress and hair suggest that the portrait is a good likeness. She was an attractive young woman, musical and beautiful, yet she remained at home through all the years of her father's financial difficulties and did not marry until nine years after his death when she was forty. The man she married was learned and musical, a man twelve years her senior. The Reverend

Thomas Mackreth was the widowed rector of St Wilfred's Halton. He and Bessy were married in 1841 and she spent the rest of her life teaching music, training the choir and playing the organ in her husband's church.

———

Elizabeth (Bessy) Mackreth continued the work of her father and grandfather. She extended the enjoyment of music down to the poorest levels of society. Her life in the impoverished country village three miles east of Lancaster revolved around her husband and his ministry at St Wilfred's, the Sunday school and the village school, which after 1863 became Halton National School.

Her story comes from four different sources: her own parish journal *Annals of Halton*, the reports in the *Lancaster Gazette* of her dispute with the local mill owner John Swainson and the letters exchanged between them, the records of Halton National School and the oral evidence of Bill Hosfield (known locally as the Halton Historian). She emerges as something more than a country vicar's wife. Clearly retaining the resolute character caught by Master Lonsdale in his portrait, she became a champion of the poor. For Elizabeth Mackreth, who never had children of her own, the village children of Halton were her family and, like her grandfather and father before her, she gave her children the gift of education.

She immersed herself in the life of the village from the start and kept her parish journal for twenty-nine years. Her entries in the *Annals* are often brief, sometimes only one or two a year, written up in moments of respite from a busy life that was as full of teaching and music as her father's had been.

> 1843 – In February this year, a family named Clark, residing in a very small house, in the Back Alley, were attacked with Typhus fever; the house could not be ventilated, and for fear of the fever spreading the medical man recommended that the school-room

Miss Langshaw (Bessy), c. 1820; drawing by R. Lonsdale.
Reproduced by permission of Lancaster Museum Service.

should be fitted up as a hospital. Beds were provided for them there, and every comfort and help that could be given. The fever was very severe.

Ten families lived in Back Alley; many sickened and five people died. Bessy too suffered bereavement. In the same month, her younger brother George died in Cambridge. She first appears in the *Annals* a year later when she erected a font that is still in the church, in his memory.

> 1844 – A stone font was erected in the Church by the Rector and his wife, to the memory of her brother, the Reverend George Langshaw, Fellow of St. John's College and vicar of St. Andrew's the Great, Cambridge.

In 1848, stone for building the Little North Western Railway was quarried at Halton on the opposite side of the River Lune. Gangs of men crossed each day in an old boat. During a winter storm it capsized and several lives were lost:

> Some of the men wore heavy boots and fustian jackets with large pockets, which made them sink at once . . . What a night that was! And until all the bodies were found the anxiety and distress was terrible . . . they came to the Rectory for 5s to buy quicksilver; they put it into a loaf of bread, and felt sure that where the loaf sank they would find the body. They tried putting gunpowder into bottles, and contriving that they should blow up under water, that the disturbance might bring the bodies to sight. There was no end to their attempts until the last was found.

A year later a footbridge, 'the latter part on planks only,' replaced the hazardous river crossing. In the same year 'an organ was placed in the church. The price of the organ built by Messrs. Holt of Halifax was £165. It was opened on Sunday, the 14th April . . .' (It was left to her husband's successor, who took over the *Annals* many years later, to record that she was both organist and choir mistress.)

Overcrowding, insanitary conditions and ignorance caused frequent outbreaks of cholera and other diseases in the village:

> 1853 – Isaac Bradley, a boy about ten years old, died this morning at three o'clock . . . he had been bitten in the arm six weeks before by a mad dog which ran through the village . . . The doctor tried chloroform for a time. The mother was so much agitated she could not depend on herself to give it him . . . she begged Mrs Mackreth to administer it, which she did . . . It was a sad time for all and all were thankful when he was released.

Sunday school, choir practice and the many concerts and music lessons she records in the *Annals* were all held in the village schoolroom: '1856 – Jan. 1 A large tea party in the schoolroom. The entertainment consisted of songs, glees and recitation. A very pleasant evening.' It was in that year that a public confrontation between Bessy and the owner of Halton's two cotton mills, John Swainson, occurred. The *Lancaster Gazette* of 22 March 1856 reported:

> Richard Carpenter, his wife and their son were charged with assaulting Thomas Newsham . . . John Swainson who was also lord of the manor of Halton . . . had caused the case to come to court. He stated that he had been obliged to dismiss Carpenter from his employment . . .
>
> After hearing the evidence of defendants, plaintiffs and several witnesses the chairman of the magistrates . . . said Mrs Mackreth was waiting to speak as to the character of the defendants. She had great pleasure in stating that Richard Carpenter, the father, had always been a good character, and his son was a regular teacher in the Sunday School . . .

Halton Rectory, c. 1840.
Reproduced by permission of Bill Hosfield.

Mr Swainson said that if he had any notion that persons would come to court to speak as to the good character of the man, he would have brought plenty who would have told a different story.

The magistrates found that there was no evidence against Mrs Carpenter or her son, but convicted the father and ordered him to pay a fine of a shilling and costs . . .

As a result of this, John Swainson ordered all his employees in Halton not to have anything to do with Mrs Mackreth and he wrote to her two days later requesting that 'as from this day you will cease to hold any communications with the people employed by me; and further that you will not intrude yourself on the inhabitants of the houses belonging to me.'

To which Bessy replied:

Sir,
My first impulse was to return your extraordinary note just received as I would gladly forget its contents and I feel sure that

you yourself, sooner or later, will deeply regret having written it . . .

[With] reference to my future conduct in this village, I have only to say, that I hope to discharge my duty, as I have hitherto endeavoured to do, as the Wife of the Clergyman of the Parish.

John Swainson published his letter to Bessy and insisted that his people obey his instruction and have nothing to do with her or allow her into their homes. Bessy responded by publishing her reply to him, adding a note of her own to the villagers:

. . . if by entering your houses, any of you should think I am likely to bring you into trouble, I will refrain: you know where to find me, and I shall continue, as usual, your friend
Elizabeth Mackreth
Halton Rectory
March 29, 1856

They needed a friend. The cotton mills had been built on the banks of the Lune at Halton in the mid-eighteenth century to spin raw cotton from the West Indies. Agriculture in the area was poor, mainly potatoes, there was no coalfield and Lancaster's port had never recovered from the economic stagnation since the turn of the century and the bank crash of 1826. The town had turned to industry and by 1856 many local people had no alternative but to work in the mills. Conditions were often grim. The long hours and deadly atmosphere depicted by Elizabeth Gaskell in *North and South* (1855) caused industrial disease for which there was no cure and no compensation. Children as young as three worked in the mills.

For the children who could escape work there was an education in Halton schoolroom, where Bessy trained the choir and organized the concerts, glees and entertainments that relieved an otherwise grim existence. The *Annals* continue: '1859–Feb. 10. Concert in the schoolroom – very successful.'

In 1863 the village school became a National School, regulated from London. A dark brown morocco leather folder lined with royal blue velvet contains thirty-four reports on Halton National School by HM Schools Inspectors, starting in 1863. The reports give the number of children in the school – during Bessy's time there were usually about eighty – whose ages ranged from five to twelve. The inspectors found faults – usually with the building – but the reports were seldom less than complimentary about the education.

HM Inspector's Report, 24 June 1863

A well conducted village school doing good service. The Clergyman of the Parish bears the chief burden of expendi-ture . . . a high state of efficiency . . . the school is a highly satisfactory one.

The reports were addressed to the Reverend Thomas Mackreth as the school manager. He funded it but did not run it; that was left to the principal teacher, an assistant mistress and an apprentice, known as a pupil teacher, usually an older boy who had done well at school.

A principal teacher was required by HM Inspectors to keep a school log book, with a brief entry for each school day. The one for Halton runs from 1863 to 1925. It is a heavy, leather-bound book. The exquisite copperplate handwriting of Mr George Richmond, the principal teacher, records:

1863
Monday August 3 Mrs M [Mrs Mackreth] visited. Examd sewing
August 24 Mrs M visited – taught singing and gave notice of
    Annual Feast – to be Saturday.
Sept 25 Dr. and Mrs M visited. Examd. Reading and Writing
Nov. 2 Mrs M took the girls in sewing this afternoon.

St Wilfred's Church, Halton, c. 1860.
Reproduced by permission of Bill Hosfield.

Bessy visited the school every week. She examined the girls' sewing and heard children read; she taught them music and she and her husband gave them feasts. It was their school. The log reports absences, many at potato-planting and harvest time; and half holidays – such as the annual Collop Monday, when children went round the village begging for slices of ham which were fried and the fat kept for cooking pancakes next day, Shrove Tuesday. There was egg-rolling and an annual Coffee Feast provided by the Mackreths. Throughout all these activities, year in and out, 'Mrs M's' name appears every week in the log book. She visited, heard the children read, examined the sewing; and she taught singing: 'How Lovely are the Days of Spring,' 'The Scare-Crow,' 'Gloomy Looks the Sky Today,' 'Yankee Doodle.'

Mr Richmond's log book continues:

1864

May 18 Very Hot. Took the 1st and 2nd to Dr. Mackreth's garden
    and worked under the shade of trees. Dr. and Mrs M present.

June 17 Mrs M visited. Wet. Singing for recreation.

Sept 19 Dr. Mackreth sent a basket of apples.

Sept 27 Mrs M – Singing.

1865

Jan 23 Swept the school chimney with a rope and straw.

Feb 21 Mrs M visited with the Rev. Binyon [curate at the Priory and father of the poet Laurence] – took the young children in poetry.

Bessy was now sixty-five, still on every page of the log book:

March 30 Holiday to see launch of new Iron Ship – Warrington – at Lancaster.

Dec 8 Mrs M visited – music.

1866

May 1 The Rector and Mrs M gave every child a prize for a wild flower arrangement.

May 8 Everything went on cheerfully today.

August 11 Annual Feast at the Rectory.

October 9 Mrs M visited – singing.

And so life at Halton village school continued, the visits, the singing, music, the feasts, the interest taken by the rector and his wife in the education of the children. They practised their Christianity. Bessy would have supervised her husband's household, as well as nursing sick villagers, teaching at school and playing the organ in St Wilfred's – tuning it as her father had taught her – and taking choir practice in the schoolroom, perhaps giving the children a note with the pitch pipes she kept in a compartment in her piano.

In October 1869 the Reverend Mackreth, now aged eighty, did not sign the Inspector's report as usual. He had already made his will,

Teachers and children outside the National School, Halton,
c. 1870. Reproduced by permission of Bill Hosfield.

leaving his furniture and books to his wife. Bessy's visits to the
school became fewer during the early months of 1870 and in June
her husband died. He had never owned the house they lived in; the
living and the rectory belonged to another clergyman who became
rector in July. Bessy left and took her leave of the children who had
been her life.

> 1870
> Monday Sept 19 Mrs Mackreth (widow of the late Rector) came
> to make her farewell visit to the school – she was much affected
> on her departure, having taken a very deep interest (along with
> the late respected Rector) in the support and working of the
> school for many years.

Her life had come to an end. Within three months her husband's successor wrote in the *Annals*:

> 1870 – Dec. 9. Mrs Mackreth, widow of the late Rector, died at
> Grange, and was buried at Halton by the Rector. Admirable as a
> wife, and beloved for her kindness in the parish. Her character as

wife of the late Rector was most estimable. She took great interest in the Choir, which she trained, and also acted as organist.

If square piano 10651 had indeed belonged to Bessy, and came with her to Halton when she married, it would have been more suitable for the schoolroom than for the rectory, for all the singing, choir practice and concerts. If it had been the schoolroom piano, it might not have been included in the sale of the contents of the rectory in July 1870 but left where it was. But nowhere in the subsequent school managers' minute book was there any reference to the replacement of an old piano.

—•••—

Light catches the edges of the worn keys in the middle register of square piano 10651. They are all slightly dished around middle C. Ivory is soft, but keys still need a lot of playing before they wear so much. The four notes below middle C are as dished as the four above and the C below is as worn as middle C. It looks as though someone with a strong left hand once played piano 10651.

Master Lonsdale had drawn Bessy from the left, showing the firm line of her jaw, her even features and dark eyes. His sitter's gown, blue surely, has a satin collar and muslin fichu, all caught so sensitively in his drawing. Her abundant dark hair is rolled into a pleat at the back and arranged in curls on top of her head. In 1820 when the portrait was drawn, Mr Langshaw's daughter would have done her own hair. Bessy rolled it from right to left and pinned it with her left hand . . .

Bessy was not a woman who had taken up music as a trivial pursuit or as a gateway to marriage. Her abilities as an organist and pianist gave her as interesting and useful a life as it was possible for a respectable, middle-class woman to have in Victorian society. She worked hard, thought for herself and did not hesitate to do what she thought was right. She loved and respected her husband, but she was not controlled by him as so many wives were. When she stood up in court in Lancaster and spoke out in defence of Richard Carpenter, the chairman of the Bench was the Reverend Thomas Mackreth.

Bessy inherited from grandfather and father the certainty that education is the key to a better life. Mr Langshaw's legacy to her had been far greater than the mere provisions of his will. He had taught her music and how to play the piano and the organ. He had also shown her how to teach. Whether or not she had ever owned the square piano, she inherited the philosophy her father had absorbed from his own father and the Wesley family: whatever you do, do it with all your heart. She put all her efforts and generous spirit into her teaching and so passed on to hundreds of children the gifts her father had given her.

Bessy's father, Mr John Langshaw, lived through the most rapidly changing phase of the piano's history. He was three when J. C. Bach wrote the first sonatas in England for harpsichord or piano, and five when a square piano was first played at a concert in London. As a boy he listened to his father playing music of the English baroque on the organ. He learned Handel's Lessons on a harpsichord and played some of the first square pianos to emerge from the London workshop of John Broadwood. He composed music for piano in the old style of Corelli and Geminiani and arranged new music by Haydn. He witnessed the rise of the concert virtuoso and the emergence of the six-octave grand piano on which Beethoven composed some of his greatest keyboard music. In 1832, when Mr Langshaw died, the salon music of Chopin was played on modern, iron-framed pianos and harpsichords had not been made for thirty years.

He had seen the phenomenal rise of the square piano, and its popularity lasted for most of his lifetime. By the middle of the nineteenth century it had been replaced by the upright as the most popular domestic instrument, and Broadwoods made their last square, number 64,161, in 1866. For 150 years, they received almost no attention from scholars and musicians. Now, at last, after being so long dismissed as troublesome fledglings, square pianos are being reassessed as musical instruments with a unique value as historically reliable guides to the music and culture of their day, though it is still rare for them to be used for recordings of keyboard music.

Many square pianos from Mr Langshaw's early days, being wooden-framed, warped beyond repair. Some have ended their days as dressing tables or cutlery cabinets, or even as chicken incubators. Square piano no. 10651 was spared. It has been restored and there is plenty of life left in it.

Mr John Langshaw was not a fictional character from a nineteenth-century novel but a modern man who struggled to live a civilized life in a fast-changing society that made no concessions. He was no Jane Austen hero whose inner conflicts, such as they were, were the counterpart of women's sensitivities, and neither were his dilemmas the dramatic storms of a Mr Rochester or Heathcliff; his personal passions remained private. His difficulties were determined by the external pressures of the real world. For much of his life Britain was at war. He lived through a time of unprecedented social upheaval, when society in the early years of the Industrial Revolution was changing more quickly than people could adjust to. Social attitudes lagged behind a bewildering redistribution of wealth. He had seen respectable wealth shift from land to money; when he died material consumption had become a virtue. Mr Langshaw was a man of his time. He was a musical modern: he embraced the piano from its early days in London yet he was steeped in the Ancient musical tradition of his father; he belonged to the Georgian era yet he felt the familiar pressures of the modern world, shortage of leisure, uncertain work, social insecurity, family.

He did not live in a remote part of Britain into which the realities of the French Revolution, the American and Napoleonic Wars, slavery and a harsh penal code never intruded. His boyhood in the 1770s was spent in a town whose prosperity was based on the West Indian slave trade and where public hangings took place on the way to school. In his youth in London he was introduced to the exaggerated splendours and foibles of Georgian high society. At the same time as he heard the finest musicians of the age play some of the most sublime music ever written, he had to hazard the squalor of filthy streets where young men ran for their lives from roving press gangs.

As a professional musician in Lancaster Mr Langshaw worked for a living in the shadow of a castle prison crammed with French prisoners of war and felons from the Manchester of Luddites and machine wreckers. Disease and death were indiscriminate familiars. He and his wife experienced the hardships of raising a large family and the heartbreak of child mortality. He knew the bite of economic decline and the consuming anxiety of financial ruin. He felt the sting of a social caste system that humiliated professional musicians and treated them as servants. In a social climate that compelled musicians to sacrifice their art in order to become gentlemen, he trod the only path to gentility open to a musician of humble birth and 'no great Superfluities,' by becoming an organist in the Established Church. He remained true to his calling throughout his life, not, as some did, 'only to keep other professional men at bay,' but because he was a musician through and through. As organist at the priory church of Lancaster he was compelled to work within a framework of petty officialdom and indifference. As a composer he struggled with little success to get his music published. Like J. S. Bach he could say: 'I have been unable to do my work without vexation and opposition.'

Yet through all his trials in the early years of the Industrial Revolution in northern England, Mr Langshaw made music. He made it from first to last, for himself and for everyone around him. Introduced to it by his father, he learned to play and maintain the priory organ until he knew the instrument inside out. At sixteen, helped by the Wesleys in London, he could play Handel's most difficult Lessons – 'Jack laughs at difficulties' – and he was the only man in Lancashire who could teach them too. By the time he was twenty-one, in 1784, he had discovered pianos. He began to distribute them in the part of northern England where he lived (and once even as far as Boston), and he continued to promote them there for the rest of his life.

During his life he bought about one hundred pianos from Broadwood, mostly squares, for his family, friends and patrons in and around Lancaster, where he taught them how to play them. His ambiguous social status had drawbacks for him personally but it did give him access to a wide range of people in whom he fostered a common interest in the piano. By the values of his day he was not successful, neither rich nor securely elevated to the gentry, and when it came to listing his life's achievements he did not think he had done much of interest, or that his Broadwood distributorship was worth mentioning. Only the lens of history shows that he was a man whose influence lasted well beyond his lifetime: the pianos he supplied and taught upon brought social and cultural change he could not have envisaged.

In his youth, music had existed in separate spheres; the harsh cacophony of the streets contrasted with the harmony of the drawing-room. During his lifetime the distance between the two became narrower. The piano, which symbolized the feminine ideal when he was a young man, became the Victorian focus of hearth and home, even eventually for working-class homes.

Mr John Langshaw was more than part of an enterprise that became a global industry, more than a Country Friend of Broadwoods. Together with the other organist music-masters and a few music mistresses who first promoted the piano, particularly the square piano, in their sphere of influence wherever they were in the world, he formed a bridge which a good many crossed, from an era when music was the exclusive preserve of a wealthy, privileged few to the time 150 years later when even the poorest households had a piano in the front room. Like the aqueduct that still bestrides the Lune Valley, Mr Langshaw's bridge has remained standing and it has never ceased to be used.

EPILOGUE

THE MUSIC ROOM

IN THE MIDDLE of Lancaster there is a music room; it was there at the time of the two organists. In their day it stood alone, while today it is surrounded by a higgledy-piggledy confusion of more recent buildings, warehouses and shop backs. It is a surprise to come across the narrow building wedged in between the others at the back of Sun Street. The sound of traffic recedes as one walks across the yard towards the tall, pale pilasters. An Ionic arch on the ground floor has been glazed to form a shop window. A door next to it on the right leads to a dark inner staircase. At the top of the stairs on the first floor is one room, a large square room, with three Georgian windows.

The room is filled with light from the windows, which makes the plasterwork on the walls stand out in strong relief. Zeus and Mnemosyne's nine daughters – the Muses – cover the walls of the music room: Calliope the eloquent; Clio the historian; Euterpe the musician; Urania the astronomer; Melpomene representing tragedy; Polyhymna: rhetoric; Terpsichore: dancing; Thalia: comedy; and Erato: amorous poetry. Apollo looks down from the fireplace; Ceres floats across the ceiling.

Imagine then, there is very little furniture in the music room, just a small sofa and a square piano to the left of the windows. The lid of the square is raised and a chorus by Haydn, arranged for piano duet, is open on the music stand. It is late afternoon. The rays of the sun slant in through the windows across the piano and in the delicate rearrangement of motes and beams other figures begin to appear.

The first is an impatient-looking man who rubs his hands together briskly, walks towards the piano, sits at one of the two stools in front of it and plays a chord or two, listening to assure himself that the instrument is in tune. A second figure, a young woman in a long blue dress, joins him at the piano and sits on the right-hand stool in front of the primo part of the duet. As Mr John Langshaw and his daughter Bessy begin to play, the two parts come together and we hear his arrangement of 'The Lord is Great' from the *Creation*. Their music brings others into the room, a strange mixture of people from many different eras, yet they all seem to belong here around this piano with its soft, faraway sound; I know them all, and I am grateful to them all.

Close by the piano stand Kelvin McGowan and another man, both of whom had rescued it at auctions many years apart, and Jean Armstrong, who kept it safe in her house for thirty years. Martin Roberts of the Early Music Agency stands next to them; 'Square pianos are a minefield,' he mutters, as he did the day he introduced me to early keyboard instruments. David Winston, who gave this square piano its voice back, is here from the Period Piano Company and looks on approvingly, as do the piano tuners Mr Goldman and Mr Drake, and the man who tunes the square piano now, John Tyrell. Dr Roy Massey, who first told me about organists and their apprentices, is here, watching one of his eighteenth-century predecessors perform. Robert Deegan arrives from his workshop in the Tonnage Warehouse on Lancaster's St George's Quay. I thank him for allowing me to try his harpsichords, and Dr Micaela Schmitz for teaching me how to play one.

Lucy Coad, another fine restorer, gave me much technical help. She shared her great knowledge of square pianos with me and I learned from her that a dust cover is also a baffle and that writing on a piano's wrest plank is not as uncommon as I had thought. She saved me from numerous technical blunders; any that remain are entirely my own. Other piano specialists who helped me are here too: Alan, the gaffer from Ladbrook's workshop in Birmingham; and John Taylor, a buyer and seller of old pianos who made me laugh with his stories about piano characters and directed me to Clementi. Mark Bebbington took time from a busy concert schedule to play early Beethoven on the square piano for me and demonstrate how serious an instrument a square piano is in the hands of a sensitive pianist. Thanks also to Colin Coleman who found Langshaw's duet arrangement of 'The Lord is Great,' and to Paul Guppy for sending me the Whitehaven psalm settings and for reviving the 'Icicle' ballad and performing it with Lancaster's Gladly Solemn Sound.

In another group are all the librarians and archivists who, without exception, entered into the spirit of the search for the piano's story. Thanks to Julian Pooley, Robert Simonson and Jenny Waugh, and everyone at the Surrey History Centre who helped me through the labyrinth of the Broadwood Archive. The Bodleian librarian was ever helpful, as were Jennifer Loveridge, Susan Wilson and Andrew Ottaway at Lancaster Library; they assisted me when I visited and responded willingly to the most time-consuming telephone enquires, sending photocopies and information. The librarians at the Kendal Record Office photocopied many of the Soulby Collection of handbills, and Kate Newman at the Lancashire Record Office helped me to find Bessy's *Annals of Halton* and the National School records and responded to numerous enquiries, whether I was actually in Preston or not. Emily Wood at Glasgow University Library helped me to trace Mr Langshaw's 1824 autobiographical letter to John Sainsbury. Theresa Jones at the Worcester History Shop and Tony Ashcroft in Wigan never abandoned my telephone enquiries either. Alan Davis at Leigh Archives never failed to find whatever obscure reference I asked of him. The British Library's music librarian helped me to find some of Mr Langshaw's published music, and the inter-library loans system, as operated by my local library in Stourbridge, saved me many a journey. I thank them and the many other librarians and archivists who were always ready to go into their catalogues to confirm or reject a possible lead for an unknown researcher on the other end of a telephone.

Dr Peter Nockles introduced me to the Wesley papers in the Special Collections Department in the University of Manchester's John Rylands Library. Dr Naomi Nelson and her staff at the Manuscript, Archives and Rare Books Library at Emory University, Atlanta, Georgia, were warm in their welcome and allowed me the peaceful surroundings in which to read the very moving Wesley-Langshaw letters. Professor Philip Olleson kindly helped me with the identification of Samuel Wesley's Sonata per il Organo. Betty Shannon and staff at the Shilton Library and Kevin Farmer of the Barbados Museum delved enthusiastically into their country's rich archives to find Miss Andrews and Hindsbury House. Dr Karl Watson and Linda Bowen of the University of the West Indies helped me through the National Archives. Linda took me to Maynard's Plantation where Miss Andrews had ended her days, and Richard Seale showed me round the former Harmony Hall where she had lived.

John Berry first directed me to the Wesley-Langshaw letters and the Reverend Arthur Wainwright of Emory University, Atlanta, allowed me to use his annotated edition of the letters; he and Professor Don E. Saliers gave me valuable time and shared their insights over a generous lunch at Emory. I am indebted to Dr Andrew White of Lancaster, whose history of the city directed me to Emily Langshaw's sketchbooks and other important local sources. Clive Holden at Lancaster Royal Grammar School gave me an insight into John Langshaw's schooldays, and local Lancaster historians Cicely Adelson and Bill Hosfield allowed me to use information from their researches on music in Lancaster and the history of Halton. Verity Smith, archivist at St James's Church, Piccadilly, provided interesting material on the organist there in John Langshaw's day. Susan Palmer at Sir John Soane's Museum, Rosalind Francis at St Bride's Printing Library and Rab McGibbon and Helen Trompeteler at the National Portrait Gallery all helped me identify material from the two organists' time in London. I thank them all for their help, for permission to reproduce documents and pictures and for making research such a pleasure.

Churchwarden James Glenn MBE introduced me to the Langshaws in Lancaster priory churchyard, and John Leyland gave me information on All Saints in Wigan and a tour of the church. The rector of St Wilfred's Church, Halton, the Reverend Derek Raitt, took the trouble to find and photocopy extracts from *The Annals of Halton* for me. Curator Sue Ashcroft allowed me access to uncatalogued material in the Austin-Paley Archive and Heather Dowler of Lancaster City Museum provided the illustrations from it. Anthea Dennet gave me an unforgettable demonstration of the Langshaw barrel organ at the Judge's House Museum in Lancaster. Katherine Walker opened up St John's Chapel for me, and Dr Colin Parsons gave me a private recital on the Langshaw baroque organ. Joan Davis, churchwarden of All Saints, Llanfairwaterdine, and Richard Lewis, the organist, kindly demonstrated their church's large, working barrel and finger organ for me. John Budgen, organ builder, helped me to understand the way music is pricked onto a barrel and how a barrel organ works. I am grateful to them all for welcoming me to their churches, for the music, and the knowledge so generously imparted.

The music room is filling with people.

Here are many friends and well-wishers who gave me encouragement in various ways and hospitality: Walter and Prophecy Coles in London, Frances Withers at St Columba's in Woking and the Sisters at Our Lady of Hyning in Carnforth. Catherine Brown helped me to get started on typing and Mary Emery allowed me to use her cottage in Devon to write the first three chapters. In

Barbados Jean Robinson showed me Great House hospitality, and Michael Gibbons, 'Mr Pianoman,' recalled his forty years with West Indian pianos one memorable morning in his premises on the outskirts of Bridgetown. The friendship of Andrew and Sheila Hatch opened many Barbadian doors to me. I thank them all for making the research of this book the interesting journey it became.

Others who belong in the music room are Tania Coles who guided me through the early stages of finding a publisher, and Michael Green of Birmingham University, whose immediate enthusiasm encouraged me to think about the broader social effects of Mr Langshaw's square pianos and who read the first draft. Deirdre Elliott read two drafts and allowed me to discuss ideas and structure with her. I wish to record my thanks to her mother, Molly Huband, who, though no longer here, as my teacher many years ago encouraged me to think I could write stories. In the early stages Dr Mimi Waitzman was enthusiastic about the book and allowed me to play the Broadwood 1807 grand piano during a guided tour of the Benton Fletcher Collection in London. I thank most particularly Julia Rochester, my editor at Corvo Books, for having enough faith in a few early, disorganized chapters to commission the book, and for leading me through the process of writing and shaping it; and my heartfelt thanks to Caroline Pretty, who reinvigorated my thinking about the book and whose patient copy-editing helped me to take it forward to publication. I would also wish to thank Jan-Erik Guerth, my American publisher at BlueBridge, for his considerable help in bringing the story of Mr Langshaw and his square piano to North American readers. Madge Hope gave the practical help that made writing possible. Greatest thanks go to my family for leaving me to get on with writing and especially to my husband, Michael, who listened to readings as the book took shape and read the final draft and who lived for many months uncomplainingly in a ménage à trois with me and Mr Langshaw.

Standing slightly apart in the music room is someone who seems to belong as easily with the Langshaws and their circle as with all the people from the present day. Dr Tim Austin could not have been more generous with his time and help. He gave me the Austin Archive on long loan and his meticulous research saved me many a return to find a forgotten reference. Every phone call or e-mail from him contained another golden nugget about his ancestors. He moves easily among them: Sarah Langshaw, who, at ninety, sits knitting on the sofa with her three little girls whose time with the square piano was so short; Catherine, her youngest daughter, who stands beside her with Charles Merriman and their eleven children; and a dynasty of doctors, surgeons and lawyers.

Three George Langshaws, once separated by 120 years, now stand together within range of the square piano. One of them, Mr Langshaw's brother, is eighteen, bright-eyed at the thought of Cambridge and, who knows, a bishop's lawn sleeves. His nephew, the rector of St Andrew's the Great, stands next to him, and his great-nephew George, Mr Langshaw's grandson, whose house in Ockham, Surrey, I came across during a visit to the Broadwood Archive, is there too.

With them are four other John Langshaws for whom time in this music room no longer matters: Major John Langshaw, the colliery owner, eldest son of Mr Langshaw, glances in the direction of a lady standing nearby who holds a sketchbook in her hand. There is Mr Langshaw's brother William's son, another 'Jack,' the black sheep of the family who was deported to Australia in 1833 for stealing a portable barrel organ. Next to him stands a twenty-one-year-old John Langshaw, Pearson and Emily's brave son who died of fever in India in 1866 after rescuing a colleague from a flooded river. From the twentieth century, there is John Langshaw Austin, Mr Langshaw's great-great-great-grandson. He created in 1942 the intelligence section which prepared all the detailed information for the Allied D-Day landings. In his hand he holds one of his own maps, the Enemy Order of the Battle in the West, 10 June 1944. In peacetime he became White's Professor of Moral Philosophy at Oxford.

Another organist of Lancaster Priory, Pearson Langshaw, listens to his father and sister play the square piano, hoping that they will play something by Bach, his favourite. Next to him his brother-in-law, the Reverend Thomas Mackreth, who has ridden over from Halton, listens to his future wife play. Pearson's wife, Emily, has just returned from a sketching trip to Morecambe with her sister Marianne and holds her book open at a drawing of Morecambe Terrace they made together. Beside them stands a beautiful woman from an earlier age. Elizabeth Langshaw is dressed in the latest fashion of her time, a gossamer-light gown and a wide-brimmed gauze hat. She watches her brother, and the niece who was named after her, playing the square piano, so like the one her husband-to-be, Thomas Green, would buy for her in 1813. She looks down at little Fanny Langshaw, Pearson and Emily's daughter. The girl holds a note she has just written to her papa in which she promises never to have her ears pierced. Fanny takes the note over to Pearson; he has promised to give her £5 when she is eighteen if she keeps her promise. Fanny's daughters, Ethel, Sybil and Hilda, who lived on at Heversham House until 1967, are here too, checking dates and making the notes that they will add to their family history.

Time has no meaning in the music room.

Towards the back of the room an important group has arrived from London. John Broadwood and his sons, James Shudi and Thomas, look surprised to find that they are here because of one of their plain square pianos. Next to her tall, stern-looking husband stands John Broadwood's young wife, Barbara. She fidgets with some new lace at her throat, the gift of her father, old Burkat Shudi, and, remembering a piano-tuning appointment for her husband, quickly jots it down between *carrats* and *mussels* on her shopping list. William the porter, hat in hand, and Fraser the keymaker stand behind their master.

It is getting dark outside. In the music room someone has lit the fire and the candles on the piano. Reflected flames and figures mingle on the window panes. An elderly clerical gentleman has taken a seat just inside the door at the back of the room. The Reverend Charles Wesley has his two sons Charles and Samuel with him and they all listen appreciatively to the music. The young men's uncle is there too, the Reverend John Wesley, and his disciple William Langshaw, who rode on horseback from Wigan. The Reverend Charles Wesley has been up since five this morning; nonetheless he carefully notes in his memorandum book those present at this recital. A line from one of his own poems enters his head: 'Though absent in body, yet present in spirit,' he thinks as lights from the fire turn in the room.

As I too turn and look around at everyone in the music room it seems to me that the square piano belongs to all of them and that establishing mere ownership is less important than finding all these people who have, at different times, played a part in its story. In the reflected firelight, Muses and people mingle in the flickering moment that is the here and now as a final figure comes into the room. It is the Reverend Charles Wesley's old friend. He stands, barely discernible in shadow at the back of the room, supporting himself on a homemade crutch. His eyes are hidden behind a pair of thick lenses held together by an ingenious wire frame across the bridge of his nose. Though he can hardly see, old John Langshaw has come to hear his son's composition and judge the merit of the instrument he plays; and he leans forward, listening, as the piano plays on.

APPENDIX I

MR JOHN LANGSHAW'S BROADWOOD PIANO PURCHASES

The following list of pianos bought from Broadwoods by John Langshaw is made from entries in the Broadwood Journal, Letter Book, sales ledgers and porters' books (GPF: grand pianoforte; SPF: square pianoforte).

The Broadwood Journal, Bodleian Library, Oxford

1784

October 4	Thomas Scott, Wigan, a Piano-forte, ordered by Mr. John Langshaw	21	-	-
Nov. 6	John Langshaw, for a pianoforte	21	-	-

1785

April 8	Mr. Langshaw, for a piano forte in a plain case	21	-	-

The Broadwood Archive – Surrey History Centre, Woking

1795

Nov 28	A Piano forte and Case add to Mr. Burrows	16	5	6

1796

May 11	A Piano forte and Case add	16	5	6

1800

Mar 5	GPF No. 1784 and 1785 for John Baynes, Boston, New England	181	10	-
July	GPF No. 1724 and 1786	114	3	-

1801

May 2	To a Piano Com ff & Case	20	17	-

1802

May 20	To a Piano forte with Pedal & Case	23	9	6
Sept 10	A Piano forte add. Ff and DP & Case	23	18	-
Dec 14	A GPF No. 2490			
Dec 30	SPF No. 7077	27	3	6

1803

Feb 15	SFP No. 6742	27	3	6
Mar 31	A Best SPF	32	6	-
May 3	A GPF	64	14	-
May 18	A SPF Orn.	27	1	-

1804

May 3	Langshaw Mr Lancaster	24	-	-
June 1	Langshaw Mr Lancaster	34	-	-
July 2	Langshaw Mr Jn. Organist Lancaster	24	-	-
Dec 18	Langshaw Mr Jn. Organist Lancaster	24	-	-

1805

Mar 8	Langshaw Mr Jn. Organist Lancaster	57	4	-
Octob	Langshaw Mr. Jn. Organist Lancaster	24	8	-

1806

Octob 24	Langshaw Mr. Jn. Organist Lancaster

1807

July 27	SPF 10651	24	-	-

1808

Aug 29	To a Small Piano forte James Green	24	19	3
Octob 1	To a Small Piano forte	27	13	-

1809

Feb 27	To a piano forte with a drwr. Cov. and Case	29	18	-
Mar 15	To a Small piano forte add. & Case	25	4	-
Octob 10	To a Small piano forte add Case repaired	23	4	-
Nov 3	To a Small Piano forte add & Case	25	4	-
Dec 22	To a Best Piano forte etc	32	16	-

1810

Feb 23	To a Best Piano forte Duke of Hamilton	28	7	-
April 3	To a Best Piano forte, case made deeper	31	10	-
April 6	To a Best Piano forte with drws	31	10	-

1811

July 17	To a piano forte	26	16	-
Nov 7	To a Best Piano forte	33	3	-
	for Thomas Taylor, Hanley, Staffordshire			
Nov 23	To a 6 Oct Upright Grand Piano forte	108	8	-
	Sent Mr. Chippindale, Skipton, Yorks			

1812

May 21	To a Piano forte and Case	26	16	-
July 9	To a Best Small Piano forte and			
	Drws & Case	33	2	-
Aug 24	To a 6 Oct Grand piano forte Cover & Case	72	6	-

1813

June 12	To a Square Piano forte, Case	26	16	-
	Sent to Mr. Green at Miss Naylor's, Warrington			
June 29	To a Grand Piano forte & Case	72	6	-
	Sent to N. Grimshaw Esq., Preston			
Nov 30	To a Grand Piano forte & Case	59	6	6

1814

July 15	To a Best Piano forte and drs and Case	33	3	-
Sept 10	To A Best Sq Piano forte and drs & Case	33	3	-
"	To a Sq Piano forte & Case	26	17	-

1815

[No transactions recorded this year.]

1816

April 19	2 Sq Piano forte DA / New Case / Sec	52	11	-
Sept 20	To a Sq Piano forte, Wire and Strings	26	9	-
Dec 14	A 6 Oct Grand Piano forte and			
	Cov & Case (for Mr Crompton)	76	6	-

1817

Feb 3	A Sq Piano forte DA and Case	26	-	-
May 8	A Sq Piano forte Best & Case	32	15	-

1818

April	A 6 Oct Grand Piano forte			
	Cover & Case	75	18	-
May 21	A Sq Piano forte with drs and Case	30	13	-

"	A Sq Piano forte & Case (for Col. Fletcher)	24	7	-
Oct 2	A Sq Piano forte & Case	26	-	-
Dec 29	A 6 Oct Grand Piano forte & Case (for S. Harrods Esq)	73	16	-

1819

Jan 30	A best Sq Piano forte And Case Sec	30	6	-
Mar 23	A Sq Piano forte & Case Sec	24	-	-
June 8	A 6 Oct Cab. Piano forte and Case	51	19	6
Sept 25	A Best Sq Piano forte with drs and Case	30	13	-

1820

Jany 3	A Sq Piano forte and Sec. Case	24	-	-
July 8	A Sq Piano forte Best with disc. and Case	31	14	-
Aug 31	A Sq Piano forte and Case	24	7	-
Sept 26	A Sq Piano forte and Case	24	7	-
Octob 12	A Sq piano forte & Case	30	13	-
Nov 24	A Sq Piano forte Wires and Case	30	16	-
Dec 12	A 6 Oct Sq Piano forte and Case	35	-	-

1821

May 3	A 6 Oct Sq Piano forte with Drs and Case	35	-	-
June 4	[Illegible entry]	35	-	-
	[Illegible name] 60 Poland Street	38	3	-
June 23	A 6 Oct Sq Piano forte and Case	38	3	-

1822

[No entries]

1823

Dec 29	A Sq Piano forte, leather for hammers etc	25	1	-

1824

June 10	A Sq Piano forte and sec'd Case	24	-	-
May 1	A Sq Piano forte and Case	30	-	-
May 28	A Sq Piano forte and Case	30	13	-

1825

April 9	A Sq Piano forte and sec'd Case	24	-	-

1826
[No piano purchases, only sundries such as spare strings.]

1827

————————————————————————————— [Obscured entry]

————————————————————————————— " " and Case   40 - -

————————————————————————————— and a gold curtain

for a Cott. & Case   36 8 6

1828
Jan ————————————— cloth and Case   44 5 6

1829
Feb ————- ————- G[rand Piano forte] ...
Cover and Case   128 10 -
April 15   A 6 Oct Sq Piano plate and Case   [Illegible]
July 8   A 6 Oct Sq piano forte Plate and Case 30 13 -

1830
[No entries]

1831
June 16   A Sq Piano forte Plate & Case   30 13 -
Dec 29   A Best 6 Oct Sq Piano forte Plate and Case 43 5 -
               to Col. Fletcher

Mr John Langshaw died on 5 December 1832. The final payment in 1833, by the executors of his will, cleared his account and ended his forty-nine years of business with Broadwoods.

1833
Sept 2   By Cash pr. Exors.   3s 10d

Assuming Mr Langshaw bought at a similar rate in the years between 1785 and 1794, for which records are missing, and in the later years where records are damaged, the total would have been well over one hundred pianos.

APPENDIX II

LANGSHAW PEDIGREE

John Langshaw of Wigan (d. Wigan, 1773), pewterer, married Ann Aspinall (d. 1761)
Nine children, including
    John (1725–98), the first organist, married Mary Haydock
        (1733–1800), daughter of George and Mary Haydock
    William (1734–1825), the Wigan Methodist
    Ann
    Mary
    Elizabeth
    Jane (d. 1769)

John Langshaw (1725–98), married Mary Haydock (1733–1800)
Nine children
    John (*Jack*) (1763–1832), Mr Langshaw, the second organist
    George (1764–82)
    Mary (1766–69)
    Ann (1768)
    Elizabeth (1770–1851) m. Thomas Green
    William (1772–1829) m. Catherine Beloudey
    James (1773–84)
    Joseph (1775–85)
    Benjamin (1775–97)

John (Jack) **Langshaw** (1763–1832), married Sarah Grundy (1774–1865)*
Nine children
    Elizabeth (1800–70) m. the Reverend Thomas Mackreth
    John (1802–83) m. Jane Fletcher (cousin)
    Sarah (1804–16)
    George (1806–43)
    Edmund (1808–69)
    Jane (1809–17)
    Frances (1812–24)
    James Pearson (1814–96) m. Emily Sharpe (1814–94)
    Catherine (1817–1905) m. Charles Anthony Merriman

*Of Mr Langshaw's nine children only the two youngest, James Pearson and Catherine, had children.

APPENDIX III

BROADWOODS

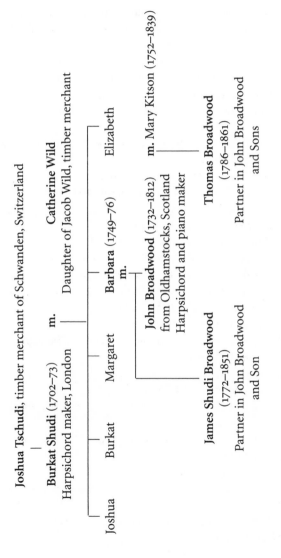

Joshua Tschudi, timber merchant of Schwanden, Switzerland

Burkat Shudi (1702–73)
Harpsichord maker, London

m.

Catherine Wild
Daughter of Jacob Wild, timber merchant

Joshua

Burkat

Margaret

Barbara (1749–76)

Elizabeth

m.

John Broadwood (1732–1812)
from Oldhamstocks, Scotland
Harpsichord and piano maker

m. Mary Kitson (1752–1839)

James Shudi Broadwood
(1772–1851)
Partner in John Broadwood
and Son

Thomas Broadwood
(1786–1861)
Partner in John Broadwood
and Sons

SELECT BIBLIOGRAPHY

Unpublished sources

Original spellings, abbreviations and punctuation are as they appear in the Broadwood records, the Wesley-Langshaw correspondence and all other quoted material.

Austin-Paley Archive, Lancaster Maritime Museum, ms. LM 86/129

Austin Papers, Lancaster University

Barbados Births Index, RL1/58 (1758–1805), Barbados National Archives, Lazaretto

Barbados Parochial Register of Burials, vol. 17B, RL2/17 B(2), p. 741, Barbados National Archives, Lazaretto

Barbados Wills, RB/44(2) (1801–1947), Barbados National Archives, Lazaretto

Samuel Bradburn's Diary, 1751–1816, Diaries Collection Box 1002, 2 vols., Methodist Archives and Research Centre, Special Collections, John Rylands Library, University of Manchester (MARC)

Broadwood Company Books, Bodleian Library, Oxford

Broadwood Company Records, Surrey History Centre, Woking

Census Enumerators' Returns, 1841, 1851, 1881, 1901

Charterhouse School Records, London Metropolitan Archives: Pensioners' and Scholars' Records/ACC/1876/PS/1–3, 4/20

Chippindall papers, V20, Lancaster Library

Lucy Coad, 'Restoring Square Pianos,' Broadwood Symposium, Surrey History Centre, Woking, 25 February 2006

George Pike England, letter to Adam Cottam of Whalley, 14 January 1813, ms. DDX336/27, Lancashire RO, Preston

Halton National School Log Book, 1863–1925, ms. SMHn1/1, Lancashire RO, Preston

Halton National School HM Inspectors' Reports, 1863–1910, ms. SMHn1/3, Lancashire RO, Preston

Lancaster Library Scrapbooks, ms. 588–261

Lancaster Priory Church Records, Baptisms, Marriages and Burials, ms. PR 3262/1/4, Lancashire RO, Preston

Lancaster Priory Churchwardens' Accounts and Vestry Minutes, ms. PR 3262, Lancashire RO, Preston

Langshaw Folder, ms. 4078, Lancaster Library

John Langshaw (1725–98):

- Letter to William Pinchbeck, 29 October 1773, ms. D/Lons/LI/1/72-file, Cumbria RO, Carlisle

John Langshaw (1763–1832):
- Letter to Adam Cottam, 5 May 1813, ms. DDX 336/28, Lancashire RO, Preston
- Letter to John Sainsbury, 3 January 1824, ms. Euing R.d 87/120, University of Glasgow

John Langshaw's (1763–1832) published music:
- Air, 1802, ms. h.61.h(8), British Library, London
- Air, 1805, ms. G.295.q(3), British Library, London
- Ballad, 'Dear Boy Throw that Icicle Down,' Carr Collection, RDW511, Lancaster Library
- 'The Lord is Great,' Haydn arr. Langshaw, 1802, author's collection
- Psalm Settings, Hargill Collection, Whitehaven 1800, ms. DH/329, Whitehaven RO, Cumbria

John Langshaw, Will, 17 January 1831, WRW A 1832, Lancashire RO, Preston

Sarah Langshaw, Will, 19 April 1851, MF 91/8 Ps 565, Chester RO, Chester

Stephen Mackreth, Map of Lancaster, 1778, Lancashire RO, Preston

Christopher Nobbs, 'Historic Broadwood Pianos,' Broadwood Symposium, Surrey History Centre, Woking, 25 February 2006

Martha Sharpe, letter to William Whittaker, 11 February 1828, ms. 6877, Lancaster Library

Simonson, Robert, 'The Archives of John Broadwood and Sons,' Broadwood Symposium, Surrey History Centre, Woking, 25 February 2006

John Hanson Sperling, Notebooks on Organ Building, ms. 79:9, 1–5, British Library, London

Charles Wesley, *Notebook*, Black folio 4:59, 55–58, Methodist Archives and Research Centre, Special Collections, John Rylands Library, University of Manchester (MARC)

Charles Wesley, *Hearers of Chas. and Sam.* (1777), ms. DDCW/6/59, MARC

Charles Wesley, *Notes on the Subscription Concerts of Charles and Samuel Wesley*, ms. GB: Lam MS-L Wesley, C, microfilm 134, Royal Academy of Music, London

Anonymous description of Charles Wesley, c. 1780, ms. DD CW6/85A, MARC

Wesley-Langshaw Correspondence, John Wesley Mss., Manuscript, Archives, and Rare Book Library, Robert R. Woodruff Library, Emory University, Atlanta

Wigan Borough Court Leet Rolls, transcript, vol. 2 1692–1834, Roll 162, Leigh Archives, Wigan

Published sources

Adorno, Theodor W., *Introduction to the Sociology of Music*, trans. E. B. Ashton (New York, 1976)

Annals of the Parish of Halton, 2nd edition, 1828–69, moo23556 LC class EO2 Halton, Lancashire RO, Preston

Apollo's Cabinet: or The Muses Delight. An Accurate Collection of English and Italian Songs, Cantatas and Duetts (John Sadler, Liverpool, 1754–56), D.379, pp. 226 and 227, British Library, London

Bach, Carl Philipp Emanuel, *Essay on the True Art of Playing Keyboard Instruments* (1753, repr. New York; trans. and ed. W. J. Mitchell, 1949)

Baines, Edward, *History of Lancashire* (Liverpool, 1824–5)

Baker, Frank, *Charles Wesley: As Revealed by his Letters* (London, 1948)

Barbadian Newspaper, obituary of Elizabeth Georgiana Andrews, June 1855, Shilstone Library, The Barbados Museum

Barbados Business and Central Directory, 1887, Shilstone Library, The Barbados Museum

Barnes, Alan, and Martin Renshaw, *The Life and Works of John Snetzler* (Otterup, 1994)

Bartohold, Kenneth Van, and David Buckton, *The Story of the Piano* (London, 1975)

Billington, W. D. (ed.) *Captain Dewhurst and his Diary* (Bolton, 1981)

Boeringer, James, *Organa Britannica: Organs of Great Britain 1660–1860*, 3 vols. (Lewisburg and London, 1983–89)

Boston, Joseph Noel, and Lyndesay G. Langwill, *Church and Chamber Barrel Organs* (Edinburgh, 1967)

Boswell, James, *A London Journal 1762–1763* (London, 1950)

Brewer, John, *Pleasures of the Imagination: English Culture in the Eighteenth Century* (London, 1997)

Bridgetown Business and Trade Directories, Shilstone Library, The Barbados Museum

Burney, Charles, *A General History of Music From the Earliest Ages to the Present Period*, 4 vols. (London, 1776–89; repr. New York, 1957, 2 vols., ed. Frank Mercer)

Chetham Society Papers, New Series, vols. 26, 31, 58, 59, Lancashire RO, Preston

Clark, Christopher, *An Historical and Descriptive Account of the Town of Lancaster Collected from the Best Authorities* (Lancaster, 1807)

Clementi, Muzio, *Introduction to the Art of Playing on the Pianoforte* (1801; repr. New York, 1974)

Clinkscale, Martha Novak, *Makers of the Piano 1700–1821* (London, 1993)

Cole, Michael, *The Pianoforte in the Classical Era* (Oxford, 1998)

Collinson, Thomas Henry, ed. Francis Collinson, *The Diary of an Organist's Apprentice at Durham Cathedral 1871–1875* (Aberdeen, 1982)

Colt, C. F., with Anthony Miall, *The Early Piano* (London, 1981)

Crombie, David, *Piano: Evolution, Design and Performance* (London, 1995)

Cross-Fleury (R. K. Rigsbye), *Time-Honoured Lancaster: Historic Notes on the Ancient Borough of Lancaster* (Lancaster, 1891)

Cumming, Alexander, 'A Sketch of the Properties of the Machine Organ' (printed by E&H Hodson, London, 1812), 07899.f.47, British Library, London

Defoe, Daniel, *A Tour Through the Whole Island of Great Britain*, 1724–26, 3 vols. (repr. New Haven, 1991)

Dictionary of National Biography, all editions

Dolge, Alfred, *Pianos and their Makers* (1911; repr. New York, 1977)

Ehrlich, Cyril, *The Piano: A History* (rev. ed. Oxford, 1990)

Elder, M., *The Slave Trade and Economic Development of Eighteenth-Century Lancaster* (Halifax, 1992)

Engramelle, M. D. J., *La tanotechnie ou l'art de noter des cylinders* (Paris, 1775; repr. 1971)

Fetis, F. J., *Biographie universelle des Musiciens, et bibliographie general de la musique* (Paris, 1860–65; repr. 1962)

Flanders, Judith, *Consuming Passions: Leisure and Pleasure in Victorian Britain* (London, 2006)

Gartner, Heinz, *John Christian Bach: Mozart's Friend and Mentor* (Portland, 1994)

Gaskell, Elizabeth, *North and South* (London, 1855; repr. 1986)

— *Wives and Daughters* (London, 1866; repr. 1996)

— *Life of Charlotte Bronte* (London, 1857)

Gore's Advertiser (Liverpool), obituary, John Langshaw, March 1778

Grove's Dictionary of Music and Musicians, all editions

Hadfield, C., and G. Biddle, *The Canals of North West England*, 2 vols. (Newton Abbot, 1970)

Harding, Rosamond, *The Piano-Forte: Its History Traced to the Great Exhibition of 1851*, 2 vols. (1935; 2nd edition, London, 1979)

Hewitson, Anthony, *Northward: Historic, Topographic and Scenic Gleanings* (Preston, 1900)

Hipkins, A. J., *A Description and History of the Piano-forte and of the older keyboard stringed instruments* (London, 1896)

Holmes, Edward, *The Life of Mozart Including his Correspondence* (1845; repr. Folio Society, London, 1991)

Hoyos, F. A., *Barbados: A History from the Amerindians to Independence* (London, 1978)

James, Phillip, *Early Keyboard Instruments* (London, 1967)

Kassler, Michael, and Philip Ollesen, *Samuel Wesley (1766–1837): A Source Book* (Aldershot, 2001)

Lancaster Gazette, various articles, Lancaster Library

Lancaster Observer and Morecambe Chronicle, 'A Note on the Re-Building of St. John's Church Lancaster,' 16 June 1905

— 'The Parish Church. Its Organs and Organists,' 2 December 1921

Leppert, Richard, *Music and Image: Domesticity, Ideology and Socio-Cultural Formation in Eighteenth-Century England* (Cambridge, England, 1988)

Lewis, Roy, and Angus Maude, *The English Middle Classes* (London, 1953)

Lippincott, Louise, 'Tuscher's Drawings for the Shudi Portrait,' *Burlington Magazine* 131:1039 (October 1989)

Loesser, Arthur, *Men, Women and Pianos* (New York, 1954; repr. 1990)

McVeigh, Simon, *Concert Life in London from Mozart to Haydn* (Cambridge, England, 1993)

Malloch, William, 'The Earl of Bute's Machine Organ: A Touchstone of Taste,' *Early Music* (April 1983), p. 172

Maunder, Richard, 'The Earliest English Square Piano?' *Galpin Society Journal* 42 (1989), pp. 77–84

— 'The Square Piano Re-discovered,' *Early Music* 35:2 (2007), pp. 298–300

Mobbs, Kenneth, 'English Upright and Grand Pianos,' *Harpsichord and Fortepiano* 2:1 (2006), p. 44

Mould, Charles, 'The Broadwood Books,' *English Harpsichord Magazine* 1:1&2 (1974)

Murray, Athol Laverick, *The Royal Grammar School Lancaster: A History* (Cambridge, England, 1952)

Nex, Jenny, and Lance Whitehead, 'Musical Instruments Making in Georgian London, 1753–1809: Evidence from the Proceedings of the Old Bailey and the Middlesex Sessions of the Peace,' *Eighteenth-Century Music*, 2 vols. (Cambridge, England, 2005)

Olleson, Philip (ed.), *The Letters of Samuel Wesley: Professional and Social Correspondence, 1797–1837* (Oxford, 2001)

— *Samuel Wesley: The Man and his Music* (Woodbridge, 2003)

Orde-Hume, A. W. G., *Barrel Organ: The Story of the Mechanical Organ and its Repair* (New York, 1978)

Ottenberg, Hans-Gunter, *Carl Philipp Emanuel Bach* (Oxford, 1987)

Parakilas, James (ed.), *Piano Roles* (New Haven, 2001)

Picard, Lisa, *Dr. Johnson's London Life* (London, 2000)

Plantinga, Leon, *Clementi: His Life and Music* (London, 1977)

Pollens, Stewart, *The Early Pianoforte* (Cambridge, England, 1995)

Rennert, Jonathan, *William Crotch 1775–1847: Composer, Artist, Teacher* (Lavenham, 1975)

Robson's Commercial Directory and Street Guide to London (Westminster Library, London, 1831)

Rohr, Deborah, *The Careers of British Musicians 1750–1850: A Profession of Artisans* (Cambridge, England, 2001)

Rude, George, *Hanoverian London 1714–1808* (London, 1971)

Russell, Francis, *John, 3rd Earl of Bute: Patron and Collector* (London, 2004)

Russell, Raymond, *The Harpsichord and Clavichord* (London, 1959; revised and repr. 1973)

Sainsbury, J. S., *A Dictionary of Musicians from the Earliest Times*, 2 vols. (1825; repr. New York, 1971)

Schofield, M. M., *Outlines of an Economic History of Lancaster 1680–1860*, Transactions of the Lancaster Branch of the Historical Association (Lancaster, 1946)

Schomburgk, Sir Robert, *History of Barbados* (1848; repr. London, 1971)

Simmonds, Paul, 'The Pantalon Clavichord. Resonance from the Eighteenth Century,' *Harpsichord and Fortepiano* 2:1 (2006), p. 38

Sinclair, D., *History of Wigan*, 2 vols. (1882)

Swindlehurst, Marjorie, *John Wesley and Wigan* (Wigan, 1991)

Todd, Janet, *Sensibility: An Introduction* (London, 1986)

Treasure, Geoffrey, *Who's Who in Late Hanoverian Britain, 1789–1837* (1974; repr. Mechanicsburg, PA, 2002)

Turnbull, Gerard, *Traffic and Transport: An Economic History of Pickfords* (London, 1979)

Tyson, John R. (ed.), *Charles Wesley: A Reader* (Oxford, 2000)

Uglow, Jenny, *Hogarth: A Life and a World* (London, 1997)

— *The Lunar Men: The Friends who made the Future 1730–1810* (London, 2002)

Venn, J. A., *Alumni Cantabrigiensis*, 10 vols. (London, 1954)

Wainwright, Arthur W., and Don E. Saliers (eds.), *Wesley/Langshaw Correspondence: Charles Wesley, His Sons, and the Lancaster Organists* (Atlanta, 1993)

Wainwright, David, *Broadwood by Appointment: A History* (London, 1982)

Wallace, Robert K., *Jane Austen and Mozart: Classical Equilibrium in Fiction and Music* (Athens, GA, 1983)

Watson, Karl (ed.), 'The Journal of Sir Henry Fitzherbert, Kept while in Barbados in 1825,' *Journal of the Barbados Museum & Historical Society* XLIV (1998), p. 116

White, Andrew (ed.), *A History of Lancaster 1193–1993* (Keele, 1993)

— *Lancaster: A History* (Sussex, 2003)

Williams, John-Paul, *The Piano* (London, 2003)

Wilson, Ben, *Decency and Disorder: The Age of Cant 1789–1837* (London, 2007)

Winstanley, Michael, 'The Town Transformed,' *A History of Lancaster*, ed. A. White (2001)

W. W., 'The Wesley Family Concerts 1777–1785,' *The Royal Academy Club Magazine* 84 (June 1929), pp. 7–11

www.aam.co.uk/features/aam, Weber, William, 'The Original Academy of Ancient Music'

www. priory.lancs.ac.uk/judges, 'The Langshaw Barrel Organ'

INDEX